In the
moment

In the
moment

CELEBRATING THE EVERYDAY

Harvey L. Rich, M.D.

with Teresa H. Barker

Sunday, April 4, 2004

wm **William Morrow** *An Imprint of* HarperCollins*Publishers*

HarperCollins books may be purchased for educational, business, or sales promotional use. For information please write: Special Markets Department, HarperCollins Publishers Inc., 10 East 53rd Street, New York, NY 10022.

FIRST EDITION

Designed by Shubhani Sarkar

Printed on acid-free paper

Library of Congress Cataloging-in-Publication Data

Rich, Harvey L.
  In the moment: celebrating the everyday / Harvey L. Rich with Teresa H. Barker.—1st ed.
    p. cm.
  ISBN 0-06-019968-7
  1. Conduct of life. I. Barker, Teresa. II. Title.

BJ1581 .R515 2002
158—dc21

                                 2002023031

02 03 04 05 06 JTC/QW 10 9 8 7 6 5 4 3 2 1

To Jane, Josh, and Aaron

who have shared with me
the celebration of life's adventures

HLR

To Steve, Aaron, Rachel, and Rebecca

L'chaim—to life!

THB

contents

Introduction

When I first thought of writing a book on the topic of the celebration of life's daily moments, I had in mind the complexities of our fast-paced, high-tech lives. I thought that explaining the role of celebrating moments, in the face of the "hot" kaleidoscope of events that flood and sometimes confuse us, was a good idea—an important idea. Now, after witnessing the devastating attacks on the World Trade Center and the Pentagon, after witnessing the mass grief and loss of innocence suffered nationwide and beyond, I am even more convinced that celebrating life's moments is an important antidote to what is poisoning our very humanity.

My first thoughts after the attacks that shook us and the world were that my book was trivial and paled against such a backdrop. Then I listened to my friends, colleagues, and patients and heard this sentiment expressed about their own lives and their own work. The realization that our sense of our selves, our lives, and our work was so easily shaken made me see that this topic was even more important and more timely, because the role of celebration in our life, and in humanity itself, is that of an identifier and a marker of what *is* of value about our individual and collective existences.

To celebrate life's moments is the big work of even seemingly small events. A dinner together, an achievement at school or work, the smile of a baby, the touch of love—all are moments to be celebrated. It is both the small and the large events of life that lend value and texture to our lives. If we don't put effort into celebrating these moments they can be lost, and the very texture of living goes with them.

To celebrate is to integrate. Celebration integrates our lives lived in the world with our lives lived in the interior of our minds and hearts—our being. If there are two themes that will pervade this book it is that of *integrating* all elements of our life and *connecting* within and outside ourselves, across the generations preceding us, and into the future. The function of celebration is to do all this, and in doing so, to help us create our own legacy and a legacy of our time— our changing, disturbing, dangerous, wonderful time.

(The Universal Search)

I celebrate myself and sing myself.

WALT WHITMAN, "SONG OF MYSELF" (1855)

I grew up in a home where people came to die. Some came to sit for a while, some to stay. They all came to be with my mother. Long before I understood the psychological undercurrents that draw us toward one another for comfort and meaning, I was an apprentice to my mother. She created a home so vibrant with life that it was in her care, or at least in her presence, that many of her closest friends and family members came to pass some of their last days.

Some memories rest just inside the mind's eye. When I close my eyes, I can see with my young-boy eyes my mother listening to the many visitors to our home, and those she visited on her daily rounds around town and in our neighborhood. I can see her, still a young woman, listening intently, rolling her eyes in wonder, laughing at the bittersweet moments of their immigrant lives or the ironies of their survival, crying at their losses, nodding and shaking her head as she absorbed their stories.

Mom was wise, but not especially so. The child of Austrian immigrant parents, she had only a high school education. She spoke simply and did not pretend to offer amazing insights into life. What she did have was an amazing capacity to listen and engage. I don't even recall that she asked many questions, and yet the stories emerged from our frequent visitors.

Theirs were lives with a few exceptional details in common. This was in Chicago, in the late 1940s, and they had all emigrated from other lands and other lives before the shadow of Hitler's evil had totally covered their world. Some had come from hardship, some from comfort. They all had come to stay alive. Those left behind were dead; there was no going back. They all had to learn a new language and new customs. Some had to learn to be poor. They all had to learn to be free.

Many had made marriages, not so much the fruit of romance as the hard crust of economic and family survival. They had children and they loved them, but their children's lives were rooted in American ways and words so different from their own that in the end, they sought out one another—especially my mother—to tell their stories.

People were drawn to her, not for advice, but because she created a space, in her presence, where each one felt heard and valued. She seemed to know, intuitively, that they needed to tell their stories; that there was something to be gained from the telling, and from the listening. She was an ardently self-motivated and self-taught student of living life. As she listened, they grew stronger, better able to face the rest of their day, or the rest of their life, or, sometimes, even the end of their life.

She felt no need to judge, and did not do it. Where I, as a child, would find fault, she would bring explanation, illuminating the complexity of human behavior. When I would ask selfish questions, like "What did they do for you?" she would tell me that once, long ago, they had done something good for someone else. She was wise enough, but the quality that drew people to her was her sense that there was meaning in the telling and the listening. She allowed them to retrace their lives. She saw merit in those lives.

My mother was not a social diva. She didn't throw lavish parties or organize special events. If I had asked her about "celebration" she would have shrugged and said she did it like everybody else—on the holidays. She would have been wrong. My mother was the master teacher of the celebration of everyday life. With her talent for listening, talking, and tending relationships, my mother instinctively provided the structure in shared moments to celebrate the lives of those around her. She was an expert, a *celebrant*. She was not a priest or a rabbi; she was a woman who simply had it in her—deeply in her, as if in her genetic code—to celebrate life in all its vicissitudes.

In this mélange of the young and old, the hearty and ailing, many of whom spoke only Yiddish, I grew to be a witness and a listener, a student of life stories rich in detail, character, humor, and sorrow. These stories spoke deeply of the beauty, if not glamour, of everyday existence. These lives reflected a promise of something lasting, meaningful—and only sometimes joyful—to be discovered in the way we live and share our lives. I didn't know it then, but I was an apprentice to her in this way of life; I grew to be a celebrant, too.

It would take years for me to recognize the value of my mother's kind of wisdom and those simple lessons of my childhood home. I would discover over the next several decades, through my work as a physician and a psychoanalyst, with patients and in my life, that the power of celebration as my mother practiced it—the telling, the listening, the reflection, the participation and sharing in the moment—shapes us in the deepest and most profound ways, not only by its presence in our lives, but also by its absence.

• CELEBRATION REDEFINED: THE INSIDE STORY •

When we hear the word *celebration,* we typically think of an *external event*—an activity, a ritual or a ceremony—something that happens around us. From the moment we are born, to the day we die, cultural, religious, and family celebrations mark our passage through life. Event and ritual are a prominent part of celebration, but they are only one part of the much deeper, richer meaning of celebration in our lives.

Celebration, as my mother lived it, and as I use the word in my work and in this book, is an *internal experience.* It begins with the recognition of something special in ourselves, and beyond ourselves. Celebration is our interaction with the moment, our experience of ourselves in the context of the moment, and the power of that interaction to define us, both to ourselves and to others, and to shape our identity, our sense of possibility, even our destiny.

Celebration is a mental experience with both conscious and unconscious dimensions. At a conscious level, celebration offers us a way—possibly the only way we know—to hold the moment, to engage in it fully and experience it fully, to experience ourselves and others in that context and feel grounded in the scheme of life and history. At an unconscious level, the celebrated moment imprints itself on us, adding to the hidden store of impressions that shape our thinking and color our view throughout life. In celebration we enrich our lives with the experience of our shared history as well as the shared moment. We may share a moment with others or with the memory of others, with God or simply with our own inner self. To do this in an ongoing way brings many of these enriched moments together to add depth of feeling and meaning to our daily lives. Our capacity to celebrate enables us to experience the deeper dimensions of any moment—at work, in love, or at play—as part of a human experience greater than ourselves.

Celebration may be joyful, or not. It may be reflective, solemn, or even sad. As we experienced in the aftermath of the terrorist attacks on home soil on September 11, even moments of horror or tragedy are celebrated in the way we engage them, find meaning in them, and bring meaning to them through our individual experiences and the experiences we share with others. (5

After the attacks, as a nation we moved quickly from the role of stunned victim to the role of determined activist, through rescue operations at the crash sites, through generosity with contributions of our volunteered time, money, and other resources, and through a military response aimed at breaking the network of global terrorism. In media reports and pictures that changed hour by hour, day by day, we witnessed our collective interaction with the moment. We saw ourselves, as a nation, transformed from shocked, grieving people under attack, to strong, caring, resilient people devoted to freedom. In subsequent days, we have seen debate over details of our ongoing collective response, debate befitting our celebrated identity as a nation that seeks to balance public safety with freedom of speech and other civil liberties.

Celebration shapes our individual lives in similar ways. The way we define ourselves and others, and the way we feel known by them, shapes our experience of everyday life at work and at home, in every relationship. For instance, depending on your previous experience, in a moment of achievement you may feel joyful and deserving, or you may feel guilty and undeserving. In a moment when you are confronted with someone else's need, you may welcome the opportunity to help or resent the expectation. In a moment of adversity or disappointment, you may experience yourself as a helpless victim, or as a problem solver, a survivor, even a hero. The way you define or celebrate yourself shapes your perception and your reaction to everyone and everything.

• WORLDS APART, THE COMMONALITY OF CELEBRATED, UNCELEBRATED LIVES •

It was in Angola a few years ago, immersed in a culture decimated by war, that the concept of this deeper quality of celebration took shape in my mind as such a defining influence in our lives. I had traveled to Angola as part of an effort by the World Bank to better understand how to help this struggling country make more effective use of economic aid. In a briefing prior to my departure, World Bank specialists explained that despite ample funds and expertise directed toward Angola for economic recovery, the effort was foundering because the people seemed too depressed to participate productively in the opportunities offered.

The statistical report alone offered a grim context for economic recovery. Thirty years of civil war had left more than half a million people dead, and nearly four million more people without homes, living in the streets or in minimal shelters. More than 150,000 children were now orphans. Everywhere, virtually everyone was sick or suffering. Sick and maimed men, women, and children languished in the roads and shelters and fields. The sight of dead or dying people of all ages was not uncommon. Even the desolate earth held the threat of more violence and death: more than ten million land mines planted by the military lay ready to explode at a touch.

Families, communities, and the culture of an entire people had been decimated by war, hunger, and disease. The basic rural, agrarian lifestyle had been destroyed by the forced dislocation of the people and the threat of the abandoned land mines in many fields. Many urban centers had been severely damaged or destroyed, and those that were intact were overburdened by rural refugees. The traditional social order of family and community leadership had been compromised or completely lost in some areas. Even the collective memory of a time when Angola had been Angolan had been wiped out by four hundred years of colonial exploitation.

(7

Facts and figures offered a concrete measure of the misery there, but a formula for recovery was more elusive. Money alone was clearly not the answer. I traveled to Angola to learn from the people; if possible, to identify what was needed to enable them to use new material resources and economic opportunities provided by the international community more effectively to increase their own productivity. As a witness to this cultural devastation, and as a student of it, I would learn two seemingly contradictory, but equally important, lessons about the nature and power of celebration.

First and most obvious, the destruction of the people and their way of life had been so complete, the loss and pain so debilitating, that they had lost the capacity to celebrate or affirm their lives in a way that we might recognize as recovery. The traditional sources of ritual and cultural teaching—the tribal shaman or medicine man, the death rituals, spiritual practice, music, dance, and tribal arts, for instance—had been wiped out or severely disabled in the war. Without these key elements of cultural survival, the struggle for individual survival was made even more difficult.

The second lesson emerged more slowly. As I continued my work there, listening and observing closely, I saw a different facet of their spirit. Despite the devastation and hopelessness of their situation, the Angolan people showed enormous courage, determination, and dignity. Young children laughed and played in the rubble of war, despite their obvious hunger and suffering. Young mothers, mostly widowed or abandoned, labored to exhaustion to tend their families, ignoring the odds that their elderly parents and babies would die like so many others died around them. In one instance, an elder statesman spoke confidently of the work he and others were doing to bring about recovery, even though he knew that the task would extend far beyond his own life.

Everywhere I looked I saw people determined to live, to rise above conditions, to embrace life, however short or hard that life might be and whatever obstacles might stand in the way. They affirmed one another, lived completely in the moment, and found the courage to continue despite their adversity. Immersed in this landscape of misery and death, they invested themselves in life.

What made it possible? How could they do it? To understand this seeming paradox—the cultural depression following such war trauma, alongside the determination to live and, in some people, the will to recover—I had to return to the basic biology and psychology of our humanity. The will to live, to survive and grow, is innate. It is biological. That fundamental aspect of humanity remained alive amid devastation and shock from war and violence. The ability to define oneself in the context of a nation or a culture or a socioeconomic system requires more than mere biology. It requires the personal history of being celebrated for oneself in one's own right, and in the social system. All whom I met, no matter how miserable, were trying to survive. Those who had enjoyed the privileges of a good start in life, however modest it might have been in material comforts, were better able to envision a future for themselves, and plan and participate in creating it. Even the parliamentarian who knew he would not live to see the recovery completed acted with a sense of his place in the future of his country.

As I listened to the stories of the survivors and the emerging voices of leadership, I heard in their different stories a common message. In essence, it was that the traditional sources of community-centered ritual and cultural "knowing"—the shaman, the community-centered rituals and creative expressions using music, dance, and art—would be the most effective connecting points through which to deliver aid in a way that was meaningful to the people. It was through these connections that the people felt valued and celebrated themselves and one another as individuals and as a culture with a history and a future. If economic aid were to be effective, this rebuilding of personal spirit would have to be addressed before anyone could expect the people to be able and willing to focus more productively on the high-end tasks of developing economic recovery and rebuilding society. Like the elder statesman, the Angolans who held the key to recovery for themselves and for their nation were those who, even under these harshest of circumstances, were able to recognize something special in themselves and beyond themselves, and who lived to tend that ember of possibility, moment by moment, day by day.

Upon my return home, I was still filled with the suffering I had witnessed in Angola and the lessons I had learned from these traumatized people whose desire and capacity to celebrate life held the seeds of their recovery. I was reminded, too, of my mother and the way she and her community of family and friends, faced with adversity, had invested themselves in the detail and texture of the most everyday moments, creating lives that were rich and full, even in the context of struggle.

As a psychoanalyst and a consultant, I have seen firsthand the devastation of spirit in individuals, as well as whole cultures, when celebration has been denied or distorted. My patients include many adult men and women, and adolescents, who cannot define themselves in their own lives, in their families, in marriages or friendships, or in their societies. These people, including many whom appear successful in their work or school environments, feel desperately empty, unable to celebrate themselves or anything else in life. Time and again, a patient's suffering can be traced back to their experience of having been uncelebrated in childhood or in other critical junctures or relationships in life. Whether their troubles have arisen in the context of relationships or personal endeavor, those who have felt uncelebrated in their life or their work find it more difficult to celebrate themselves and others.

To have been celebrated is to be able to celebrate. To have not been celebrated or not invited into the celebration of life is to be unable to celebrate oneself and life itself.

The pattern is consistent, evident in failed marriages and damaged relationships, emotionally isolated or abused children, dysfunctional families, self-destructive behavior, or a more generalized cynicism about the mystery and miracle of life. Even at a societal level, the history of celebrated and uncelebrated lives defines the quality of relationship between management and labor, between dominant and minority races and religious groups, between men and women. Those who celebrate themselves and others create connections and generate possibility. Those who celebrate themselves at the expense of others, or those who deny celebration to others, generate conflict and suffering. And those who are unable to celebrate themselves or others struggle and suffer deeply.

We all struggle, to greater or lesser degrees, with fear, anger, helplessness, loneliness, loss, problems attaching, problems letting go, abandonment, betrayal, chronic idealization, chronic cynicism, power gained, power lost, having, not having, achieving stability,

10)

achieving change, love, indifference, ennui, or frantic overinvolvement. In these moments, we feel a sense of disconnection and dissatisfaction, and a yearning for a more deliberate, meaningful experience of life.

Sometimes we struggle with incongruity. We go through the motions of a celebratory moment but feel emotionally shortchanged by the celebratory process. This is the obligatory family holiday gathering that only renews old wounds and inflicts new ones. This is the celebrated professional or scholastic high-achiever who inwardly feels empty or unsatisfied.

When a mother says to her son, "But your father brags about you to everyone," and the boy does not know of his father's feelings directly from him, there has been a successful celebratory moment in the father's bragging, but a failed celebratory process between father and child. In the same way, to acknowledge the divine or spiritual in our lives, but not include such acknowledgment in the daily rituals of life—or to engage in rote ritual, but not practice what we preach—is to successfully stage the external event, but fail to provide celebratory process. It is simply not enough to think good thoughts. To be effective, celebration must be put to work in our lives.

Contemporary life inundates us with events and rituals designed to entertain and engage us—supposedly to celebrate us—and yet, we know intuitively that these ritualized events are not, in and of themselves, genuine celebrations of ourselves. I have seen a child glow with excitement over the simplest gift from a close friend, while another child grows bored and petulant at his own extravagant birthday party, entertained, but at a deeper level, unnourished by the superficial show.

We experience a similar disconnect in adult lives, when work, family, or friendships are more draining than sustaining; or when spending on clothes, homes, cars, electronics, and other accoutrements fill lives in which close and loving relationships are missing. At one time or another, we all experience moments that either make us feel inwardly rich, whole, and celebrated; or cut off from that experience, and uncelebrated.

We struggle to find the balance between our work and personal lives—between commitments to family, friends, community, and ourselves. If we are parents with children at home, we wonder how best to make their childhood the kind that will fortify them for life; if they are grown, we search for new ways to relate to them and their life choices. Some of us are rich in family traditions. Some of us feel trapped by them. Most of us struggle at times to breathe new life into traditions that seem rote or stale in the context of contemporary life.

The same tools and trends that have made us more efficient in so many practical ways have changed the very nature of human interaction and shared experience in those realms, and often distanced us in important human ways. We can buy everything, from groceries to cars to underwear to vacations, from print or on-line catalogs or services, without ever speaking to a human. Increasingly, E-mail and automated telephone answering systems have taken the place of more traditional means of communication. Even in our recreational pastimes, computer games and virtual reality, in many cases, have eliminated the need to play with a partner.

Necessity, which we call the mother of invention, also is more importantly the catalyst for human contact and collaboration. The more we use conveniences that eliminate our need for one another, the more limited become our opportunities to know ourselves in relation to others, and to know others in a way that brings meaning to their lives and to our own, even if it's just for a few minutes in passing.

Maggie, whose three adult children and six grandchildren live in Dallas, Seattle, and Omaha, far from her Boston home, longed for a closer relationship with her grandchildren, especially as they reached school age. Periodic visits were the best they all could do; phone calls were more frequent but always felt rushed and a bit superficial. Nobody, including Maggie, seemed able to maintain correspondence through letters. It was nobody's fault. Everyone loved everyone. Everyone missed everyone. But time and distance trumped good intentions, and Maggie felt cut off from the family she had always envisioned sharing life with as a loving grandmother. Then one day, after a yoga class at the community center, a friend invited her to attend a beginners' computer class down the hall. There Maggie discovered E-mail, and with that, began to correspond with her faraway grandchildren in a way that clicked in their active cyberspace lives. The steady flow of messages back and forth, over time, gave Maggie the opportunity to share her thoughts and memories with each grandchild, and hear back about their days in greater detail. Their face-to-face visits were no more frequent than in the past, the phone calls were still rushed, but their ongoing E-mail conversation gave Maggie's relationship with her grandchildren a new, more intimate, dimension.

As we become technologically advanced, we need to go deeper in the way we address the impact of technology on our human family, near and far, and the quality of life for humankind now and in the future. Technology itself is not the enemy. The way we choose to use it either distances us from others or brings us closer.

We must ask ourselves:

How can we use our resources to strengthen our connections with others rather than insulate ourselves from the challenge of closeness?

THE UNIVERSAL SEARCH

How can we use information and technological prowess to enhance our search for self-knowledge, rather than to avoid looking inward?

As our families spread farther and farther apart to accommodate work demands, divorce, and other adjustments to modern life, how has distance changed the core experience of our relationships and our ability to share our lives in meaningful ways with family and community? How can we bridge those gaps?

In this context of contemporary life, how can we create those environments, within ourselves, our families, and our communities, that welcome us as we are, that give us a place to grow, and that help us to avoid the lie that we are connected when in fact we live a disconnected life?

• Celebration at Our Fingertips, or at Arm's Length •

Each of us yearns to live a celebrated life: to celebrate life and to feel celebrated. We want to love and be loved, to know joy and be able to weather adversity. In solitude and intimacy, and in the grand scheme of things, we want to feel that our lives have merit and meaning.

For most of us, it does not take psychotherapy or psychoanalysis to learn to do this. For most of us, any lack of celebration in our lives will respond to our attention. Every day affords us new opportunities to embrace life in the fullest, most affirming way. We can do this by consciously engaging with life and life events through our interactions with family, friends, coworkers, and others; in our most practical relationships and our most spiritual ones; and in the way we are attuned to our inner selves.

Mrs. K, the kindergarten teacher at my son's elementary school, greeted each child each day with a handshake, a straight look in the eye, and a genuine inquiry into their well-being. She took just that moment, but it was long enough to ask and to listen. She made the others wait if the response needed time to be heard or if she had some wisdom to impart. Day in and day out, she greeted them with her eyes focused and her smile warm and her whole being excited about the day that lay ahead for both of them together. It was a ritual that enriched the lives of everyone who came through her door, including Mrs. K.

Linda, a highly respected and beloved manager, heads up the research and development division of a major international technology company, where her staff repeatedly outperforms the competition and shows the lowest turnover rate in the industry. She has earned a reputation for discovering talent and cultivating it by creating a corporate climate that celebrates individuals for their professional contribution and their personal qualities alike.

Isaac, whom I met in war-ravaged Angola, worked as a photographer for the local township at community events, but he was quick to explain to me (through an interpreter) that he was "really an artist," although circumstances in his country were so harsh, that no one had any interest in discussing art. Even so, he continued to paint, continued to see himself as an artist. He wanted to show me his paintings so that "someone else can see what I have learned about life." It was Isaac's capacity to celebrate his life, and life itself, amid the worst of human misery that carried him over the seemingly insurmountable obstacles to survive, to live, to understand some of his world, and even to have moments of joy and connection in an impromptu encounter such as ours.

Leah and Sam retired from successful corporate careers to become inner-city high school teachers. As teachers, they were gifted and passionate, but their most inspired piece of teaching came in the form of notes they began to send home with the children, complimenting their thoughtful turns of phrases or interpretations of ideas, or praising them for their thorough science lab reports. The children had never before received such personal, positive notes as these. The notes got their attention, and the attention of their parents. This simple recognition changed the way they thought about themselves as students, which proved the more powerful lesson needed before they could open fully to learning all that was available to them in the classroom.

Celebration, and the yearning for it in our lives, is universal and instinctive. We are born with it. We can do a lot to encourage this instinct or we can blunt it in many ways. Sometimes our history impairs our search; sometimes it offers us grounding for new exploration. I believe that we all wish to learn how to celebrate our lives.

For the Angolan people, social and economic recovery depended on creating a mechanism for individuals to be recognized for their existence and their contribution to society. For my patients, psychological recovery calls for tracing the thread of celebration through their lives, to find the origins of neglect that have denied them celebration of their existence and the value of their individual participation in life.

For any of us, if we can overcome inner obstacles and choose to bring that richness into our lives and the lives of those around us, then the celebrated life is within our grasp.

Celebration offers this if we recognize its intricate dimensions, the power it wields in shaping who we are, and how we can use it consciously to infuse everyday life with meaning that sustains us. By enabling us to merge what is meaningful in our past with the reality of a given moment in our lives today, celebration is the most valuable psychological tool we have for meeting challenges in life, and living fully and richly in the present.

(The Elements 2 of Celebration)

That far land we dream about,
Where every man is his own architect.
ROBERT BROWNING, *RED COTTON NIGHTCAP*
COUNTRY (1873)

Our fondest memories and most moving life experiences are more than a mental picture gallery to enjoy when
time allows. Throughout life, these memories and life experiences
have something to teach us about ourselves and our world.

These are internal lessons about the internal experience of
celebration and its power to shape us, hurt us, heal us, enrich
us. Whether your memories and experiences include a midnight
Christmas mass, the birth of your own child, or the summer you
spent as a kid at your aunt's house, picking strawberries from
her garden and smelling her home cooking, the magic that
transformed those experiences into something deeply meaningful and memorable to you is always available to transform every-

day life into a rich, full, satisfying experience. That magic is the internal experience of celebration, and the way this internal process creates a unique and powerful interface between you and the moment.

Twentieth-century scholar Rabbi Abraham Joshua Heschel called the Sabbath an "architect of time" in the way its rituals provide structure, purpose, beauty, and access to a spiritual experience of time. Beginning with the naming of the Sabbath, each step in the ritual—the lighting of candles, the blessings said over the bread and the wine, the shared meal and reflections—draws us into the moment, and heightens our experience of it.

In the same way, celebration of everyday life is the architect of our inner lives. It creates the blueprint for our mental life, the template for our outlook and behavior. Just as an architect arranges basic building materials to become working, stable structures, celebration designs and orders our mental life, using the pieces of information, sensations, experiences, emotions, and responses that our mind collects from our experience of a moment. These pieces are stored randomly in the mind, some up front in our conscious mind, but many more in the vast recess of the unconscious. As we encounter a new experience or task, the elements of celebration allow us to open the stores of memory and even forgotten experience, and order these random pieces into a sensible relationship with one another to build a meaningful structure for understanding our experience.

The passage of time does not, in itself, make the moments of our life meaningful and celebrated. However, if we are willing to suspend our interest in other goals of the day, or the hour, or the task, and allow ourselves to simply *be* in the moment, then we can purposefully experience the texture of it: the sound, sight, color, emotions, and the presence of others with us or remembered in the moment. We can experience the sense of history evoked by the moment. We can loosen the barrier between the conscious and unconscious and in doing so let the two mingle, and deepen our experience. We can bathe ourselves in all of that, elevating the moment from a blur that races past to a moment that nourishes us.

Five elements of celebration give us access to this richer, more meaningful experience of any moment:

In celebration, we recognize the moment. We recognize a moment when we turn our attention to it. We must look for what is special. We're accustomed to taking our cues from our calendar of holidays, but the celebration of life calls upon us to recognize that which is special in any moment.·

One day I was working at my desk in my home study when my son walked in and sat down in the armchair next to me. "You know," he started, showing no sense that he was interrupting me, "I've been struggling with a problem." Teenagers are not known to live by the same sense of time as their parents. Conversations are sometimes rare and often untimely. However, this was about to be one and I needed to recognize the moment and put down my work and listen. This was a special moment for both of us.

We push hurriedly through dozens of interactions in a day, countless moments when we might pause, in conversation with someone or simply in thought by ourselves, and recognize what is special. This is the first step into celebration.

In celebration, we name the moment. We name a moment when we consciously identify it. In naming the experience, we build in a handle with which to hold, turn, inspect, grab onto the experience. By naming, we place the new experience into the infrastructure of our mind. We may name it in familiar ways, calling it a "birthday" or "anniversary," or a holiday, such as Christmas, Passover, Kwanza, or Ramadan. Sometimes we recognize the moment solely with the power of our attention. We stop what we're doing, turn off the TV, step away from our work, as I did with my son, or otherwise indicate to someone "I am listening to you" or "your feelings matter to me." Or, by contrast, when we deny someone our focused attention we may communicate that "You are not important to me" or "Your ideas are not valued."

In celebration we share the moment. This may be a deliberate sharing, as it is when we engage in conversation or song, dinner with our family, or on a larger scale at a religious service, community festival, or other organized event. Or sharing can be of a simpler kind. In sharing, we use one another as interpreters, filters, scaffolds, and safety nets, so that we are not overwhelmed by too much—too much information, emotion, sensation. We feel held in the moment. Sharing lends depth, texture, and meaning in history and time for the new event. And what if we are alone? A moment can be shared with one's inner self or those whose memory we hold inside ourselves, or with our God.

In celebration, we open ourselves and bring ourselves forth most fully into a thoughtful and sensory awareness of the moment. When our minds are open fully to the senses, to memory and to wonder, to pain and to joy, and to those who share the moment with us, our conscious interaction with the moment loosens the barriers to the unconscious, allowing us to experience the moment in a deeper way. We draw upon unconscious aspects of genetic and biological history, our nature, and the history imparted to us of our own life and the lives of our people and our culture.

In my home growing up, my mother kept a kind of kosher kitchen, observing the spirit, though clearly not the letter, of the traditional Jewish dietary laws. In the years following the dropping of

THE ELEMENTS OF CELEBRATION

the strict kosher laws in our home, my mother continued to "kosher" all meats—even pork—by soaking them in brine. As I grew into a cynical critic of my parents, one day I teased her by asking her why she tried to kosher the pork by soaking it in brine, when it was, after all, pork, and verboten by kosher dictates. She looked a bit pained by my question but answered in a manner that put me back in my place, both literally and figuratively. She said, "This tradition is not to make holy the meat that cannot be made holy according to kosher laws. I do it because generations of Jewish women for five thousand years have been doing this to remember their heritage and their God. Doing this connects me to them, and *us* to that heritage. God I will leave up to you."

Through this kitchen tradition, my mother celebrated a connection through time and heritage to these women of faith, and placed herself among them.

Acknowledging mystery and awe. The sense of enchantment at discovery, awe in the face of mystery, wonder at the immensity of the universe in which we live, are all natural parts of our mental life. Through our openness to mystery and awe, we locate ourselves in a scheme of life and history. It is at once to surrender, humbly, to that which is larger than ourselves, and at the same time to feel ourselves part of the grandeur of life. The celebrated moment contains a sense of awe and humility in the face of that which is mysterious to us and is greater than our own existence.

We only have to listen to the uniform voices of a great choir singing out the praise of the greater powers of the spirit in our lives to understand. We are lifted above our own mortality by the melody and the uniform control of voices singing in unison and by the sense of shared worship. To witness the great migrations of birds or fishes who move over immense distances to complete their cycle of life and continue their species places us in the greatness of evolution. Our life is important and central to the celebratory experience, but it is only a part of a great mystery of life itself, and particularly of the evolution of the human life and mind.

If you think of a holiday or experience that has great meaning to you, you will find these five elements in some form. Where any of these elements are missing, you will find an experience that falls short of being meaningful in the way you might wish. If any of these elements are routinely missing in your experience of life, then be concerned. Life can be better and richer and contain deeper meaning. If you recognize this missing element, you are prepared to fill the void.

• **CELEBRATION AS ACCESS TO SELF-KNOWLEDGE** •

For most of my career as a physician and psychoanalyst, *celebration* was never a word I would have thought to use to describe the process of psychotherapy or psychoanalysis. Anyone familiar with therapy or analysis knows it is hard work, sometimes uncomfortable and even painful work, to examine your innermost life and come to terms with what you find. Introspection is challenging. Memory delivers pain as well as pleasures.

That said, *celebration* is now the best word I can use to describe the work and healing of therapy. Psychoanalysis and psychotherapy are ultimately about helping people discover and create their own life story. Psychotherapy, and to a greater extent psychoanalysis, create, replace, or repair the missing emotional framework for celebrating the life of the individual, and in so doing they repair a damaged emotional life.

As we journey together through psychoanalysis, we examine the past, and we see how the past shapes our present and our future. Patterns emerge. We can see how we spend our lives trying to gain what was lost or deficient. We see our compulsive efforts to undo injustices, which ironically lead us to repeat the injustices in our lives. We see the motivations behind what before we simply called bad habits. We supply text to our lives and our behavior, where before there was only action. We create choice where before there seemed to be none. In short, we learn to celebrate our textured lives.

One way to look at the talking therapies is that they represent a celebration of the individual and the individuality of the patient. People come to therapy to heal psychic pain. That pain can result from recent traumas or long-ago formative traumas.

If we can look at the life of each person as a tapestry, then those who seek therapy or analysis are those whose tapestry has rents or threadbare edges. For those who have suffered rents in the tapestry of their lives by virtue of the stresses and strains on the fabric of their life, we must find the loose ends of their story and reweave them on the worktable of therapy or analysis.

We talk. We poke around in the tear and say, "Oh, there is a loose end. How did you drop that one?" We pick it up and hold it in view and continue to look for others. "There is a match." We can now connect one end of the tear with the other. We can begin to close the rent.

Sometimes we find out that the fabric of the story is not well constructed. The threadbare quality speaks not to stress and strain but to insufficiency in the construction of the tapestry from the outset. In those cases, our job is a bit harder. We must move into the basic construction of the tapestry and find the colors and lines of the story and weave new fabric—the fabric of the new relationship—into the place of the old to reconstruct the tapestry.

To bring the metaphor into the reality of the therapeutic experience, we are looking to recognize the moments, present and past, in a person's life. The very exercise of therapy is a recognition of the individual as being worthwhile. But then we go into the story of the person and we name the moments—the formative and deformative moments—of their life. We share their hurts and the manifestations of their hurts. We bring ourselves to the moment of sharing and we see a person become stronger, healing before our eyes. We acknowledge the mystery of their life and the hurts and healing of their life. We stand, together, in awe of the process we have created and shared. This constitutes a celebration of the person.

When we find a person who cannot do those things with us in therapy, but who wants to heal, we must create what is missing or we must remove the obstacles to sharing—to celebrating—so that a celebration can take place.

GEORGE: "JUST A BASTARD"

George was a very successful man who came to therapy because he felt "a bit depressed," he said, and he was drinking "a bit too much." George warned me that he doubted therapy would help much. He was, as he put it, "simply a bastard," and that was all there was to it. He really didn't like his wife or his two children. Because they got in the way of his life, he resented them. Marriage and family had seemed like a good idea at some earlier time, years ago, but now he felt it had been a mistake. However, divorce would have shattered his image and ruined his career, so he lived this resentful life and stayed away as much as possible.

"I wasn't cut out for this bonding thing," he said that day. "I'm just a bastard who should have lived alone," he asserted with some pride, in his frank self-analysis.

George told me, in passing, that his two children were not getting much quality attention from him or his equally unhappy and troubled wife, so in order to settle them happily away from him and the tension at home, he had searched far and wide and found the perfect boarding school for each child. One child loved music, so he had found a school with a rich music curriculum. One was very athletic, so he had searched out the school with the most promising sports opportunities.

When he finished his description of himself, which was more like a character assassination, I said, "That was a really considerate, loving, and devoted act you did in finding just the right school for each child."

He scoffed at my suggestion. Considerate? Loving? Devoted?

"I'm getting them out of the house," he retorted.

"There are many ways to get children out of a house. You chose to find the best fit for each one. Why is it so important to cast yourself in the worst light?" I asked. "Are you afraid of being called loving and considerate?"

George had never been approached with this thought, and he first reacted with hostility to my invitation to share this side of himself, then suspicion. It clearly pained him, and he responded by pulling back, with curt, dismissive, short answers. However, in the course of our conversation that day his defensive, critical demeanor began to soften. In the course of analysis, George began to recognize that he was a sad, needy man with a capacity for harshness, and a man with the capacity to be loving, considerate, and devoted. We turned our attention to this aspect of George's life. The issue was not simply that he had a capacity for caring that begged to be used and recognized, but also that the recognition itself—my pointing it out in that first conversation—had pained him, eliciting a hostile, defensive response. The focus of his treatment would be to understand that pain, beginning with its origins.

George had been born into an ambitious, distinguished "all-American" family, with a prominent father and dutiful mother who was also the chorus of praise to his father's life. George's life was supposed to be an elaboration of that chorus of praise for his father's life. George's life was not his own to be lived and celebrated for who he was.

A talented youth, George excelled at academics, but not sports. His failure to be a star athlete was seen as a disappointing blemish on his father's reputation. How could his father, a former athlete, have an athletically inept son? Yet his academic achievements were begrudgingly valued as "at least something" about which his father could boast.

When he was older George was told, "At least make a good marriage." It was unclear who chose his wife. He couldn't remember, but he did recall the sense of approval in his father's face. She had the right credentials.

It was funny, George said, how his accomplishments in life, which far exceeded his father's, were always held up as second best. No matter how far he climbed in the national levels of his profession, his accomplishments were held wanting against his father's local achievements. George had always felt that he was deemed "good enough, but not quite as perfect." The shadow of his father eclipsed his life and the recognition of who he was. George had swallowed his anger so early and so thoroughly that he could not see that his view of himself as "simply a bastard" was the product of that anger turned inward against himself.

The conditions of George's history had created the impoverished and self-punishing climate of his interior life. He had defined himself this way for all of his adult life, but he had never explored the deeper emotions that made it so difficult for him to express love and feel loved. Finally, in the celebratory process of analysis, George was able to come to terms with destructive feelings that originated in his childhood experience, and which had only been amplified when he married and began a family of his own.

George came to recognize his long unresolved anger about how his parents had shortchanged him in his rightful expectation to be honored for who *he* was. He also recognized the damage that their parenting *and* his hidden anger had wrought in shaping his sense of himself and his relationship with his wife and children. His vocabulary for emotional expression had grown, and now he had the words to name and describe those early feelings of being uncelebrated, and their ripple effect in his adult life. We shared these moments of self-discovery, and in doing so placed George's life thus far in the context of the larger story of his parents and extended family, and his roles as son, husband, father, and professional man.

He was finally able to recognize and own his feelings—the full range of them—and with his newfound capacity to feel love and hate and regret and remorse, came the capacity to share and to celebrate others. It was too late to save George's marriage, but in time George was able to transform his desiccated life into a celebrated life and overcome an uncelebrated childhood by building a framework for celebration in his adult life.

• LISTENING FOR THE SUBTLE SOUNDS OF CELEBRATION •

We encounter the nuances of celebration constantly in our lives. If we are alert for them, we can discover in conflict the opportunities to learn more about ourselves, which we can then use to help one another.

Sherry and David had been married for several years, had two school-age children, and had drifted into traditional patterns for dividing housework that placed the responsibility for cooking meals almost entirely on Sherry. As her career began to require a greater commitment of time and energy from her, she began to resent the continuous kitchen duty, and responded by announcing "cold cereal mornings" when she would not be cooking. The children didn't mind, but on those days, David would sulk and often skip breakfast entirely, a reaction Sherry found "childish," inappropriate, and infuriating. Finally, in exasperation one day, she confronted him.

"Why does this always have to turn into such a big issue for you?" she asked. "What makes you feel so entitled, that I should have to fix you a hot breakfast every day?"

David was embarrassed and defensive, but her question had struck a deep chord. Surprising even himself, he was able to explain instantly why it felt like a big issue. David's mother and father had divorced when he was five years old, his father had dropped out of his life, and his mother had found a job that demanded long hours, often through mealtimes. Whenever his mother was unable to be home for breakfast or dinner, he was expected to help himself to a bowl of cold cereal. This he did, and from that time on, through his days away at college, and his years living on his own as an adult, he looked at cold cereal as a lonely meal of last resort. Whenever he was "reduced to eating cold cereal" those old grim feelings from his childhood welled up, a mix of feeling unloved, abandoned, and helpless. He knew Sherry didn't mean it that way, he said, but he couldn't help how it felt.

Sherry was taken aback by this explanation. She thought about the "meaning" of cold cereal in her own childhood. It was quite different from her husband's. In her childhood, in a mostly happy, bustling, two-parent family of five, the family typically sat down together for breakfast, and sometimes it was for cold cereal—she could still recall the lineup from which they got to choose Cheerios, Wheaties, cornflakes, or Rice Krispies. The kids read the backs of the boxes and together solved riddles and sent entries in for contests that would net them secret decoder rings or other prizes. When Sherry was hungry after school, she would fix herself a bowl of cereal and enjoy her snack in the peaceful quiet of the early afternoon kitchen, before the others descended for their snacks, or her mother began preparing dinner.

"For me, cold cereal meant being independent, not needing to wait for anybody to fix me anything. Getting things for myself and feeling happy about it," she said. Her husband's sulking attitude, however, exacerbated Sherry's feelings of resentment that she was "stuck" in an unfair division of cooking duties.

Their breakfast menu wasn't really the issue. Cold cereal was an emotional trigger, a moment loaded by David's and Sherry's different histories, their expectations of family life, and their respective needs to feel affirmed in their marriage and family life.

• MOMENTS: THE BUILDING BLOCKS OF EMOTIONAL EXPERIENCE AND MEMORY •

The elements of celebration offer five ways to access the intricate dimensions of a moment. But how does a moment, as fleeting and seemingly inconsequential an increment of time as it is, come to have such complexity and power in our minds?

First, moments contain content: sometimes action and sometimes not, sometimes thought and sometimes not, and sometimes feeling and sometimes not. We can all remember moments when someone's silence "said it all": when our failure to act was a decision to allow others to have their way; or when an absence of feeling was as important a cue to our emotions as a rush of feeling might have been.

In the cereal story above, Sherry's childhood "cold cereal moments" were happy family times or moments of independence she relished; David's were anguish, created by his parents' divorce, his father's abandonment, and his little-boy feelings of loss and helplessness.

Second, every aspect of a moment is subject to interpretation, adding to our opportunities for understanding, misunderstanding, or missing cues. Children, for instance, are quick to assume (mistakenly) that they are responsible for a parent's unhappiness— including alcoholism, depression, or divorce—and even for a parent's neglect or abuse of them. We may worry that a friend's silence means we offended them in some way, or that someone else's laughter is aimed unkindly at us. Sherry had assumed that her husband's reaction arose from a sense of entitlement, and further, that his unhappy demeanor was a sign of unhappiness with her. Neither interpretation was true.

Finally, we live a moment in two dimensions—the conscious and the unconscious. Conscious perception is a mechanical function, enabling us to access information, emotion, logic, and reason to think and act in a rational way. The unconscious absorbs our experiences in a different way, creating a vast background of sensory impressions that are formless, timeless, and without judgments or values attached.

We occasionally catch glimpses of the unconscious. A song on the radio triggers a vivid memory from years before. A feeling of déjà vu startles us with the uncanny feeling that we have lived this moment before. These expressions of the unconscious aren't always tidy and easily named, but under examination, they are always illuminating.

David's reaction to the cold cereal moment was, on a superficial level, an expression of mild annoyance; at the moment Sherry confronted him with her feelings and asked him to explain himself, his unconscious memory was roused, and it opened like a new wound.

Once these underlying feelings came forward into conscious awareness, the couple had something to talk about—a way to work through the issue, rather than remain trapped by it.

The power of a moment is neither inherently good nor bad. It is shaped by the detail and complexity of the moment, our vulnerability or openness to it, and the way we process that experience mentally. In our mental life, *experience and emotion stored in the unconscious are not dormant.* They continue to color our conscious experience of the moment. They continue to have force and pressure us toward action or decision or choice.

While we would like to think that we can respond rationally to the moment and that we make rational decisions and choices and actions, the fact is that a purely rational response is impossible. We can hope to take rational elements of the moment into consideration, but we are also always influenced by unconscious memory and associations. Our conscious and unconscious together shape our experience of a moment, and by the same token, a moment leaves its imprint on us in both ways.

Each moment offers a choice. We can recognize it or we can pass it by. Our ability to celebrate life depends on our willingness to be open to what the moment has to teach us, to be vulnerable. To the degree that we close ourselves off, for whatever reason, our experience is curtailed, and so is our access to the celebrated life for ourselves and our ability to create that for others.

I'm reminded of the experience so many people describe, myself among them, after visiting the Vietnam Veterans Memorial in Washington, D.C.—the long, low monument called "the Wall." The design is very simple. A small dip in the earth brings us to the wall, and draws us into the vortex of names of those who were sacrificed in that war. As we descend into the structure we read the names individually at first, then more collectively. We are drawn into a human tragedy that has individual names and a collective humanity. People grow silent. They become worshipful. They leave mementos. They trace the names of those they knew and those who died before them. Some weep.

Why is this slab of chiseled stone so moving? It affects us so powerfully because in that moment we experience part of history, and human tragedy, and human sacrifice, and human courage, and the span of human history that demanded all of this from all of us. At that moment we are in the midst of celebration. It cannot but be moving. The Wall is far greater than its simple architecture. As we move through it and ascend the slope, most of us feel changed by the experience.

There are those who see the Wall as nothing more than a monumental slab of stone covered with names. They may even be annoyed that others find it so moving when they feel nothing. And others may avoid visiting the Wall at all, dismissing it as "nothing to see" or "too depressing." These are people who don't recognize the value of the emotional experience of the Wall, or they suffer from an inability to celebrate this deeper experience. In this and every other moment in life, we can access the richer dimensions of experience only to the extent that we are open to the possibility they hold for us.

Each of us comes to a moment with our own history of associations and expectations. Life is composed of moments—past moments, present moments, and anticipated moments. We move forth from the womb into the world with an invisible tether to our origins and our personal history. That tether can give us a sense of safety in a scary world or it can be a constraint. To understand our response to a given moment we must go back and discover the lens through which we first saw the world, the template for celebration that we were born into, and adjust it to see ourselves anew.

(**Origins**)

The little world of childhood with its familiar sur-
roundings is a model of the greater world. The more
intensively the family has stamped its character
upon the child, the more it will tend to feel and see
its earlier miniature world again in the bigger world
of adult life.

CARL JUNG, *PSYCHOLOGICAL REFLECTIONS*

(1953)

Creation stories tell of epic beginnings, but they
also illuminate the most intimate origins of our lives. Genesis, in
the Bible, is the story of every family on your block, every person
you know. It is a story that plays out at birth for each of us, and it
was your story, in the beginning.

In Genesis, God creates heaven and earth, separates light from
darkness, names day and night, fashions man and woman, gives
them a garden, and lays down a few rules. Through this divine or-

ganizational process, God brings order to chaos and meaning to the first moments of time.

In our own Genesis, history and family organize the formless chaos of new life, creating light and darkness, order and meaning, naming us, placing us, and recognizing our new contributing role in the family story. This creation story, unique to each of us, is passed down through the generations and opened to a new page at the moment of our birth. It creates our first experience of ourselves in the world, and it becomes the foundation for our view of the world. It remains hidden from view and resistant to change, yet clearly defines the shape of our experience and understanding. Every child has an innate story, yearning to be heard and recognized. It is a story of their individual nature and their place in culture and social history. The celebration of our life unfolds from these origins.

There are those who suggest that a child is a tabula rasa when born, a blank page, which remains to be filled out by life experience. That is not true. Children are born with the encoded nature of their genetic being, and they are born with the history of their culture and their family infused into their very conception, and as the context into which they are received. This becomes what is innate and in each of us yearns to be heard and recognized, to be named and known in relationship to others—to exist.

In the beginning, as infants, we experience ourselves as one with the universe, literally. Neurologically, we are babies without borders. There is no "me" and "them" or "it." We are one with all that surrounds us and all that is in our interior. We are our heartbeat, and the heartbeat of those who hold us. We are the surface of our skin, and the surface of the skin that cradles us in arms that are relaxed or anxious. We are the natural gifts and perceptive skills, or lack of gifts and skills, with which we are endowed. We are the way our parents anticipate our birth, greet us, hold us, name us, and tend us. We are the context and the expectation—some say the destiny—they create for us and have for us. In psychology, it has been called the *nurturing surround,* but that surround also includes the interior of our being. It is this environment that, from the very beginning, shapes our sense of who we are and how we fit into the family story.

Newborns "inhale" their environment; they take it *all* in. They don't screen anything out; they don't give any single experience more weight than another, but they do notice experiences that repeat and repeat over and over again. In this early period of neurological development they don't discriminate in their understanding of this mass of details, but they do gain a great deal of information in a less than organized and useful manner. "Oh, that smile of pride and joy *is me.*" "That soothing sound I hear," coming from Mother's voice, *"is me."* "That feeling of safety and calm security, in which I am being held, *is me.*" "That tension I hear or feel *is me,*" also.

To the degree that our surround is truly nurturing, we are filled with a love and a *knowing that we exist and that we matter,* which enters every cell of our being. It generates the first neurological and psychological connections of our being—our sense of ourselves. We are filled with a physical and psychological sense of confidence that the world coming into view is a hospitable place, where we have our own particular place to live and grow, to thrive, and to have our own dreams and aspirations.

• THE FAMILY TEMPLATE FOR EMOTIONAL GROWTH •
This beginning—this entry into our nurturing surround—is our initiation to the celebratory process, and the point at which personality, history, cultural history, and the history of our parents' lives, their joys and traumas, are communicated. Before a word is ever exchanged, the way we are anticipated and welcomed into the world,

and sustained there, becomes our first taste of the celebrated life, lending order and structure to our world, and creating a lens through which we look out upon the world and make sense of it.

As we grow and can think and respond more purposefully with individuals and particular parts of our world, we move out of our universal one-ness and into a new, interactive relationship with the world around us. We begin to recognize certain faces as familiar others. Then, those faces begin to have recognizable personality qualities that we can predict. If we smile and the other smiles in return, we remember this interaction. If we cry, then the other reacts in a particular way, and we remember that, too. Although their reactions are more a reflection of their own personality than anything we bring to the moment, we experience moods that become attached to our view of these people and everyday surroundings.

This is how memories begin. They are rudimentary at first, but they are associated with faces, functions, and feelings. The constellation of our world begins to take on character. These assembled characters, with their tempos, and sounds, and tensions, and mannerisms, and idiosyncrasies are all relating to us and to one another. We no longer simply inhale a sensory experience of our surrounding environment; we purposefully interact with it. We remember and recognize, we anticipate and expect. We continue to take in the atmosphere of the family, and we always will, but now we join the family in progress as a full participant in the action and negotiation process.

Family is the organizing theme around which our consciousness grows, from the earliest childhood stages of brain development. It is where we begin to define ourselves relative to others, and as part of the larger story of family, community, history, and humankind. At the deepest level, it is where we first discover ourselves. This family template for celebration of the individual, and of life itself, colors our experience in every other realm that follows—friendship, marriage, work, and community. Our ability to celebrate ourselves and others, to create meaning and find satisfaction in life, begins here, in these earliest of communications.

• A PARENT'S SMILE, A PARENT'S SIGH: EARLIEST CONSCIOUS AND UNCONSCIOUS DIALOGUE •

Even in the earliest and most ordinary moments, parents communicate and children inhale meaning that has deep and lasting effects. Some of these early preverbal communications are conscious and clearly stated. A baby cries to make its needs known; when parents or others discern the need and satisfy it, they communicate the presence of a caring world. A baby smiles, and when we smile back, we convey the mutual pleasure of recognition.

As we communicate with our children consciously, we are also communicating unconsciously through the same smiles and ministrations, as well as through our pauses, hesitations, muscular tensions, and voice. We convey the meaning of our lives that is contained in the vast storehouse of our personal unconscious memories and experiences.

"Look what I have made!"
"Am I good enough?"
"Can I provide enough?"
"Will I ever be free again?"
"Will this child lift me out of the hopelessness of
my life?"
"Will this one survive?"

All these thoughts, and many more, may never be spoken, but they are very much communicated and have a profound effect upon the psychological formation of our children.

You can see this kind of communication at work between any young child and parent or caregiver. For example, at the age of about fourteen to nineteen months old a child begins to toddle away and explore the world. Some parents watch that and adore it. Other parents are compulsive about stepping in front of their child and making themselves the focus of the discovery, or fearing the hazards of adventure in their child's life. As a child's explorations and self-expressions widen, from toddler through teenage years and beyond, a parent's responses infuse the moment with meaning and emotional color.

BRANDT: THE SELF-FULFILLING
PROPHECY OF SUCCESS

Brandt, at thirty-two, was a glass-half-full kind of guy. He was confident and charming, a dream come true for his mother and father. He was the fulfillment of their love, their lives, and their individual and collective destinies. His earliest efforts to communicate were rewarded by a consistent effort by his parents to listen, understand, and respond. Brandt came to expect the world to greet him this way. When it didn't, as it won't sometimes, this rebuff did not confirm some insecure sense of himself; he shrugged it off as an annoying reality of the moment. More often than not, Brandt met with positive responses from others, in large part because he acted in the manner of one who expects it. This genuine expression of his sturdy sense of himself drew responses that only reinforced his confidence.

The colorations of a child's experience are created by the parents' frame of reference to experience. We celebrate the moments of our lives with the tones established by our history. A child whose parents are anxious or fearful will find their moments of helplessness treated differently by their parents than by those without that history. A mother or father who is anxious, dismayed, or disappointed by their child's forays into the world communicates those feelings to the child, even if only unconsciously. In a context of fear, a child's experience of discovery then carries with it the emotional tint of anxiety or reprimand or recrimination, dark emotional colors that stunt the sense of wonder and awe in exploring life. For the child, it's the difference between experiencing helplessness as only a momentary state, or experiencing a moment of helplessness as a slide into hopelessness.

RAUL: CHANGE AND A SHADOW OF FEAR

Raul was overwhelmed with panic following the announcement that his company would be downsizing, and he and his departmental colleagues were to be let go. He felt helpless, rejected, and doomed; he was frozen in certainty that there was nothing he could do to alter his destiny. Listening to his colleagues around him, Raul realized that although they were unhappy about the turn of events, he alone was experiencing such deep despair. His sense of helplessness was only compounded by the paralysis it imposed on him.

Raul turned to his friend Sid and asked why he didn't seem as devastated by this news. Sid responded that he was unnerved by the loss of his job, but that his family had taught him that, while the paths of life change directions, they are continuous; there are no dead ends. He said that his grandfather had lost everything in the Great Depression, only to come back into greater wealth and, more importantly, greater happiness afterward. His grandfather had often said that in those hard times he had learned some valuable lessons in business and life, and had changed his priorities, placing family equal to or above business. It was family that had sustained him when business failed, and it was family that helped him keep business concerns in perspective.

Raul realized that his family lessons had been quite different.

His despair echoed his parents' anxious history as refugees from a revolution they had narrowly survived, and the lingering cast of dread they had never found a way to resolve and move beyond. Both Raul and Sid faced the same moment, and in their different responses were the echoes of the earliest celebrations of their lives. For Sid, this was to be only a bad moment. Raul was reliving the history of his family, as it was imparted wordlessly from birth.

WANDA: THE MAGIC OF A MOMENT

Wanda, in her forties, struggled with low self-esteem and a certain dourness that undermined her personal and work relationships. She once had told me of a moment from her childhood in which she twirled, dancing, into the kitchen, where her mother was finishing washing the dinner dishes as the family watched the Miss America pageant.

"I want to be Miss America!" she sang out to her mother as she glided, dream-filled, across the room. Her mother had missed the magic of the moment, as she typically did, and delivered an unsympathetic piece of advice: "Darling, you're too tall and not glamorous enough for that, but don't worry—I'm sure there are other things you can do."

Why did her mother have to do that? Why couldn't she just embrace her daughter's momentary dream? Why did a sour fact have to replace a starry-eyed fantasy? It costs us nothing to embrace an enchanted moment. Our reluctance to do so, or our aversion to it, can cost a child a great deal.

LARRY: LIVING ON THE ANXIOUS EDGE

"I don't get it," Larry said, with reluctant resignation. "I don't get why everyone else just goes through life and lives life making their mistakes, having their successes, and not torturing themselves the way I do." Larry tortured himself about everything, but the main part of his life that brought him to consultation was his work as a financial analyst for a small law firm specializing in tax law for an elite group of investors.

Larry was, in his own words, "an incurable procrastinator." He couldn't get anything done unless he was absolutely under the gun. Only when he had to "produce or else" could he get a project completed. Without that threat, he was paralyzed.

As Larry told his story to me, it quickly became apparent he was paralyzed in many aspects of life, particularly in his emotional life. Larry couldn't say *or* do anything for fear of the consequences. He also couldn't describe specifically what he thought would befall him, how he envisioned those paralyzing consequences. He just *knew* that his world would unravel in some catastrophic way if he spoke his mind or showed his initiative. At the deepest level of his existence, Larry hesitated his way through life, deadline to deadline. He was smart, analytically minded, humble, and yet he was completely in the dark about what had been hobbling him in life. He lived between the vague fear of catastrophic consequences at work that would befall him if he didn't act, and the vague fear of catastrophic consequences in his head if he did act.

Larry's excessive procrastination was a memory of sorts. It was a memory of the chronic tensions and disparaging conversation between his mother and his father, which had surrounded him as a child, and held him throughout his life. His father was an ambitious risk-taker, but when things went wrong, he was quick to blame others, often his wife. Larry's mother had a quality of panicky hesitation that discouraged risk taking and feared failure—the result of her life as her husband's scapegoat. Larry embodied both; his talents placed him at the center of the world of high-risk finance, but his procrastination made it painful, and almost impossible, to fully engage in his work, his family life, or his inner life. The celebration of Larry's birth contained the cacophony of conflicting parental histories. It played out in a form of paralysis—procrastination—in the unfolding story of his life and ambition.

Larry progressed in analysis to the point of being able to see the patterns of emotion and behavior that were a part of him, and how those now were becoming apparent in his children's lives. One day he arrived with a pained smile on his face. A conversation with his son had reminded him of something about himself, and while he was pleased that he was able to see these patterns in and around him now, and was developing new responses to them, he was also concerned by what he saw.

"My son, Jeff, received a great honor at his graduation last week," he said proudly to me. "When I went up to him and hugged him and told him how proud I was, and he should be, to have received this recognition from his professors, he shrugged it off, saying that 'they had to give it to someone; it was no big deal.' It made me cringe to see myself being reflected back to me by my son. I asked him why he couldn't just rejoice at his honor, and not belittle it. Funny enough, I was in the midst of one of my worst procrastinations. I had come up with a very creative solution to a problem at work, and I couldn't get it off my desk and into my boss's hands. So here, my report is still sitting on my desk, and I'm telling my son to be proud of his work!"

As I listened to Larry, an old—a very old—image came flooding into my consciousness. I was two years old. It was 1946, those sad days after the war when my mom was trying to find our distant relatives in Europe. I was standing in the doorway between the dining room and the kitchen of our one-bedroom apartment in Chicago, where the four of us lived. Her back was to me as she stood at the sink preparing dinner. There was the icebox next to me—a *real* icebox. There was music coming from the radio; there were no televisions. I started to move and dance to the music. As clear as the day—the moment—it occurred, I saw her turn to me with the biggest smile one could hope for. Her smile was particularly important, since I had seen the sadness on her face so often as tragic news came in about our relatives. But I can see her smile. She was beaming, shining, as she leaned down toward me and began to clap her hands in time with the music and my dancing. She sang, *"Tanzen, tanzen, tanzen"* (dance, dance, dance) in Yiddish. I bathed in the glow of her smile as I danced to the music. The joyful flashback hardly took a second, and then I was back in the moment, with Larry. He continued to speak of his struggle to just hand over his solution to his boss.

"What would your mother have done with some wonderful moment in which you came into the room singing or dancing?" I asked.

"She would have grimaced at the interruption, the burden, of another active moment by another active child," he said sadly, but matter-of-factly. Nor would his father have been tolerant. In fact, there was no one in Larry's childhood who welcomed his self-expression. No one celebrated his creativity: his thoughts, his energy, his feelings, his *being*. And now he was seeing the cost, not only to himself but to his son, the next generation. The legacy of uncelebrated inspiration had been passed on.

The echoes of family history, of those early smiles, grimaces, and uninspired comments, always affect us. Brandt, who was so beloved by his parents, trusted and expected a good reception in life. Raul was trapped in repeating and reliving his family history. Wanda's enchantment withered, with lasting effects, in the harsh light of reality as proffered by her mother. Larry avoided the disappointment that he, like Wanda, had learned would sadly, painfully, but inevitably, await him. He was further chagrined to see that he had passed this legacy to his son.

• FINDING OUR PLACE IN THE FAMILY STORY •

A child is witness to the family drama, inhaling it from birth, but that is not sufficient. Children hunger to be part of the story. They must see themselves as part of the drama, part of a bigger story, into which they have been placed. This is not a theoretical construct for a child. The world is full of mystery and wonder, and children see it clearly, love it, and want to be part of it.

For the musical child amid a family of scientists, it is the obligation of the scientists to celebrate the music. For the shy child in the family of extroverts, the child must not be made to feel wrong or bad in his or her shyness. The family must recognize the nature of the child and invite the child to join as he or she can in the discourse of the family. The athletic child in a family of scholars is not dumb; the scholar in a family of jocks is not a bookish nerd. The challenge for both the family and the child is to find their place with each other. It is a parent's obligation to celebrate the child's nature.

This new existence—the child's life—changes the family story by its very being. If this larger family story is to change in directions that we would not have wished or sought, then so be it. This new life, this celebrated life, *if permitted,* will develop its own promise and seek its destiny to the fullest. Whatever the intellectual skill or natural talent or spiritual purpose, it will be developed and added to the family story and the story of humankind. What parts will be happy or heroic, and what parts will be about sadness and loss, is not for us to know. The important point is that *it is a child's birthright to be honored within the family story and to bring new dimensions to it.*

This meshing and weaving of stories—the new child's story with the larger, older story of the family—is a negotiated process, and as with any negotiation, some compromises must be made. Sometimes there is a great fit between the dreams of the family and the personality of the child. When that is the case all goes swimmingly. But often the fit is not so smooth or equitable, and the child, lacking the clout of seniority, loses too much. It is during this process of mixing and negotiating dreams and realities that we first experience the celebrated or uncelebrated life, and this becomes our lifelong template.

• THE CELEBRATED CHILD: INVESTED WITH EMOTIONAL ASSETS •

In this formative context of family, the celebrated child is that child whose individual qualities are recognized and appreciated by the family as a new dimension to the family story, making the individual qualities of the child special qualities. They are special simply by virtue of being recognized and valued as that child's contribution to the family and the family story. Celebration is a process, and a celebrated child from a family in which this process is practiced emerges with the capacity to adapt securely grounded in the context of relationship, family, culture, community, nationality, and what is most important, in the process of changing times. The celebrated child is not rigid and defined by his or her environment, but rather, contributes to the definition of that environment. They can stand upon their own story and, from that point, center themselves in any moment and contribute to defining the moment.

The description that comes to mind is "durability." These are durable people. That does not mean that problems, misfortune, and even agony does not enter their lives; it means that they can handle whatever comes their way. They will handle life in their own very characteristic fashion, but handle it they will. They will bend, but not break. They will move on, recovering from whatever blows come their way, and they will gain from living through the episodes of their life.

Our innate nature affects our durability. E. James Anthony wrote about three types of newborns, characterized by their nature and temperament: rubber babies, steel babies, and glass babies. Rubber babies feel the impact of life upon them, but they absorb it. Steel babies are impervious to life, resistant more than resilient. Glass babies are fragile and can shatter under pressure. We can see a similar pattern in the way we are, to some extent genetically predisposed throughout life, to be more or less durable.

But nature alone does not determine durability. Life experience has an effect, tempering glass, softening steel, and unfortunately, pushing even the most resilient rubber to its limits. No, durability grows with a child's comfortable sense of self and of fit within a context for life that encourages and supports durability.

For this to come to pass, this *knowing of self and context,* a child must feel a resonance between what they sense of their inner selves and the recognition of that same self by others. They must feel that what is being celebrated in the real-life context is a close match to the unformed elements of themselves that they *know* internally. If that resonance exists, then they can feel truly supported and known. It is in this constant back and forth—the resonance between who we feel we are on the inside with who we see ourselves to be in our effect on the outside world—that we slowly build an internal armature called "self."

The celebrated child, emerging from the family that tells its story and embraces the child as a new dimension to that story, comes out of that experience with a consolidated sense of self. That sense will include the capacity for loving, working, and playing, to paraphrase Freud, without inhibition, impairment, or the need to create compulsively repeated and emotionally costly ways of dealing with life. These people know their place in the universe of humankind. They know they are part of the great story of humankind, and that they, themselves, are a chapter in that story.

The qualities of the celebrated child—apparent in adulthood, too—speak to this durability.

The celebrated child is capable of generous acts. If we have been celebrated, we find it easier to be unselfish. This capacity to be generous is much more than giving money to charity. We can place others' interests before our own, an essential ingredient in deep love and nurturing. We can imagine ourselves in someone else's circumstances and empathize. The difference between empathy and sympathy is telling. It is easy to pity or sympathize with someone in a wretched situation. To empathize with that person, we must be capable of finding in our own experience the capacity to feel what the other must feel, and respond as if it were part of our experience. Some version of this greater emotional complexity is required in order to deeply love and deeply nurture.

The celebrated child has a healthy perspective. If we have been celebrated, we can see ourselves and others in a realistic but compassionate light. We can laugh at ourselves and enjoy humor. We can understand allegory and metaphor and symbol, having learned them early on in the unfolding story of family. We have learned that we are only part of a larger story, though an important chapter in our own right. We don't take ourselves too seriously, but keep a sense of our proportion in the world, neither too grand nor too insignificant.

The celebrated child is adaptable. If we have been celebrated, we can manage a world that is constantly changing. We can take the newness of an experience and make it our own. We can continue the process of exploration and discovery in both our internal and external lives, based on the changes occurring inside and outside of ourselves. We retain the sense of exhilaration from that wonderful time of discovery in childhood. Our sense of self is not based on an external identity, because we have a secure internal identity that includes the unconscious whisper "you will be all right." We have that security because we know we are part of a grand story that has continued despite small moments of disappointment or setback, even tragedy, in individual lives. We have a sense of history—our own history.

(49

Finally, the celebrated child has a full range of emotions. If we have been celebrated, we know the full range of emotional colors. We can laugh and cry. We can fear, or be angry, or love. We can acknowledge our emotions without fear of bad consequences. We can express and receive emotions without fear that someone else will be upset or that the world will become disarranged. We can fully embrace and appreciate our emotional life.

GIL: AT EASE, SURROUNDED BY LOVE

Gil, my college friend, seemed an odd duck. He was not handsome, he was not athletic, he was very smart, but a complete nerd. Gil was also an exceptionally talented harpsichordist. Gil didn't seem to know he was a nerd. He didn't seem to know he was not handsome, though he did know he was not athletic. Gil entered any gathering as if he were the guy for whom everyone was waiting to start the party. At a social gathering, he approached girls as if they were dying to date him. He spoke to jocks without being embarrassed by his tall, gangly, cranelike stature. He was an amazing contradiction of what I saw and what I would have expected. If I were Gil, I thought to myself back then, I would be a bit more low-key.

The contradictions were explained when I visited Gil's family one school holiday. Gil's father, a machinist, was an average-looking, macho kind of guy. His mother was a traditional 1950s mother and wife. They literally surrounded him with their love. That first evening, and every evening during our visit, the three of them gathered around the harpsichord and sang as Gil accompanied them. They sang opera duets and choruses. His parents listened as he played a Bach harpsichord sonata. His father practically swooned in joy at his son's talent. Gil was the joy of his parents' lives. Gil's ability to move about the world with such ease and confidence was not only a natural gift but also the gift of a celebrated childhood from his parents.

AMY: CHERISHING DIFFERENCES

Amy, aged six, looked up at me and studied my face.

"You look like my parents. I don't. I look like my birth parents. They were Cambodian, but they couldn't keep me," she said matter-of-factly.

That grabbed my attention.

"But, you know," she continued, "I *feel* like my adopted parents. I have two families. I'm learning one now when I'm little, and I'll learn about the other when I am older. My parents said so."

Amy's parents had done a good job. They managed to celebrate her differences, which could not be denied, as well as her belonging to them, her adoptive family. They told her who she was, even though it was a complex story, and they held out the happy anticipation of some consolation of her history in the future when she could understand and use it well.

JOHN: LOVE ENOUGH FOR A SON

When my friend John called, he wanted to talk with me about how to "handle" his son's recent disclosure that he was gay, and his "coming out" to the extended family.

"What needs to be handled?" I asked.

"I guess it's my reaction to his coming out," he said.

"What is your reaction?" I asked.

"Well, I'm scared and proud—mostly proud," he said. "I am scared that he will live a lonely life. But I am so proud of how he presented it to us. He said that he had always been taught to look inside for his inspiration. He said that he had been doing so for several years regarding his sexuality and now knew that his sexual interest and the completion of his soul would be with another man. He said that he hoped we could be pleased with him about this, as he had come to rejoice in figuring this out about himself. I was so proud of him for the way he thought this through, and then shared it with us. Now, what should I do to show that?"

"John, just put your arms around him, and hug and kiss him, and say what you just said to me," I told him.

"I already did that. Is it enough?" he asked.

"It was enough to get him this far," I said.

The celebration of John's son had already taken place. That is what had permitted this fine young man to navigate the difficult waters of "coming out." John's uneasy feelings about his son's disclosure to the rest of the family were reasonable, including his wondering if what he had done was enough. What is enough celebration of a child? Enough is that which permits our children to grow and think for themselves and want to remain part of the family and society. John had done that.

• THE UNCELEBRATED CHILD: EMOTIONALLY UNDERNOURISHED, OVERLOOKED •

The Hans Christian Andersen tale *The Ugly Duckling* offers a timeless illustration of both the pain of the uncelebrated child and the power of celebration to heal and serve as a lifeline to healing from the uncelebrated life. In the story, a young swan accidentally hatched into a family of ducks is ridiculed for traits unbecoming a duck. He is too big. His neck is too long. He looks odd, they say. When a duck should quack, he honks. From the most superficial aspects of his appearance, to the innermost qualities that define him to himself, he is branded as ugly. His family derides him as a misfit for the very qualities that make him who he is, and, knowing no different, he withers under their judgment. The ugly duckling's tale ends happily only after he meets a kindly swan who recognizes him as the swan he is, and a fine one at that. With this new truth about himself, the uncelebrated duckling can finally appreciate and embrace a celebrated life as the swan he *is*, instead of the duck he *isn't*.

The uncelebrated child is one whose special characteristics are not marked and noted, one who is devalued in the family, or one who is raised for the honor of the parent, family, religion, nation, or whatever other theme the family story celebrates above all—above them. Theirs is a sad and angry story. I see this story of suffering and recovery in its infinite varieties, in my work with adults who were uncelebrated children, and in the lives of children today who are uncelebrated. There are as many stories of uncelebrated childhood as there are those wounded individuals, but some common themes emerge:

The *invisible child* is one who is overlooked or underappreciated, in a family's struggle for survival, or strivings for outward appearances or success.

The *branded child* is uncelebrated by virtue of being cast in a family role that confines or misunderstands the child—even when those roles might seem flattering. *The smart one, the pretty one, the troublemaker, the black sheep.* Any label is limiting and discounts the complexity and possibility every child brings to life.

The *exploited child* is assigned a supporting role in the family story, valued only to the extent that the child uses his or her energy or talents in service of others. This includes the trophy child, seemingly the most celebrated of all, for their performance in school or sports, or their compliance to the powerful family identity in the community, but actually shortchanged by the pattern of recognition based on achievement.

When there is too much emphasis on the required image or outcome of the family story, children come to see themselves as functionaries in a family system and not as important in their own right. The system may keep them functioning well enough, perhaps even thriving in terms of their accomplishments, but there is an insidious cost to that child and to the whole family.

In these and other versions of the uncelebrated child, what is lost is that special sense of personal history in which the child's life becomes a new center of action and movement and meaning. As children or as adults, some are downcast and struggle to find the energy to face the day. Some are driven superachievers. Many are people who feel drawn to marry or associate themselves with others who do not recognize their finest qualities or who ridicule what is truly special about them. It doesn't matter what gender, age, cultural background, level of social success, level of educational achievement, level of wealth they may achieve, the hurts of being uncelebrated in childhood haunt them and hurt them.

MARLENE: A "SPECIAL" UGLY DUCKLING

Marlene, twenty, was suicidal. She arrived for her visit neatly dressed, though without any adornment. Her dress was simple and plain, she wore no makeup, and her hair was combed, but not styled. A priest at her college had urged her to seek help after she expressed suicidal thoughts. Appearing resigned, she sat with her hands clasped in her lap so tightly that I could see her knuckles whiten, and she looked up at me from lowered lids and bowed head, searching my face but fleetingly. She tried to smile, but it was too much of an effort. She appeared sad but would not cry. Her voice was very soft and tense, as if she were afraid that if she raised it at all, even to a normal conversational level, she might lose control and scream.

Marlene couldn't understand why she wanted to die. She was smart and did well in school. She had friends. But she was dissatisfied with life and disconsolate. She felt that she was "bothered" by something deep.

In our first session we talked about her history—her family, her birth, her development, her social relationships. A week later Marlene returned for our second meeting having done more introspective work based on our first conversation than most people do in many months. I was struck by something very special about Marlene and told her so. When I used the word "special," she laughed wryly and said that her family had often used that word, but in a cutting way.

" 'You're something special,' they would say, sarcastically. 'Maybe you need special ed.' " She had learned to smile and join them in laughing at herself, even in the face of hurt and insult. She especially remembered the taunting she suffered one day when she was eight years old and dismantled a family clock to see how it worked.

"So, what did you do with the clock?"

"Oh, I put it back together!" she said, even now with a brittle laugh.

Marlene had been a child of exceptional intellect and talent, who, far from feeling celebrated, had been mocked for her gift. To survive in the family, she had learned to laugh at herself, but on the inside she was hurt, devastated, angry, and growing despondent. That which was wonderful about her was not considered good; it was laughable, it was bad and a source of shame. She had tried unsuccessfully to silence herself and keep her keen observations and earnest questions to herself, but endlessly she erred and spoke her thoughts, and this brought derision upon her.

The normal temptation to lash out at her parents was tempered by that fact that Marlene saw her parents as good people. They were kind and loving people in most ways. But Marlene had been their first child, the pregnancy that had forced the marriage. Her parents had been young and not ready for the burdens of parenthood, particularly parenthood of an exceptionally brilliant child. They weren't aware of their resentment of Marlene, but it was her birth that brought about their marriage and ended many of their dreams. Marlene's consequent hurt and rage turned inward, and now, as a young adult, it contributed to her suicidal depression.

The treatment of the depression was not hard. Constructing a framework in which she could begin to fully appreciate herself would prove the harder task of therapy. For Marlene, silence was a way to "hold her breath" until she found the acceptance she so desperately needed. As is so often the case, these self-protecting measures only made matters worse. She was emotionally isolated and impoverished by her silence. In the safety of therapy, her stony shell of silence began to crack.

She was wary, at first, about being "special," even in therapy. But in time, her trust in the process grew. Our labor to recognize what was and wasn't truly special about her brought order to her life and enabled her to speak out and break through her silence. She had to know more about herself. She had to go over that history buried in silence. She had to recount all the hurts and slights and injustices. For all those old names that she had been called, she had to have new names for herself, like "curious," "determined," and "creative." She had to learn to recognize jealousy and envy and call them by name. She had to know that good, loving people *could* hurt those they love. She had to know words like *dignity* and *pride* and how they applied to her. She had to learn to have pride in her talents and understand that all exceptional talent has a cost.

She broke her silence, awkwardly at first. But with increasing confidence she spoke. She spoke to her family and her friends. She spoke proudly of her observations and solutions. She was angry about the years of oppression, but forgiving. In therapy, Marlene was able to repair her view of herself and her place in the world. She was able to build an inner structure for celebrating her life and use it, literally, to save her life.

Celebration can be either positive or negative in its impact on a child's self-esteem. As a child, Marlene had been too ready to blame herself for not fitting in and for the tensions that created the discordant background music of her family life. We had to change the meaning of "special" for Marlene. That which was unique to her—special—had been used to celebrate her *not* fitting into the family. In analysis, carefully, we managed to celebrate what was truly special about her and what was appropriately and wonderfully ordinary.

The specialness of which we take note in a child's life need not be early evidence of extraordinary talent or intellect. A smile is special, an early sign of recognition and interaction, a physical milestone, an early form of communication—all are special. After all, what is more amazing and mysterious than the capacity of a child to communicate and learn? The significance of this quiet, daily form of marking the characteristics of a child is most apparent in its absence. A child whose simple milestones of life are ignored or taken for granted *knows* he is being taken for granted, and *feels* that he is being taken for granted. It takes a measure of purposeful intention to recognize and name what is unique—special—in a child. It doesn't have to be above average; it simply has to be recognized and named:

> *"You are so alert to directions when we travel about the town or city."*
>
> *"You have such a great laugh."*
>
> *"You see things in an artistic manner; that is a true talent."*
>
> *"You ask such interesting questions."*

Children valued only for how well they serve the family myth remain uncelebrated for whom they are as individuals. In the course of seemingly celebrated lives, they suffer deeply.

WILMA: POLISHED FAMILY, TARNISHED CHILDHOOD

Wilma had lived what most people would consider a fairy-tale life as a child. When she first came for a consultation, it was during what should have been a happy time, she thought. In her midthirties, Wilma had it all. Her five-year-old son, Sam, was lively and beautiful, her husband was successful and devoted, and she was at the height of her career. They had money, a second home, and their health. Lately, though, she said, she would wake in the middle of the night thinking, I hate myself, I hate myself.

At first those thoughts, or the hangover of those thoughts, would quickly disappear after awakening. Then the thoughts would return, and her days felt labored. She was becoming rote and uninspired as a worker, mother, and wife, even to herself. Then the crying started. She would cry and cry and cry. She hated this, and she couldn't explain it. She went to a psychiatrist and got drugs. She stopped crying but felt just as rote, like an automaton, in her life.

After another year, she was desperate to understand what was happening to her. She came into therapy, and eventually analysis. She stopped the medication and, within a few weeks, started to cry again.

"I can cry again," she said. "It feels kind of good and bad at the same time." She was ready to revisit her story for clues to her sadness.

Wilma's childhood story was one of wealth and privilege. She was an only child. Her parents had hoped for a boy, but they got a very pretty and very bright little girl instead. She became a darling decoration for her father, a famous university president. They lived in the president's mansion for most of her childhood, and she was always on display. Mom was also on display as the president's wife. They had a lot of student help at home in the mansion. Drivers conveyed her back and forth to private school, because school was far away and Mom and Dad had their duties. Everything revolved around her father's career and position. Wilma was a truly privileged and uncelebrated child. She was surrounded by the accoutrements of a celebrated life; it simply wasn't hers.

Wilma remembered, now that she was crying again, how as a child she would cry and cry and cry at night when she would go to sleep. She thought that she didn't want her mother to leave the room, but even when she got used to that, she would continue to cry. She would hear her mother entertaining people in the sitting room, playing the piano. Mom was such a good pianist. Wilma loved to hear the music, and she would cry herself to sleep.

Wilma didn't want to go to boarding school, but the local schools "wouldn't do," her parents said. Specifically, they felt she needed the refinement of the nuns. She hated going away and wanted to be sick and stay home. She really couldn't make herself sick, although she did break her leg once. Mom and Dad did not come to the hospital to visit. They had their duties. When she was sent home to recover she was conveniently located enough to get some attention from them.

Wilma once had received a small gift from the kind old gentleman assigned to drive her. Mother made him take it back, because, she said, it would spoil her. She angrily told Wilma that she must always remember she was privileged to be the daughter of her father, and without that, she was "nothing but a nothing." Wilma remembered pleading, "Yes, Momma, I know that, but I could have hidden the present from everyone and taken it back to school with me," she said. "You are a selfish child!" Mother had scolded.

Wilma actually was a very "good" child. She was compliant, naive, eager to please, and enjoyed the accompanying reputation. When she finally moved away and lived as a working woman, life began to open up. She had an affair, got married, got divorced, got married again. All this time her career was moving upward.

She really had no interest in having a child; there was no strong draw toward motherhood, even in the face of her friends' children. Finally her husband expressed interest. She dawdled for a while but finally went along with his wishes. Motherhood was okay, but she was at sea as to what to expect or what to do. She became a good copycat. She watched what others did and did the same.

Wilma and Sam, her son, had never been close. They related as cohabitants in the same house. Sam needed Wilma and Wilma enjoyed the idea of Sam. But almost from the beginning, Wilma was depressed. Sam was a "perfect" boy—handsome, intelligent, and thoughtful—but as time went on he grew stubborn and had, as she complained, "a mind of his own." Sam made Wilma feel incompetent, and Wilma did not like feeling that way. Wilma had an idea of what a son should be like. In time, Sam seemed to sense this and seemed to make every effort to sabotage Wilma's ideal. When Wilma would have ideas or make plans for a good time with Sam, Sam would ruin their time together. He threw tantrums that Wilma could not tolerate; bedtimes were an ordeal. Wilma didn't think she was a very good mother, and she hated that in herself. But she also did not think Sam was a very good son. She was in effect asking her son to do what she had done—celebrate the family myth rather than his own being—and he refused.

In analysis, Wilma eventually realized that motherhood was painful in large part because she was reliving the hurt of her own childhood. She had been conceived reluctantly, received reluctantly because she was not a son, and deceived to think that she was adored and valued when in fact, she had been her parents' prop. She had been groomed to fit into the picture. Her talents, her inspirations, her opinions, her impulses, her longings and dreams had never been recognized, never been given priority.

Wilma maintained an icy detachment in therapy, and it took quite some time to move past her armored shield of politeness and correctness. Once we did, we discovered a cauldron of anger and bitterness. In her picture-book childhood, she had never had a chance to really discover who she was—neither her goodness nor badness. And now, her child was challenging her to be somebody *real*! She simply couldn't. To be real would be to explode the world she had crafted so carefully from her earliest childhood. We knew intellectually that it was the world of myth, but in her heart, it was the real world, the whole world. She had come to believe that without that myth she was "nothing but a nothing."

Her inner world was a secret world, even to herself, and her experience had taught her that it was best it remain so. The idea that I felt it was important to get to the "real" Wilma was horrifying to her, yet she was intrigued and stayed in analysis.

It was not easy for Wilma to open up about her feelings, or even be in touch with them herself. We used a lot of teasing humor to navigate her fears. But as we explored her secret inner life, she found it easier to open up at home with her husband and son. She began to sit and play with her son, and let him see her flaws and insecurities. She shared her history with her son, explaining how in her own childhood she had been raised to honor the family myth of prestige and status, and keep her anger and sadness to herself—no tantrums allowed. She created a more open, accepting space in their relationship for honest expression of feelings. Her son easily moved into that space, reassuring her that there was a lot of love left. It was not too late—for either of them. Wilma had felt obliged to be the celebrator of the family myth without which she felt she did not exist. In the safe and searching environment of therapy, Wilma learned to appreciate herself as an individual in her own right, and subsequently to allow her son the same opportunity.

MICHAEL: A SUPPORTING ROLE
CREATES MASTER MANIPULATOR

The uncelebrated child or adult will use anything in their natural armory of skills, talents, and temperaments to try to gain that sense of personal recognition that is missing. Drama, religiosity, silence, and anger: these can all become instruments of manipulation to gain attention, or they can be instruments of revenge, to give hell for the injustices of the past. Serial sexual liaisons are a common pattern for men and women trying to satisfy the longings of an uncelebrated childhood. For the uncelebrated boy or girl for whom ambition holds no allure, as they grow into sexual maturity they may discover that sexual interaction, a successful seduction, gives them a momentary celebration of themselves. Typically, they satisfy their repressed anger by dumping the lover; it works for the moment. Eventually, however, compulsive sex—like any other compulsive behavior—grows empty, boring, sad, and lonely.

This was Michael, impeccable in dress and demeanor as he stepped into my office for the first time. Only his broad, confident smile showed an edge of something hidden, an edge of cynicism. A project manager at a major advertising agency, he was in his early thirties, articulate, bored, and a bit blasé as he described the concern that had prompted him to seek help.

"I have traveled everywhere I could have wanted to travel, and done all I would ever want to do, and yet," he paused, "I have never known joy."

Michael was gay and currently in a relationship with Jake, a loving, thoughtful partner, who had issued an ultimatum: either Michael give up his fast-track social life and "settle down" or Jake was leaving. Michael had mixed feelings. He appreciated their relaxed and stable life, but he missed the fast and glamorous life he had left behind.

It was Jake who had pointed out to Michael that despite his sleek, sophisticated life of travel, clothes, and the social circuit, he showed very little satisfaction and joy in life.

"He is right," Michael said. "I can barely hold on to that idea. But I know he is right."

In the months that followed, Michael told his story. He was no misunderstood ugly duckling, nor did his family story overshadow his own as a child. However, throughout Michael's childhood, he had been celebrated only to the degree that he used his intelligence and creativity to polish his mother's image in the community. He was the middle of three children, and at an early age his mother had made it clear that he was her favorite, the chosen one to accompany her on her social and shopping rounds, and the one who was expected to "rise above" his unremarkable father and other siblings, by virtue of his considerable charm and talents.

However, in his own realm in elementary and middle school, he had been a sad, unpopular child because he was, in his words, "fat and nerdy." One of Michael's earliest memories, from about age five, was of going to sleep praying that God would take him that night. He wanted to die. If not that, he wanted to awake transformed into a desirable, popular boy. At school, he routinely gave gum and candy to other children to curry favor.

His parents didn't want to hear about his woes. His father was unapproachable, and his mother simply assured him that he was "better than the rest of them" and that as long as they had each other, he would be fine. Michael said he ceased telling her about his misery and his prayers that God would take him, because she either didn't hear him or, when she did, she became irritated with him. He sensed that his misery was a burden to her.

Finally, in high school, he took charge of his fate. He lost weight, worked out, wore stylish clothes, and became very popular. He pulled away from his mother, and she reacted with criticism or stony silence. In college, he was a stellar student, graduating summa cum laude, but discounted the honor; he believed his success was the result of charming his teachers, much as he had charmed his way through most of his life. In graduate school, he came out as gay and began what would become a pattern of casual sexual relationships.

His choice of advertising as a career disappointed his mother, and his coming out as gay appalled her. She was absent for each of his graduations and rarely spoke with him when he called home. His work eventually brought him to a major city, where he found a thriving gay community, and eventually to Jake. Now he was confronted for the first time with the opportunity to settle in a neighborhood and with a partner that felt accepting and comfortable, and he wasn't sure he knew how to do that—or *whether* it was right for him.

As Michael told his story, I felt that I was hearing a most fluent and thorough summary of a life, but a story missing all the colors. It was like looking at a sepia photo of old times. I drew his attention to the gap between style and content.

"Your inability to reflect upon yourself doesn't match your otherwise eloquent presentation," I said. "We'll have to find out if this is defensive, meaning you simply don't want to go there, or if it represents something you *can't* do—a natural mental skill that has been withered in you for some reason."

I sensed a warm and honest man under the habit of seduction and manipulation. The fact that he had been able to drop his defenses long enough to fall in love, his honest distress at Jake's interpretation about the joylessness of his life, and his fluency at the telling of his story were positive signs. Michael had genuine advantages, too: he was smart and capable in many ways. However, here was a man who could accomplish much on his own merits, yet he felt he had to use manipulation and seduction to gain his ends. He had worked determinedly to erase the emotional coloration of his internal life. Michael clearly used his external good looks and charm to distract himself and the rest of the world from his internal colorlessness.

As we explored Michael's history of relationships, from family to friends to lovers, he characteristically described himself as the "user" in relationships that failed. He avoided any acknowledgment that he had been disappointed by someone meaningful to him. This turned out to be a natural pattern for Michael, to see and use manipulation and seduction instead of feeling disappointment or, unthinkably, anger.

Michael was never angry and never really happy. His lack of joy was like a droning sound that masked whatever other sounds entered that range. With the chronic drone of joylessness, he could not feel disappointed. Without disappointment, he had no reason for anger. Afraid of disappointment, he had made sure that in work, friendships, and love relationships, he was in charge and never the passive victim of another person's failure to care.

As we worked in analysis to bring emotional detail to the text of Michael's story, we also were able to begin to repair his hurt as a child whose rightful celebration had been co-opted to serve others, most notably his mother. By recognizing his genuine talents and skills, we were able to name them and help him see the exceptional young boy he had been, and man he was now. He grew to appreciate that he had not received his high academic honors through seduction, but through talent and hard work. Michael was a creative, talented, even brilliant man, but we had to revisit the manner in which he had been celebrated as a child, in order to repair his sense of himself and his ability to celebrate himself and others.

As he began to see the effects of his history on his current life, he took some bold steps. He left an unsatisfying job to start his own business. It proved more difficult for him to be a partner in a love relationship based on commitment, rather than seduction and manipulation. In time, however, he put his energy and talent into overcoming the old foundations of mistrust and fear, learning instead to love his partner without reservation.

Michael had been an uncelebrated child not in the sense that his talents went unrecognized but in that they had been subordinated to the service of his mother. His father's ineffectual presence had left him abandoned to his fate in the family. Michael used joylessness to protect himself and others from his disappointment and rage. By revisiting his life story together, we had been able to name and repair the foundation of his character on which he could build a new life, one with a wide range of emotional colors—including joy.

• MISSING STORIES, MISSING PIECES: DISCOVERING AND REPAIRING OUR HISTORY •

So many people don't know their own Genesis story. Some have no story of their youth. Why not? Why can't they remember anything that happened before the age of ten? Why don't they know much about their parents' or grandparents' struggles and dreams, their setbacks as well as their accomplishments, even when those elders are alive and available? Why don't they have a sense of their life as *a part of* that larger story rather than *apart from* it? Why is there often no concern, or even curiosity about it? The loss is tremendous. They have lived life, sometimes quite successfully, but without a sense of being rooted in a history—a story.

Celebration invites us to revisit our life stories, and in doing so, recover our life stories and the stories of our families. But there are people for whom the stories are missing or distorted. When people are deprived of their story they are deprived of a significant part of themselves—their base, their place, their foundation. When we suffer the loss of context for our life story, we struggle in its absence, whether we are one person alone, or a nation of people in search of their roots. We can see this in the struggle of African-Americans to reconstruct the story of their heritage, which has been ravaged by slavery, brutality, and oppression. Other racial, religious, or ethnic minorities share a similar challenge in recovering lost or damaged pieces of their respective stories that are vital to their identity and voice as a people.

In the story of the Nimpkish band of the Kwakiutl people, on Vancouver Island, we can see these principles at work even in this small, isolated setting.

The Nimpkish take their name from the river that flows through their territory. The central ceremony of the Nimpkish was the Potlatch, a ceremonial dance in elaborate costume that captured the entire belief system and sense of history of the people through song, poetry in their language, and their art.

In the first quarter of the last century, the Canadian government forbade the Potlatch and the use of the Kwakiutl language. To celebrate the Potlatch or to use the Kwakiutl language would encourage confiscation of the costumes and other art objects, and be punished by imprisonment. In the early 1900s, this was in fact done. The Potlatch was held in protest of the law, and in response to it, the government arrested the chief and sent him to jail for several years, and all the art objects and costumes were confiscated and placed in warehouses far away.

Over time, the band began to lose its identity. The people remained commercial fishermen and other tradesmen. They knew they were Indians, but they didn't know much more than that. The rates of common social ills grew: alcoholism, domestic violence, family disintegration, suicide, and delinquency.

Years later, after the old chief had died, his daughter began a movement to apply to the Canadian government to get their art and costumes back, and for permission to celebrate the Potlatch. In time both were granted, with the stipulation that the art and costume would be housed in a proper museum. The band built a community center, which included a museum. Its purpose was not only to house the art and artifacts, but also to begin to teach the language and art and to tell the stories.

Enough old people survived to do both. The children learned the native language of their people by listening to their elders tell the tribal stories. The Potlatch was finally celebrated. These people began, once again, to tell their story and include their children in the story. They began to recover themselves. A new sense of personal and cultural pride and optimism replaced the rote lives they had come to know.

In a broader context, for families and peoples everywhere, family feuds or family secrets have traditionally blacked out portions of family stories. Today, we suffer a similar loss for more mundane reasons. Our families are scattered geographically, and they are scattered around the clock. If we live at a distance, we may gather only rarely, if at all, and the visits are quick and crowded. We may share the same home and not do much better. In heavily scheduled lives, we see each other briefly over a walk-through breakfast or a drive-thru fast-food dinner, and we may chat a bit in the car between destinations, but the time and setting conducive to sharing family stories has simply vanished. We can lose our history by merely ignoring its place in our lives.

Sometimes we choose to not tell the story of our family because we are ashamed or angry:

*I am a single parent and we couldn't
make the marriage work.*

*We married outside the faith and family
relationships became strained.*

*Grandpa lost everything by some foolish act;
it was a public disgrace.*

My father was an alcoholic, but he's dead now,
and we don't need to talk about it.

My brother didn't help when we needed it.
I don't care if we never speak again.

Our family was poor. We have left that behind
and don't want to look back.

We were immigrants, but we want
our children to feel all-American.

I never graduated from college, but I don't
want my children to think I'm a failure.

Missing stories wound us. People who come to therapy often do so because they are having difficulty evaluating or making sense of their lives, or effectively dealing with essential parts of living, such as loving or struggling with unfairness and injustice. Sometimes they feel that they don't matter, that they don't exist in a meaningful way to the important people in their lives—their spouses or children, their parents or friends.

"If I died tomorrow, they would be provided for and not really miss me," one patient said.

They go through the motions of life, but in time they feel an overwhelming sense of ennui—"dead air" as someone once described it. Life has no flavor. Very little is meaningful. Often they pay lip service to the idea that they love their children or their spouse. They know they should, and they do feel some sense of loyalty and obligation. But it doesn't take long to cut through that layer of social amenity and find out that they really don't have much more depth of feeling for their spouse or child than they do for other familiar people who populate their lives.

These people are in great pain, but they don't scream. They do other things, usually not happy things: they drink, take drugs, have illicit sexual encounters, gamble or play recklessly with their fortunes, break up good relationships and partnerships for petty reasons, work or do other things to excess to bring momentary happiness or interruption in the pall of ennui. But neither activity nor achievement brings comfort because neither addresses the underlying emptiness, nor the pain it causes.

What we do in therapy in later life is move backward to the origins of a person's life, and we discover in the re-creation of those origins the lens through which the world was ordered for them, and the emotional coloration of the order and meaning that were given to them in those earliest of life's moments. Once we have defined the lens through which they view life, we regrind and polish it so that the flaws and blind spots are removed or repaired. Psychotherapy and psychoanalysis are ultimately about helping people discover their story and create their story in the context of a clearer view of themselves in the world.

Whether it is through therapy or analysis, or through reflection in the context of family, friends, or faith, this therapeutic celebration enables us to embrace all aspects of our story, and integrate it into our ongoing one. Mental health can most simply be described as the ability to integrate the whole of one's self—nature, nurture, talent, deficit, love, hate, compassion and indifference, activity and passivity, and much more that is human. We cannot do this if we must keep secrets from ourselves or our loved ones. We cannot integrate ourselves in any given moment if we cannot tell the stories that the moment evokes in us. Our unconscious yields itself to external calls. If we are internally forbidden to embrace the inspiration of our unconscious, then we cannot fully celebrate the moment. If we are missing the stories of our history, then we stand alone in the moment, walled off from ourselves, and from others.

In the full rendition of our life story we find the origins of the patterns that continue to repeat themselves in our lives. It is in this fullest telling of our story that we access the inner resources needed to live more conscious and meaningful lives in subsequent circles of relationship. It is in the process of naming and sharing that family life becomes a celebration of relationships and connections that are grounded in history and anticipate a future.

(71

(Friendship: Celebration's Echoes, Patterns, and New Dimensions)

Fate chooses your relations. You choose your friends.

JACQUES DELILLE, EIGHTEENTH-CENTURY
FRENCH ABBÉ AND POET

Echoes have always held a special fascination for humans. Cave paintings in France, which are some of the earliest artful renderings of our species, are believed to have been purposefully drawn in particular chambers of the cave where sound resonated in ways that mimicked the sounds of animals and forces of nature, the elements and mysteries of the world for early humans. In specific locations within the cave, sounds echo for many seconds, lending a sense of depth and awe to the moment, just as thousands of years later, we seek to create resonance with the acoustic design of grand cathedrals and concert halls.

Echoes play an important role in our inner lives as well. The facets of our emotional life are not heard in a single note, sounded

and forgotten. They exist as facets within facets, sounds that become richly developed and appreciated only as they echo through
the first and continuing celebrations of our character through relationship with family, then friends and others.

Echoes resonate through our lives in telling ways. We often find
that certain themes in life repeat themselves. Lucky people seem to
find luck repeatedly. Unlucky people, regrettably, find misfortune
time and again. People who experience themselves as losers in the
realm of love continue to find love and lose it, and feel betrayed by
lovers. People who feel very lovable tend to find love at every turn.
The power of these echoes is often greater than any physical reality. We all know people who, under the worst circumstances, find
success or hope, and others who feel like failures despite clear evidence of outward success.

Remember Wilma, who was told by her mother that she was
"nothing but a nothing"? Wilma had a loving husband and son, and
had found great professional success, but she found "nothing" in it
for herself. Her mother's stinging words became a self-fulfilling
prophecy, an echo that resonated through the deepest chambers of
her inner life: nothing, nothing, nothing.

What are these echoes? Are they the karma with which we are
born? Are they our astrological or genetic destiny? One explanation
is evident in everyday terms. These echoes are of the early celebrations of our being, the sounds of our infancy, our childhood, and our
family. In our unconscious screening of new experiences, we open
ourselves to familiar sounds, and screen out those that do not resonate. As a result, we continually form experience to conform to our
earliest sense of ourselves. As we move out into the world, we are
drawn to these sounds, these patterns in relationships, even when
they are not comfortable. They are the familiar sounds we know of
our*selves* in relation to others.

Whether these echoes are affirming or painful, it is their familiarity that resonates and makes us feel secure in the moment and able to ground ourselves in a new context or new situation. They allow us to feel rooted in our own history, and we feel that we belong to the new context. Just as the signals of the earliest preverbal communications in our infancy led to our sense of being understood—the feeling that we existed—the echoes of that experience help continue the formation of our character in new, broader contexts. While celebration is not the only factor that determines the leitmotiv of our lives, it becomes a very central theme, which we find over and over again as we emerge from family into society, and particularly in the realm of friendship.

If our origins and experience of family life provide the first sounds of our emotional life, then friendship offers us our first acoustic chamber, our first sounding board, for the celebration of ourselves beyond family.

The true beauty of friendship, however, is in the unique experience of choice and the freedom it offers us. Ideally, friendship offers a source of essential support, refuge, and modeling of healthy relationship and self-expression. Friendship can affirm and reinforce the echoes of a nurturing beginning. We also find in friendship the sacred space to explore new facets of our character, hear and experiment with new sounds, and create new echoes of celebration that can resonate in deep and lasting ways. This may not be available to us in the family setting, or it may feel daunting to step out of our familiar role. If we are emerging from a less positive early experience of ourselves, then in friendship we often find the opportunity to break free. A friend can intervene and offer new perspectives and structures for seeing ourselves and evolving; we need not be destined to repeat the patterns of celebration we first learned in our earlier family experience.

"I felt myself *disappearing*," Kimba explained, in some distress as she arrived for our session. She was describing a rare after-work bar stop with her colleagues. They were very nice people. She liked them and they returned her affection. They sat at a long narrow table, the kind that accommodates a large group. She was at one corner.

For a moment the conversation that swirled around her left her out. It was just a moment and without malice. The person on the end of the table to her left was engaged in conversation with the person to his left, and the person to her right with the colleague beyond. Kimba suddenly felt dreadful. She felt paralyzed and unable to speak up and join in either conversation. She felt physically unable to move, held in place; she could not break her sudden and overwhelming sense of isolation. Then she looked at her hand and thought it was "faint." Literally, it seemed to be fading before her eyes. She had a frightening sense of disappearing! She knew it could not be true, but she could feel it happening! She broke out in a sweat, and this caught the attention of others around her.

"Are you okay?" they asked.

"I don't know," she responded, and managed to excuse herself to go to the rest room. When one of her friends offered to accompany her, she felt an immediate sense of relief. The panic subsided. In the rest room she looked in the mirror with a fleeting fearful thought that her image would not be returned. Happily, she saw herself in fine form, though a bit grave in expression. "It must have been the beer, without much lunch," she told her companion.

They returned and she continued to enjoy the evening. But Kimba knew it was not the beer. The feeling was reminiscent of some vague time long ago. It was a place to which she did not want to return in her thoughts. However, Kimba knew she had to face this time and this place if she wanted to free herself from its grip.

She needed to because she was passing her youth in privacy and seclusion, feeling captive, but unable to explain by what, or why.

We began our search for the origins of this "disappearing" experience. Kimba had been the second daughter of five children, sandwiched between older and younger brothers. She was a good child. She was born in the United States, to a first-generation family from a foreign country. "The old country" was a patriarchal and tradition-bound culture in which the boys were celebrated for being males, and the girls were not particularly celebrated, though they did have some sort of generic value. Social respect for girls and women was conditional upon their acceptance and success in the assigned role of females in this society; when they embraced those roles, they found approval. It was the only socially acceptable option.

At the family dinner table, Kimba remembered, the events of the boys' days were told and discussed. Father was very interested and full of advice. Mother served, and as soon as the girls were old enough, they cleared the table and did the dishes. No one asked about *their* day. The most they would hear might be a comment on their appearance or a mistake that they might have made. The fact that they were attending school was a national requirement and of no interest to either mother or father. During the day, the boys could play outside, but the girls were restricted to entertaining themselves at home. They had no context for knowing themselves in a larger, community setting. They were never seen "just hanging out" in the neighborhood. That would have bordered on indecent.

Kimba's story took a different turn. She grew into a very bright young woman and was encouraged by her teachers to continue her studies. Her father and mother wanted to arrange a marriage for her to a boy from the old country. He arrived, but Kimba decided he was not her type, and she refused to marry him. She gathered her courage and said no. All hell broke loose. She could still recall the heated conversation, as if it had taken place an hour before.

"No?! What do you mean, no?!" her parents demanded.

"I mean, I will not marry; I will continue my education," she told them.

"On your own, you will continue your education," they declared.

"Then, I will do it that way," she said.

"You will end up on the streets, a whore!" they screamed.

"No, I will end up on the streets a working woman," she responded again.

Where she found the courage to speak these words was unknown to her. But once she had spoken them, she had no desire to take them back. She moved out, on scholarship and loan, an "emancipated student" and went to college and graduate school. However, she also confined herself in her small room and thus avoided both the promise and the threat that men presented: she would neither meet a man with good relationship potential, nor would she become a whore on the streets. She had accomplished her goal of becoming a working woman, but almost as if she were cursed, she had remained afraid to take advantage of these very accepting colleagues and friends in her life at work. Instead, she had retreated to the confines of her home and lived an ascetic life.

Kimba had not been celebrated for who she was, but for who she *was supposed to be* in her cultural setting. Whatever faint efforts she made to speak of herself in the context of her own desires and her own dreams were dashed by unanimous family censure. However, Kimba's innate capacity to celebrate herself was not extinguished.

As Kimba started to engage more fully in outside friendships, she put herself forward, awkwardly at first. But with the same strength she had summoned up in breaking the ties with her family tradition, she persevered. She admitted to a few friends just how unaware she was of the possibilities "out there" in the world. They were delighted to help. And they were kind and loving.

There was a parallel process going on between her therapy and her friendships. As she developed an understanding in her therapy of the internal forces that had bound her, she felt released to move more openly into her friendships and learn from them. Her friends, in turn, were learning from her. Her sense of internal serenity and peace, a wonderful product of her childhood, was an example for them. They sought her wisdom on matters of the interior life, which she knew so well. What was developing was a reciprocal celebration of Kimba and her friendships.

She gained a new understanding of the "disappearing" act at the bar that night. It had been a very poetic form of an anxiety attack, her "before" story in symbolic form. The bar, the beer, the sensuality of the moment, the man to her left, all these elements had evoked her parents' curse and her history of never having been seen as the individual she was. Kimba had escaped the silencing confines of her family culture, but even far away from it, the echoes of her past had led her to lead a cloistered, emotionally silenced life. She had disappeared, even from herself, but her friends offered her a chance to see herself more clearly and feel appreciated by others. This family of friends celebrated Kimba for *all* that she was, including the history that had been part of her burden, and now became a valued part of herself.

• FRIENDSHIP: OUR FAMILY OF CHOSEN PEOPLE •

We each need to be seen, to feel we exist and matter, in the eyes of others. We define ourselves by how we see ourselves and how we feel seen by others. It is in the arena of friendship that we can continue to learn about ourselves, and be discovered and known by others. Friendship offers us a refuge from the ghosts that inhabit our daily world, the discordant echoes that instill doubt, insecurity, self-defeat, and despair. A friend can assure us we are not alone. A friend can see us struggle with one aspect of ourselves, and remind us of the rest.

In the acceptance inherent in celebrated friendship, we can find a simpler, uncomplicated love that wishes us well. In the dynamic of friendship we can care for others by choice, and feel the nobility of our souls. In the school of friends we can grow and change, trying out new things we discover about life and our own character. Friendship, perhaps more than any other relationship, gives us room to freely evolve, experiment, make mistakes, and make discoveries about ourselves and others.

Friendship is a place where disappointments can be used safely. In marriage the stakes are too high. In child/parent relationships, they could be crushing. In business, disappointment can be costly or disastrous. In friendship, we exist on a playing field of life where disappointment can play out and even enrich us. Friendships make life less lonely, indeed, but beyond the practical effect of filling our social calendar, they create new opportunities for us to evolve as adults, in ways different and apart from the context of family. At every age, friendships give us room to grow, and some degree of emotional safety in which to do it.

CAROL: PAST HURTS AS A CHALLENGE TO FRIENDSHIP

Sometimes the echoes of celebration resonate in hurtful patterns that make themselves visible in our experience of friendship, providing us both a mirror into our inner self, and an invitation to heal and change. If we see ourselves repeating patterns in friendship that don't serve us well, we need to examine those patterns and ask why, listen closely for the echoes, and be open to change.

Carol was dissatisfied and impatient with her life. She had seen too many people come and go in her relationships. She knew that she was a good person, and yet friends and lovers alike left her. Referred by a friend, she came, reluctantly, to psychoanalysis. Introspection was not her forte.

She arrived in simple clothes and carried herself as if she had a burden on her shoulders and was getting tired. Her smile was polite, but fleeting. She slumped into the chair and stared almost blankly at me. If I looked hard past the weary exterior, I could see a dim sparkle in her eyes that spoke both of potential cheerfulness and daring to anyone who might try to engage her that way.

Carol had had many boyfriends, and many men and women friends, socially. One at a time, all the relationships had failed. For someone as good-hearted, charming, and witty as she knew herself to be, it didn't make sense to her.

Her story unfolded from clear memories. Carol had grown up with a sister and two brothers, children of parents whose interests seemed elsewhere. Her father had shown a distaste for family interaction with any of them, typically retreating behind his newspaper to avoid conversation. Carol felt he hated her. Her mother was self-absorbed, lacking empathy, and interpreting any moment in terms of her own pleasure or discomfort. Carol recalled how her mother would often arrive late to pick her up from school, but her mother's greeting words would be angry ones, admonishing Carol that she had no right to feel upset. As a matter of fact, in the context of her family, Carol had no right to feel anything of her own, no right to claim the celebration of herself.

So Carol had learned not to depend on her parents. Further, she expressed a kind of independence by purposefully distancing herself from them in routine ways. She would not tell them anything they asked to know. She would demand what she felt was her due in terms of money, clothes, and other "parental services," but she would not give them anything. Carol carried this style of practical and angry independence into her adult life outside the family.

Out of begrudging hurt she could not offer these uncelebrated parts of herself to her friends. Her relationships with friends and potential boyfriends followed a similar path. She was an attractive friend, in the sense that she made herself available, and generally was open, friendly, and self-sufficient in her dealings with others. But her touted independent nature was a facade only. As the relationships deepened, she would transition from the independent woman they found engaging to the angry, petulant child who was ready to accuse and punish at the first disappointment. Through her disapproval, she became controlling and oppressive in these relationships. When the inevitable petty disappointment occurred— an untimely delay in returning a call, or a failure to follow through on a plan, as she understood it to be—she would become inconsolable, angry, bitter, and cold. Some friends weathered this. Many couldn't, and very few boyfriends could make it past this gauntlet. She would begin to find fault with them, pick on little aspects of their personality that were disagreeable to her, and eventually the friendship or romance would fall apart.

Carol was a needy woman who was unable to cut anyone a break when they disappointed her in the slightest. She wasn't able to celebrate them in the context of disappointment. She could do fine until she was disappointed, and then she didn't have the capacity to say to herself, This is part of them, and I have to recognize the wholeness of this person and why I am a friend. She was incapable of accepting flaws in her friends, because for her, disappointment carried so much more profound an experience of hurt.

In analysis, as we moved past the facade and into the realm of feelings, Carol eventually was able to share that she constantly experienced what she called "feeling irrelevant." One day, angry at me for a mix-up in our appointment time, she cried openly. "I cannot tolerate it," she said. "I cannot tolerate being treated as irrelevant. I promised myself a long time ago—'never again.'"

That moment gave us a particularly helpful opportunity to draw Carol's unconscious feelings—the echoes from her childhood—forward for a conscious examination of the way they resonated in her adult relationships.

"You have forgotten who I am," I said. "You are experiencing me as if I am one of your parents, but I am not. Not all social errors mean the same thing. Your sense of irrelevance is coming forth from your history, and naturally you apply it to me, but these are different circumstances. I am not one of your parents and you are not irrelevant to me. You know that."

Dry-eyed now, she acknowledged that my immediate apology and invitation to talk about it was a dramatic departure from what she had experienced as a child. "But it still hurt," Carol said after some reflection, "and the hurt is overwhelming."

In subsequent months this process repeated itself many times in many versions: any appearance of inattention on my part, a question I might ask that indicated that I had forgotten something she had told me, or my own tardiness. In the process of discussing the origins of her reaction and her hurt, and other factors at work in current situations, Carol eventually was able to distinguish between the circumstances of her past feelings of irrelevance and those of her current life, and thus see her relationships with others in a new light. She practiced a new way to describe herself: "relevant." She experienced that her friends and I genuinely cared for her. Carol made efforts to recognize her misperceptions. Sometimes her old assumption was right—people sometimes *were* self-centered and untrustworthy like her parents—but often she was mistaken on this count. As she healed her own injured past she learned to apologize and work at healing the injuries she had inflicted on friends and lovers. She learned that people can talk about hurt and not be blamed, as she had been, for feeling injured. She interposed a space between her tendency to react to history, and what was happening in the present moment.

Carol's friendships grew longer and deeper. She discovered that other people, her friends, had their own hurts. She discovered a surprising thing about herself: she had a deep capacity for empathy and helping others. With this new insight into her past and into her potential for more affirming relationships, she was able to break the old pattern and create the new types of friendship that she sought. She was now able to accept that the flaws in her friends, though disappointing, were a part of them and not an assault on her, as the echoes of her past made them seem. She was able to create this new sound, and from it, a new echo in her life that would generate new patterns for more satisfying relationships.

• A Celebration of Time, Maturity, and Change •

The beauty of friendship is that it is a celebration, not of what we do, but of who we are and how we share our humanity with another soul. We can *do* many good works and still *be* a miserable, self-centered person who cannot share our souls with anyone. It is in friendship that this will become evident. Friendship is a bond of choice. It demands deeds and work, but in the end, a friendship is not measured that way. The measure of friendship is in how the friendship has added to our mutual growth as human beings who are connected and feel a responsibility to others. The real question is whether we will find celebration in the lives of those who surround us and, just as important, bring it to them.

HANK: A ONCE AND FUTURE FRIEND

Hank was nearing the end of his analysis when he remarked that Sam, an old friend from college days, had called; he hadn't talked with Sam in fifteen years. Sam had recently moved back to town and had called Hank just to say hello. Hank told me how he had listened spellbound, and strangely sad, as Sam described his involvement in the community and how enriched he felt his life had become by virtue of that activity.

Hank had been transfixed, not because Sam's story was so impressive, but by the contrast between Sam's life and his own. Hank had led a largely self-centered life, seldom looking around himself, let alone involving himself in the community.

Their friendship had drifted apart fifteen years before, when Hank was living the party life and had grown bored with Sam's more mature "do-good mentality," as Hank called it.

"Sam was into examining life and talking about it, and I was busy trying to numb myself to it," Hank said. "He wanted a real friend. I was living and surfing on the surface of life and had no idea how to be a real friend. He was very tolerant about my partying lifestyle, but he was way ahead of me on the maturity curve, and I just wasn't ready to go there. He tried to be a sincere friend, and I just ignored it."

In the years since, though, Hank had done some growing up. In analysis, Hank had come to terms with his struggle through a sad and angry childhood as a son born into his parents' deteriorating marriage and cast as the go-between in their bitter divorce. While they ostensibly had fought over him in a custody battle, in truth, it was the fight itself that they sought. They had been indifferent to him. From his teen years and onward, Hank had used alcohol, drugs, and shallow socializing as a cover for a smoldering anger, rage, and self-hatred, and as a way to numb himself to the pain within.

Through analysis, Hank had been able to confront the past, examine it, and move beyond it. The raw wounds of his denigrated childhood had healed. He was no longer abusing drugs and alcohol. We chatted a bit about the healing aspects of friendship, and he said he was ready to look outward now, ready to *be* a friend. He felt a bit awkward about his past shortcomings but said he might eventually call his old friend back.

A few months later Hank called to share some good news. He had E-mailed Sam, told him of his regrets for his past limitations, and had asked for a second chance, as he put it. Sam had welcomed the opportunity to resume the friendship. In their conversations about the past and their lives since those college days, they rediscovered the chemistry that had drawn them together as friends so many years before. However, now each man was able to appreciate what was different about the other. Sam spoke of Hank's unabashed capacity for joy, and how that was something he had found difficult to bring to his own life; he was a generous do-gooder, yes, but he always kept his emotional expression in check. Hank knew that his own past revelry had been fueled, in part, by his painful childhood and his attempt to escape through drugs and alcohol; now he enjoyed a good time but felt drawn to develop a more thoughtful and caring response to life. Each man had something to offer his friend, and something to learn from him.

Hank could see now that with the renewal of this old friendship, and increasingly with other people, he felt capable of celebrating himself and them in a genuine relationship of friendship.

Like virtually every other aspect of life, the way we engage in friendship changes with age and experience. In childhood, we look to friends to create a social and emotional context for our lives, a peer group where we know our place, and a mirror that tells us what's cool or socially acceptable, and what isn't. On our way to adulthood, our friendships either accommodate our more individualized interests and lives, or we leave them behind. The expectations of friendship have to evolve and mature, as we do. These are the hard lessons of friendship, but one of the best lessons when looked at with hindsight. We must accept that some people don't want to play with us. We must use this tough lesson to look at ourselves and at others. It could be about us; it could be about them; it could be about circumstance. That lesson can bring a sober reality to bear upon life, and it is a most important lesson.

We take for granted that children drift in and out of friendships. One of the most challenging tasks of parenting is to guide our children through early social development and the friendship issues that arise. We always assume that we are in the teacher's role as we help young people learn to navigate these relationships, but their stories also hold valuable lessons for us.

AARON: GROWING THROUGH LEAVING — AND RETURNING

My sixteen-year-old son, Aaron, was in a meltdown. When I came into the kitchen, he was holding back tears, standing, leaning up against the sink. He had had it. One time too many now, he had been hurt and shocked by a friend's response. Not some thoughtless quip from a simple acquaintance, but a deeply felt put-down from a *friend*.

"This is simply not my group," he complained. We had looked at this issue before. We had talked it through, many times; he had examined his own actions, his expectations, and his options. He had done that. I had done that. He had done all he could reasonably do.

"This is silly," I said. "We need to look for a place where you can find a good fit for yourself."

In time, we did. We found a program abroad. He would have to live with another family for a year, in a home where only French was spoken. He would study in French and play in French. He was scared, but his fears were ameliorated by the sense of opportunity.

It was hard—really hard—at first. As he struggled to express his personality in French as he gained fluency, he was not alone. The other American students in this program were in the same boat. They sought refuge in one another's strengths—a common language being high on the list—and he came to see that they appreciated *his strengths* as he had come to appreciate *theirs*. This interdependence in such a stressful moment served as the basis of several important friendships.

We would get messages frequently. One day, a message spoke of an evening of laughter at his French family's dinner table. They were teasing the mother of the house, "much as we tease Mom," he wrote, and we realized that, without saying it, he was gaining that fluency and confidence he sought.

At the end of the year, Aaron returned. He was changed. He filled out his skin. He stood erect again and faced his old group with a self-confidence that had been withered before. He sailed into the group and through the rest of high school. It was the experience in general, but most particularly the experience of sharing and growing with his new friends, that expanded his chest and his soul.

Aaron had not so much been crushed, as he had withered, in the absence of affirmation among his hometown peers. He was fine at home after school; every day he would come home and recover. But home is not the only place a child needs to find affirmation. He needs to find both affirmation and friendship outside, hopefully among schoolmates. The experience abroad was reparative because he felt reaffirmed for his strengths and talents as a comrade. He returned to the school near home the next year and found the same old crowd, but some of the kids had matured, and he had matured, too. There were still classmates who weren't nice, but they didn't have the same effect on him anymore.

✳ **DELORES: TURNABOUT FAIR PLAY AMONG FRIENDS**
When Delores went away to college, she admitted she was too close to her family and in need of some distance. Once there, she found herself at sea in her crowded dormitory on a huge campus overrun with peers. She sought refuge by moving into a small house with only a few fellow students. Ann, one of her housemates, was friendly, and she and Delores spent comfortable times together, hashing over their daily routines. Beyond housemate status, Delores liked Ann as a friend but could not get over the feeling that Ann was holding something back, that she was not fully forthcoming about herself.

Finally, Delores couldn't remain silent; it was impossible to be close friends as long as Ann seemed remote in this sense. One evening Delores asked Ann directly, "What are you holding back? I feel we're close, but that there's something you're not telling me, and it keeps me at a distance."

Ann thought for a while and then explained. "You're so naive about life. You talk endlessly about your perfect family. I'm not saying you should or shouldn't, but it's what you do. My life's been really different, but I don't want to burst your bubble."

Delores was surprised. She had assumed that she would hear something about Ann, not about herself.

"Tell me what you mean," she said.

Ann responded, "Maybe your family is wonderful, but mine isn't so picture-perfect. My dad is an alcoholic. I've had to live with his temper and his abuse of my mother and us kids all our lives. We walk on eggshells." Her story unfolded to Delores's amazement. But what was more astonishing to her was the growing realization, as she listened to Ann, that much of her own talk about her wonderful family was defensive. She talked about them like that to surround herself with them—to avoid facing life on her own. She began to hear herself through the ears and experience of her friend. She had not lied; her family was quite "normal" by comparison. That was not the problem. The problem was that she wrapped herself so tightly in her family story to avoid developing her own story, her own life, by growing beyond it.

Suddenly, the basis of the friendship changed and deepened. It had been not only Ann who was holding back; Delores could see that she, too, had been holding back her feelings about this new, challenging life. Delores began to listen and respond to her friend. She didn't share her friend's experience, but she did have the capacity to listen. In the listening, she discovered a level of humanity in herself that she had never exercised in the protected environment of her home. She began to grow, as did the friendship.

As adults, whether we lose a friend, rekindle old friendships, or build new ones, this unique relationship offers rich opportunities to discover new facets of ourself in interaction with others who bring different life experiences to the moment. This opportunity is available to us all the time, in all kinds of friendships, from simple acquaintances, to deeply loyal and long friendships.

• NEW ROOTS, SHARED HISTORY •

In a city like Washington, D.C., where I live, it is almost universal that everyone comes from somewhere else. That means that extended families typically are somewhere else, too. Parents, grandparents, siblings, aunts and uncles, and childhood friends: they all live in a place called "back home," that place where everyone goes once or twice a year around holiday time. Or they live someplace else, where their work has taken them. Sometimes it's a half-day's drive, sometimes it's halfway around the world. In this context, nearly everyone is a pioneer of sorts, here with a purpose, but because their past is not here, they are somewhat adrift in the social sea.

This makes Washington both a tough place to live for the first few years, and a wonderful place to live as time goes on. Over the years, I have listened to many newcomers to Washington lament its shortcomings: it doesn't have this, it isn't that, and it's a far cry from that beloved "other" —the place they left behind. Then after a year or so, the comments change: Washington turns out to be a wonderful place to live, with the beautiful parks, the cosmopolitan avenues, the neighborhoods, the history and culture at every turn. What has changed in that time? Certainly it was not the city. What has changed is the sense of connection to others; friendships have developed at work and in the neighborhood, and the "transplant" has begun to put down some roots in relationships. They have begun to build a family of friends. The celebration of friendship has begun.

In medical science, one of the most critical challenges in organ transplants is to attach a blood supply and then support the transplanted organ or tissue for the period of time it needs to grow its own vessels into the body, at which point it becomes a more natural part of the body. For any of us in a new environment, friendship serves as that nourishing support structure, as we establish ourselves more firmly and begin to feel less transplanted and more a natural part of the social environment.

ROLLA: FRIENDSHIP ROOTED IN DUTY, DEVOTION, AND SHARED HISTORY

Rolla was my mother's cousin and best friend. They were about the same age but only really got to know each other in their late teens when my mother was sent one day to visit Rolla, who was sick. Mom later described it as a duty call. These two young women, only about eighteen years old, bonded quickly—and for life. Duty was the context of their first meeting, so it is not surprising that duty continued to play a prominent role in their friendship, from the most mundane favors to the most heartfelt support they exchanged as friends.

The same day she met Rolla, Mom met the man she would marry. Rolla had a boyfriend, and his buddy came along to visit Rolla that day, too. These two young women both married the young men they were with that day. They often marveled at the similarities and the differences in their destinies. They were both poor, and their husbands were caught up in the war before the ink was dry on their wedding licenses. Each couple had two children, one son and one daughter, in reverse order, at about the same time. These two friends sustained each other through poverty, joy, death, illness, great sorrow, marital disappointments, and all the exigencies life placed before them.

When they weren't working, Rolla and my mother would talk on the telephone; their phone conversations filled the moments between family duties and housework, and part-time jobs in town. Mom told Rolla everything about all of us. She began with the facts and moved right through to commentary and conjecture. Sometimes, as a child and even into adulthood, I thought that Rolla knew my sister and me better than our mother did. She was given all the raw data, but she also had just enough distance to see us objectively. It was this way all our lives.

Rolla's children were my cousins also, but they might just as well have been my siblings. The two young mothers frequently helped each other with child care. I can remember my cousin Sandy as a baby in my mom's arms. I was about three, and Sandy a little younger, when my mother, carrying Sandy, slipped on the ice and fell. Even in her fall, she turned to protect the baby, and broke her own back. There were no tragedies or celebrations without Rolla and Mom together. They laughed a lot and cried sometimes. They seldom were angry at each other, but there was that, too.

In purely practical terms, their friendship filled a desperate need for celebration and healing. They were so alone in a very scary world, and they and their husbands struggled in every way to make ends meet, and to raise their children well. Their shared lives and mutual sense of duty and devotion to each other had evolved into love, and that loving friendship became a source of healing and celebration otherwise missing in their lives of hardship. Women were not born into celebration in those days, especially those in the homes of struggling immigrants. Mom and Rolla found in each other the opportunity to deeply know and celebrate each other. And celebrate they did, for nearly fifty years. They celebrated the good times and the bad times, equally and thoroughly.

Friendships can carry us through life. Just as when we were young children, and one parent provided a safe "other" for us to discuss our struggles with the other parent, friends provide a safe "other" to whom we can bring the struggles of our lives. Through their friendship, Rolla and my mother, in effect, reparented each other, providing a link to the past and their heritage, and the unconditional love both needed so sorely to survive and thrive in the present.

Most of us find the potential for friendship greater today than ever, by which I mean that the technology available can help maximize our access to one another: we can call, fax, E-mail, use portable phones at the very moment we think of each other, or we can travel at reasonable prices over long distances to visit one another.

In this context of constant and global communication with others, we really must begin to use the word *friend* more carefully or we risk diluting its profundity. We must use the word *acquaintance* for those with whom we pass hours or days in mutual pleasure of the moment, but with whom we go no further. Friends, real friends, celebrate each other and celebrate their friendship. The celebration of love in friendship is a celebration of a love of mind, heart, and soul, having nothing to do with romance or sex. Together, as friends, we name the moments of life, painful as it may be sometimes. We share all we can in and about those moments, and we recognize and rejoice in the friendship what we have created. In friendship there is room to stretch our minds and hearts and speak without fear of the consequences to our attachment to each other and our love for each other. Our exercise of meaningful friendship is on the decline, and we are just beginning to feel the unsettling side effects. We lead such rushed lives that we can fail to take the time to recognize moments of possible connection, which can cause us to miss potential friendship.

There are so many activities that we can use to enjoy each other's company. There are so many ways to communicate a quick cute thought or moment. It is so easy to feel a part of something or some group by such mutual activity or communication. However, can we really ask for something special—to be known and appreciated for whom we are—from these people with whom we communicate through mutual activity? Can we reveal ourselves safely? Can we express through word or gesture our love for them? It is easy to *feel* friendship and not really *have* it. If we cannot say yes to those questions, then we might have a good acquaintanceship or a possible future friendship, but we aren't yet friends.

JAY: AN UNSETTLED POTENTIAL FRIEND

Jay stopped by to chat. A young friend in town for a short visit, he was troubled by something he had just begun to notice about himself and everyone else he knew at work and in his social set. He parked himself at our kitchen table and described the problem.

"Tonight, I'll go to a party at the home of a friend of mine," he said unhappily, "and I can tell you now that very few, if any, of the people who have said they'll come will actually show up. She'll invite way more people than she really wants, so that the no-shows won't be noticeable—so she won't embarrass herself. It's like overbooking a flight."

Jay was in his midtwenties, a thoughtful, articulate, handsome fellow with a budding career and active social life. He had no shortage of good-time "friends," yet he felt he had no friendships to speak of. He had grown cynical in the fruitless search. Now, he said, he no longer depended on friends for much more than what they found convenient to share in the moment.

"You sound disappointed," I said.

"Well, it *is* disappointing. It's as if everyone has amnesia," Jay said. "You can do something special with a friend, or do a friend a favor, but if you turn around the next day and ask for their attention, there is no memory of caring or sense of obligation," he stated frankly. "Forget about 'best friends' or even 'good friends.' They're fiction. They don't really exist like they did for our grandparents or our parents."

Jay spoke with the smoothed, flattened tone of a person who is

In the
moment

reporting facts and determined not to show his hurt for fear of revealing too much—maybe sadness, maybe vulnerability, maybe even tears. He did not complain; his was trying to achieve a hardened view of the subject. He displayed a multitude of hurts in his hardness, and he also displayed resignation to his acquired view of contemporary friendship. He had "dumbed down" his social vocabulary, he said, to avoid making the kind of conversation that invited emotional disclosure and the closer connection that seemed to make his friends uncomfortable. He had downsized his expectations, but still, he wanted to get a grip on this feeling of being cheated. He wanted to know: if friendship does not include some special degree of commitment, obligation, loyalty, forgiveness, mutual dependency, and a need for one another, then is it friendship at all? "And if it's not friendship, then what is it? Because whatever it is, that's *all* there is anymore," he said.

"Now, you sound disappointed *and* angry," I said.

"Yeah, I guess I am both. I grew up in a home where my parents and their friends really cared about each other, and you could tell, you could *hear* it. It looked similar to what I have—dinners together, good times, good conversation—but it was different. There was something more personal about it. They seemed to really care about each other." He added dryly: "They just don't make friends like they used to."

He judged himself just as harshly. "The worst of it is, I'm as much like the people I'm talking about as they are," Jay said. "The truth is that I have some friends who are too needy. I like them, but they're 'high maintenance' and I can't afford the time they need. I have too much to do to keep my job and do the things I like to do."

We talked about Jay's fast-paced life, a fairly normal one for most people these days, and about the conflicts it contained for him around this issue of friendship. Through contact at work, at the gym, by E-mail, on the Internet, at parties, and at the restaurants he frequented, Jay was in personal communication with more people in a single day than some people meet in a year, and yet he felt oddly unknown. At the same time, his desire for friendship was sincere, but it conflicted with his resistance to the seemingly "labor-intensive" aspects of friendship that build a relationship of commitment rather than convenience. The result was a nagging sense of loss *and* guilt, anger *and* disappointment, even in the company of sociable others. He was well aware that he was both a victim *and* a perpetrator of this shallow form of friendship. He wanted a closer kind of friendship but wasn't so sure he was capable of being that kind of friend himself.

Whether Jay wanted advice or not, little advice came to mind. What choices do we really have? There is no easy way to true friendship. If we live a contemporary urban life, we encounter so many more people than we feel we can genuinely know as friends. Yet we must put the effort into selecting and developing friendships. We must send out the signals of willingness to be open to the opportunity of friendship, much as a ship sends out sonar signals. They will be reflected back to us in ways that tell us about the next steps to take. When the early reflected signals, or social responses, tell us that we are understood and there is a willing person on the other end of our effort, we must move forward. We must put out the stronger signals of trust, and eventually, we can share a deeper, loving friendship. We still must await the responses, but each time we are rewarded with a positive and reciprocal response we must go back for more. We must also be prepared to drop the effort and move on, if the signals returned are nonwelcoming of the next step. That could be the first round or a later round. It is sad, but it is a natural consequence of taking the time to really know someone; the friendship won't always stand the test of time.

In the
moment

When I hear laments about the scarcity of "good women" or "good men," and the question "where are they?" the only good answer is that they are out there, and the only way to find them is to *be out there*. Despite the fact that the search for good friends can be uncomfortable, disappointing, or even painful at times, our job is to just be out there and be open to friendship. Young people today are more impatient with the process of being out there than in generations past. Everything about contemporary life values speed of response. At work and in personal communications, technology has made our response times faster and faster. Relationships, and specifically friendship, don't work that way. They take time. That's why E-mail is so easy, but human relations are as difficult as they have always been.

We must take the time to cultivate and celebrate friendship because, no matter how self-sufficient technology has made us, we still need those echoes to give our own lives resonance. There are many types of friendship; not every friend will be the one you would call to your hospital bed. But each friendship has unique potential as a relationship to be celebrated: mutually recognized, shared, nurtured, explored, and marveled at. We must bring our histories and our wisdom to our moments together, and feel safe sharing the meaning and mystery of these moments. Finally, we can enjoy the awe of how being a friend can help us feel expansive and grow.

(Love and 5 Commitment)

*To love another you have to undertake some frag-
ment of their destiny.*

QUENTIN CRISP

Of all contemporary adult life passages, marriage
remains the most commonly, openly, joyfully, lavishly celebrated in
our culture. Yet the failure of marriages is just as dominant on our
social landscape today, suggesting a troublesome gap between the
way we think about marriage and the way we engage in it.

When two people make their marriage vows, I believe most are
well intentioned, but many are poorly equipped to follow through
on the commitment. We have, all of us, become infinitely more sophisticated in our views about marriage and our practice of it today
than were our parents or grandparents in their days of courtship
and marriage. We tend to experiment earlier and marry later (and
sometimes, often) in life, carrying much more education, and work,
and life experience with us into our marriages. Even so, we are

really not any better equipped to deal with our vastly more complex lives as a couple than were our grandparents in their time. In some ways, we are even at a disadvantage.

In the rush of contemporary life, and the accompanying focus on material comforts and convenient relationships, we have lost, to some extent, our capacity to celebrate the *interdependence* of our lives to- gether. Now that both partners in the relationship are often self-supporting, we are less financially dependent upon each other. Now that sex without marriage is socially accepted, we can access the purely physical pleasures of sex without the complexities of emotional commitment. Now that divorce is commonplace, it may be more tempting to abandon a stale or difficult marriage than work to revive it. In purely practical terms, marriage has lost its traditional moorings.

More importantly, contemporary life teaches impatience and impermanence. Very little in our social environment or conversation prepares us for the slower-paced, interior journey of a deep, loving commitment between two people, and the unique and challenging opportunity this shared experience can offer for mutual self-discovery and personal growth.

• LOOKING TO THE HEART OF THE ISSUE •

In my line of work, I hear a lot about sex, love, desire, adultery and infidelity, marriage and commitment. For most of us, not a day goes by in which we do not, at some point, to some degree, turn to thoughts along these lines. Most of the conversation we generate about the rise or fall of a love relationship misses the point. We react to the ups and downs and ins and outs of it. We react to our partner's missteps or acts of omission, and sometimes even our own. But this review of the evidence can become a rote exercise that distracts us from the more meaningful truth.

The truth isn't about the marriage or the divorce, or her commitment or his lack of it, but about whom we are in the context of these relationships. Marriage and divorce are both simply cultural constructs, each one a context in which we express our deepest selves, whether we do so consciously or unconsciously. In the context of any of these love or loss relationships, the core issue is about what we, ourselves, bring to that context. We define its content by our actions, and shape it with our expectations. If we want to know what makes for a rich, satisfying, deeply committed love—a celebrated love relationship—or what keeps someone from such a relationship, we must look beyond the evidence, to the source: our own history, personality, and patterns of desire and discomfort. Once we begin to understand ourselves, then we have a basis from which to build and sustain a loving relationship that deepens over time, or leave an uncelebrated union and move on to a new, more promising context for our life's expression.

• ORIGINS AND ECHOES: DÉJÀ VU, ROUND TWO •

We hear of marriages made in heaven, and others made in hell, but in truth, the blueprints and building blocks for each are the same. Celebration forms the infrastructure of emotional intimacy and commitment. Whether we are talking about two people in love, in marriage, or even in divorce, the nature of their relationship is shaped by their origins, by the echoes of the celebrated or uncelebrated self that each one brings to the moment, and by their ability to heal, complement, and blend those elements in their shared life as a couple.

In marriage (which I'll use to refer to any deeply committed love relationship) we celebrate three journeys of the inner life, three stories unfolding: our own, our partner's, and the one of our combined life as a couple. Our stories grow enmeshed. Our partner's inner journey becomes part of the continuing revelation of our own, as ours becomes part of theirs. The third story, the *we* story, also unfolds not only in the practical realm of everyday life but more importantly in our inner, emotional realm. It is this shared inner life that, psychologically, re-creates conditions in which we may experience anew the original connectedness of early life, when we had a sense that we were safely held in the mind's eye of our parents.

I have spoken in earlier chapters about origins and echoes; the echoes of those all-important beginnings and earliest celebrations of our life will create our emotional template for commitment and shared love in the context of adult life. Our original context is our mother's womb; then it is in the arms of our parents and family. In this context we first learn how we are anticipated and welcomed into this life. At this time, our first experience of our own *interior context* is defined by our sensitivities and our proclivities, as well as by what we take in, and how we take it in. As babies, most of us feel committed to our surroundings; we seek the connection. However, the quality and style of our parental and familial commitment to us is variable. Some parents are patient and loving; others are not. Even where the commitment is strong, it is naturally uneven at times, and our experience is informed by that unevenness, too.

This earliest combination of our mutual context and our mutually held commitment creates the first experience of celebration, the first sound of it, in our lives. In adult life, the echo of this formative experience resounds with special power in committed love for and with another person. In this type of relationship we can feel the sense of being held—safely—and cared for and cared about, almost absolutely.

Echoes of the past resonate in marriage in our feelings of security or insecurity over issues of autonomy and dependence, control, abandonment, money, loyalty, work, and family commitment. We hear them, too, in our feelings of safety or risk at our partner's attention or inattention to the details of our lives and our well-being. Sometimes consciously, but always at the deeper, unconscious level, they connect us with our earliest experiences of ourselves as celebrated—or uncelebrated—children.

102) Lena cried angrily at her inability to challenge her husband's ongoing criticism of her housekeeping and mothering. Her friends saw her competence, and urged her to stand up for herself, and she wanted to do so. "But when he starts criticizing me, I feel about this big," she said, lowering her hand to a point about knee-high. "I can't help it. I feel stupid and scared. I know I shouldn't. But I do." Upon reflection, Lena said, those moments reminded her of her childhood, and the fear she felt when her father would react angrily over small, ordinary mistakes she would make. In those childhood moments, she had felt scared and powerless to assert herself. As an adult now, in relationship with another adult, she was not powerless, but she felt and responded that way.

Don was losing patience with his wife, whose career ambitions he had admired in college but which he now resented, since it took her away from family time with him and their two children. "I know it doesn't have to be this way," he said. "My mother worked all our growing-up years when I was a kid, but somehow she always found time for family and made us all feel special. I want that for our kids, too. And for me."

Rosemary complained to her friend that Chuck, her husband, never made her feel pretty enough. Her friend responded candidly, "But in all the years I have known you, you've always been dissatisfied and critical of yourself—your hair, your weight, your shape, your *self*—you've never seen yourself as pretty. You're always telling yourself that you're not good enough. Chuck can't *make* you feel pretty. First, you have to feel that way about yourself."

Echoes like these are responsible for our deepest hopes and expectations, and for the greatest disappointments when we are let down. When our hopes and expectations for this committed loving context are dashed, it is not only our adult self who is devastated. The young child part of ourself also must suffer the loss. This is what makes marriages and divorces so complicated, and sometimes painful.

This second chance, which we meet now as an evolved adult, invites us to share our inner journey and exploration with our spouse or partner, as they share theirs with us. If you want to understand why a marriage is or is not thriving, celebration offers a useful lens through which to see some fundamental pieces of the puzzle. Here is the great confluence of story, soul, nature, and social influence. All that I have said about celebration in our lives leading up to this point comes to bear upon this moment we call commitment or marriage. What does each partner bring to the relationship? What capacity for love is there in each person, and in the new blending of their stories, their souls, and their destiny?

If we were celebrated, we can celebrate. If we were shown the ways of love, we can love. If we were shown the ways of compromise, we can compromise. If we were shown the ways of interdependency, we can be dependent without fear. If we were shown the way to be open to another person and share ourselves, we can open up to our spouse. If we were given the language of searching and discovery, and feeling, then we can celebrate the search for ourselves in this new context of marriage and celebrate the discovery of new, unheard-of potentials in our new selves.

If celebration has been absent in our life; if openness and vulnerability have been closed off by caution or custom; if we have no language for inner exploration, discovery, and feeling; then we lack critical basic skills for the shared journey. If we fear certain depths of discovery, our fear creates obstacles to sharing and intimacy. When one of us is open and the other is not, the relationship cannot advance or deepen. If we have no words to name an obstacle or talk about it, no skills to negotiate it, and no inclination to find our way around it, then the relationship spirals down.

However, past pain does not preclude a loving marriage. We can come to marriage with a history of emotional wounds, we can face formidable obstacles in this new context, and we can set out to consciously and purposefully celebrate our union and the opportunity to heal ourselves and each other. This requires intention and it requires effort from *both* partners. It requires mutually acknowledged effort and intention to heal the hurts and limitations imposed upon us by our history. It has got to be mutual. If nothing else, marriage has to be a safe place where we can acknowledge our limitations and our historical hurts, and seek and mutually agree to help each other. The mutual agreement may be there and not need to be verbalized or even discussed. But if one person is working on it, and the other person doesn't know it, or isn't a partner to it, then it won't work. It can't work.

The celebratory process enables us to identify old damage and build a new inner structure for intimacy in the act of recognizing, naming, sharing, and embracing mystery and awe in the context of marriage.

• THE CELEBRATED MARRIAGE:
A PARTNERSHIP IN PROCESS •

Marriage is like wine. The best wines start with grapes whose flavors are made up of complex elements. Time matures the mix, blending and synthesizing those complex elements to create a new flavor. Time matures a marriage if the elements are brought together to blend and affect one another. In wine making, the art of the vintner is in the timing and tasting and adjusting the blending process. The art of marriage is also in the timing and tasting and adjusting of the blending process. Celebrating marriage day to day is the way to both taste and adjust, and taste again, making modifications as you go along to develop the blend's full potential.

What we bring to marriage is a bit like the kind of grapes that are brought to the blending and fermenting process. If the grapes lack complexity and depth, no matter how hard the vintner works, the wine cannot end up complex and unfold, over time, to create a new and wonderful flavor—it will be flat and carry at best a simple flavor—and it will lose even that in time.

If the point of the marriage is to provide a context in which to safely explore the depths of ourselves with our partner, in a mutual context, then that context must be recognized, named, shared, and the mystery of marriage must be appreciated with a sense of accomplishment and awe. A marriage that honors the complexity of each partner, and protects and cultivates the sacred space of their shared life, grows stronger, richer, and only more satisfying.

Tim's and Robin's marriage is the second for both. Tim's first wife died after a good, long marriage, and Robin had been divorced long enough to have appreciated her own life as a mother and professional woman. Tim and Robin seek to celebrate their marriages and their respective histories. You can see it in their constant devotion to his and her family (a very large group). You can hear it in Tim and Robin as they speak about their histories—their individual childhoods, their individual growing-up years, their first marriages, their losses, their children, their readiness to find each other, and their lives now together. There is a solidity built out of constant attention to these details in each other's life and their new life.

Simone and Doug are a complicated couple. They are both intense and brilliant people with highly successful individual lives. They have raised three sons and seen them all to marriage and grandchildren. No one would call them easygoing. It has not always been easygoing to live their lives. There have been conflicts, illnesses, deaths, and disappointments well sprinkled amid their joys and successes. They have had to work at sorting out their very strongly held positions in life and finding their common ground. They have talked about their differences—a lot—and at times chosen to talk less and simply let it be, but they have never stopped celebrating their married life. One gets the idea that, despite all the intensity and career problems and successes, the marriage was cared for as the highest priority.

Jed called, asking to see me because his girlfriend said he needed help expressing himself. They had fallen in love rather quickly, and Becka moved into Jed's apartment shortly thereafter when he needed a roommate and she needed a place to live. "It was better before we lived together," Jed sadly admitted. "She didn't seem to mind my mess and my obsessing about things. Now she sees everything as a big problem. When I make a mistake in our relationship, like forget to call her from a business trip during the time that I know she can talk, she sees it as a *big* mistake."

As a matter of fact, all Jed could do these days was make mistakes. He took to telling her about her mistakes, which was not his style but just a way to get back at her.

"This is not going in the right direction," I said. "Why don't you two give yourselves room to make mistakes?"

"I said that to her," Jed complained, "but she said that she didn't have time for mistakes. She was running up against the 'clock' and had to settle down and not settle for."

Jed was unable to help Becka with prioritizing what was important. Her criticism paralyzed him, and his helplessness infuriated her. The spiral was not about messes on the floor but about two incompatible pressure points that could not be named or discussed. Jed was unable to negotiate his place in relation to another person in the context of a relationship, and Becka hated any sign of weakness. Neither had the skills or patience needed to lead the merger, and despite its early promise, this start-up failed.

On the other hand, there are my friends Robert and Meg. Their marriage of twenty years has not always been smooth. They are both very intense and professional people. There were a lot of negotiations in their marriage. When asked how they made a complicated marriage work, Meg looked at Robert, as if this one they both could answer for the other. "We give each other a lot of room for error," she said. "We had to realize rather quickly that the rules of the workplace were not the same as the rules for marriage. We both work in areas where error can cost a life or a fortune, but we realized that we could not carry that into the marriage. Believe me, that lesson was not learned overnight. We were having some tough years early on and wondered sometimes if we could make it. Then we sat down and 'deconstructed' our marriage, looked at how we were functioning in our relationship, and realized that we were using the same standards for marriage as we were for work. Once we figured that out, we knew we had to change it, and we made a conscious effort to do so. It got a lot better after that."

Conflict, tension, challenge, absence, ambiguity: in one relationship they become irreconcilable differences, and the story of commitment ends; in another they are part and parcel of a long, textured, cherished story of commitment that only grows stronger.

• MARKING THE JOURNEY OF MARRIAGE •

Time and context are everything in marriage. But time and context are only experienced in our celebration of them: time, because it is an abstract concept that must have real markers to be known, and context, because we grow so accustomed to our context that we can lose sight of its existence. Marriage is a celebration of both, and an entity that evolves through the entire range of human emotions and experience.

Even the down times, fully noted, contribute to a richly celebrated marriage. It is not that we acknowledge down times for their own sake, but that we do so to mark time and context in the marriage. If we celebrate a down time now, then later, when we are at a different place and time in our relationship, we have marked that journey; we feel more deeply alive and part of our ongoing story.

The old people—the old ones of my childhood who had married for many reasons other than romance—used to snicker at the romantic movies of the 1940s and 1950s. They would say, "Who knows love like that?" They knew love as commitment to live life together and "do" life together, and "share" life together. If they were lucky they felt love and fondness for each other, but it was not a necessary ingredient. Were they right or wrong? I don't think there is a yes or no answer. They showed us something that has been lost in contemporary life but can be regained: a sense of the value of sharing time and context.

We have one advantage now that they did not have in the same way. It was very difficult to end a marriage back then, especially for women. Today, when it is clear that there is no celebration left in a marriage, when we agree that the connection is lost and the context is so corrupted that it cannot be saved, then we can formalize it with divorce. That new option—that new fragility of the bonds of marriage—is actually a source of strength in the long run. It requires that we put the effort into the work of celebrating our marriage, or suffer the grave consequences of ignorance or inattention. It also enables us to step free of a context that is lifeless or toxic, and rediscover ourselves in the process of building a new one.

• INTIMACY AND COMMITMENT: THE EMOTIONAL DIMENSIONS OF TIME •

Love, sex, and commitment require time to do well—time to "get it right." It takes time to learn the language of our partner, and to bring depth to the very special, somewhat vulnerable and sometimes scary parts of life. Unfortunately, at this point in history and in our culture, "it takes time" is not a popular concept. Time is valued these days by its brevity, not its length. This shift in our concept of time and how much of it we're willing to invest in seasoning, has undermined the one adult relationship that should, above all, celebrate emotional intimacy.

For a person who seeks to celebrate his or her love for another person, sexual intimacy can be the ultimate act, both psychologically and physically. The elements of celebration are there in our recognition of the moment, our focused attention in the act, our sharing, and if both parties are tuned to the silent soul of the other, the inherent mystery and awe that envelop us and are exclaimed in orgasm.

Despite the physical intimacy inherent in sex, however, emotional intimacy is not about sex. In fact, sex isn't even necessary for emotional intimacy, and sex without love creates more obstacles, than access, to such intimacy. Nor is emotional intimacy necessarily achieved by feelings we usually associate with it: openness, vulnerability, and trust. They are, as we say in the language of science, "necessary, but not sufficient." Emotional intimacy requires *time*. Context and commitment can happen in many circumstances— military or camp life, deep friendship, affairs of the heart, work, and religious faith—but they do not necessarily lead to intimacy. Intimacy is about all that *over time*. I don't think it matters if love comes first or not. I don't think it matters if there is marriage or not. I don't think it matters if the people are of the opposite sex or the same sex. What matters is that we are willing to invest the time to cultivate intimacy.

Our independent rush through life shortchanges us on the quality time needed to develop the emotional intimacy we assume to be part of marriage, and the seasoning needed to strengthen that partnership. In love, sex, or marriage, seasoning is of the greatest importance. By seasoning I mean time to wrestle with the substance and the meaning of the intricacies of relationship and the skills we bring to it. It takes mistakes—many mistakes—and it takes figuring the way out of those mistakes. By seasoning, I mean exploring in both directions: it is about each partner's adventure of self-discovery in the context of life with the other, and the growth and blending of each partner's interior life, to make a combined interior life. It is this interior journey of marriage that brings us the greatest reward and creates a reservoir of feeling we can tap when needed, to revive a marriage that has grown parched.

ALMA AND TED: NEGOTIATING LANGUAGE, CONNECTION

Alma called, asking whether I would be able to see her and her hus-band, Ted; they were having troubles.

"What troubles?" I asked.

Alma answered with a bit of anguish in her voice. "It's as if we live two separate lives. We share a house, but nothing much about ourselves anymore, and nothing about *us*," she said. "There's no fighting or animosity, but there's no passion, either."

They came from different worlds—not different countries, just different worlds: one rural and one urban. They met in graduate school, shared a great friendship, and eventually fell in love. Nei-ther had much family support, but each for very different reasons. Ted's family were very stoic country folk and didn't believe in talk-ing about feelings. There was a family story, a handed-down history that went so far back that among the current generation no one re-membered nor cared any longer. They had lost their history over time and through the growing disinterest of generations before. That tradition—the disinterest in their history (or the new genera-tion's chapter of the family story)—was the only tradition that was passed along.

Alma's family was steeped in their own cultural tradition. No one ever moved very far away, especially the women, and no one pursued higher education or cohabited with strangers—people out-side the culture. Against family pressures, Alma moved away to at-tend the university, and in her family's view, her idea of marriage to "that man from the country" ended all hopes that she would come to her senses and return to their clannish life.

Their friendship was what came first. Feeling very alone at school, they both were in need of a friend. Then, in the context of their friendship, they shared their thoughts, but mostly Alma's difficulties aspiring for a life unbounded by the restrictive climate of her family.

"Ted was my soul mate and best friend," Alma said, and Ted nodded in agreement.

"Was she yours?" I asked.

Ted nodded and then said thoughtfully, "She was my best friend. No one had ever been that close to me before, and I didn't know what to do with that."

They told their story. In time, Ted said, he had learned to like this new experience of sharing. "I loved sharing her different perspective on life," he said.

"He was good at it," Alma volunteered.

They saw themselves as two people allied against "adversity" (Ted's word) and "exclusion" (Alma's word). They began to feel deeply for each other and soon called it love. They were passionate about advancing each other's careers. They moved to a city unfamiliar to both of them, for highly desirable positions in different corporations. They lived together and enjoyed building their material lives as their combined salaries permitted. When they felt financially secure enough, they got married.

"It was the logical thing to do," they said.

Their families were happy that they had legitimized their union, and relations were friendly, although neither family was near nor present in their lives. Their married life centered around career advancement and material acquisition. Both agreed that children would not fit into this marriage. They liked children, but both felt that a child would disturb their devotion to their careers, and that the child should not bear the burden of their resentment. Having settled that, and being well on their way in their careers, they were on the road to living happily ever after.

Then Alma's job deteriorated at the same time that Ted's career soared. She shared her woes, and he tried, as always, to advise and "fix it." Alma found herself resenting his help and told him to keep his advice to himself. She felt that his style was more like a parent than a sharing partner. Ted felt that she expected something of him, something she wasn't making clear, and it left him feeling confused and defensive. He didn't like being forced into a position in which he felt incompetent.

Communications between them broke down. Alma worked hard to improve her work situation, and slowly she began to advance and be recognized and valued at work. She was obsessed with securing her career and never again letting herself get into the position at work that she had just been through. She was not present for Ted in the ways she had been. He began to involve himself in various sports activities after work, keeping his schedule to himself. Soon their leisure time was being spent mostly separately. They continued to live together, and financially they prospered and, in a way, enjoyed the fruits of their labors. But whatever had bonded them seemed to have been lost.

"Do you love each other?" I asked.

They both nodded yes, Alma through tears and Ted with a serious, thoughtful look on his face. Then Ted said, "I'm just not so sure what that means now, at this time in our lives. What we had is no longer what we need. What we need is no longer at our fingertips."

"What is not at your fingertips?" I asked.

"We don't have a way of telling each other who we have become, who we are *now*. I feel rejected in the one and only way I had always related to Alma, by listening and suggesting what she could do. She wants something else, but I can't figure it out, and she hasn't explained it. She hasn't yelled, but I know she has been angry at me. But I haven't done anything wrong! How can I fix something unless I know what it is? Anyway, the problems have changed—they used to be practical things you could fix, and then she didn't want that kind of help anymore. Now the issues aren't something you can *fix,* and we can't seem to talk about things in a way that allows me to be helpful. It makes me feel pretty useless, and that hurts."

"He's right," Alma said. "I did reject his help. At the beginning of my troubles with work, I just wished I had my family around me. I wanted my mother or my father, but they really would have been worse than Ted about giving advice I didn't want to hear. But I still missed them, and I can see that I got so angry with Ted because he wasn't them, and they weren't there. Then I got busy at work, which made things better, and I couldn't stop work to look up until I felt secure in my job—it's a very competitive place. He couldn't understand that, and by the time I was on my feet, he was gone into his macho sports thing, which really excluded me."

As they spoke, they felt hurt by each other but connected in their hurt. They could agree about the history that led to their hurt. They could admit love, but estranged love. They shared the same memories and the same feelings about those memories.

Sometimes a couple does not share the same memories, nor the same feelings about the same memories. This is more of a problem because they have not been sharing for a long time. The precedence of sharing deeply in their marriage is not evident. They feel estrangement without love; the marriage is over or bankrupt.

Ted and Alma did not feel like that. In their second or third session they evidenced the work they had done alone and together. They accepted responsibility equally and did not feel the need to blame. They did not say "you did . . . ," but instead they would say, "I felt this way when you did that." They remained sensitive to each other and respectful of each other's autonomy, while at the same time joined in time and context and memory. It was clear that, despite the drifting apart, they remained a viable couple, two individuals who shared a soulful commitment to each other, to their marriage, and now to the effort to revive their shared life.

The good news for Ted and Alma was that they were still committed to their marriage. The challenge was that it would take work to rebuild. It was like a brick wall built long ago; the bricks were still in place, but there was very little mortar left. It needed new mortar. The two of them would need to find new ways to share their lives, both as individuals and as a couple. Neither was good at feeling incompetent, so they would need to help each other through this challenging piece of reconstruction.

What we did in therapy was create an environment of safety again, since it had been lost in the marriage. Safety to name their respective hurts, to recognize the particular histories that they each had behind those hurts, and to remind them of the skills they had in the marriage, with which to lay these out and share with each other their own inspired sense of what they could contribute to healing each other's hurts and pains. In that space they could rediscover that which they originally had in their marriage, which was the capacity to be each other's best friend and confidant. They went on to do that, and without extensive counseling. They were ready. They wanted their loving marriage back. They used the elements of celebration to reinvest themselves in each other and in their marriage. It was marriage again in process.

Marriage is endangered by the loss of time to season ourselves in the language of love and building a relationship. We can't escape the burden modern times place on love and marriage. There are too many points at which a couple can move apart in tiny increments. The two-career couple, commuting, the overscheduled lives of parents and children, the Internet and the capacity to connect outside the marriage: all can move us apart in tiny steps that are not recognized until two partners cannot call out to each other over the chasm that separates them. Alma and Ted did *not* make choices to move apart—not at all. They used the easy things and activities at their disposal to do so when they could not confront their needs and hurts. Ted had used listening and advising as his language of love, and Alma wanted something different, a more textured response, as she would have gotten from her family during her stress and fear at work. When Ted failed to give her what she wanted, Alma began to fail communicating her needs, so they just reached out to what *was* at their fingertips—work and play.

• DIVORCE: CONTEMPORARY STYLE, TRADITIONAL PAIN •

In medicine, much of the scientific knowledge that enables us to save lives comes from our study of death and the progression of disease that precedes it. In the realm of relationship, some of the most valuable lessons about marriage can be found in the details of divorce. I say this not in a cautionary sense, to suggest that all divorce is preventable or all failing marriages curable. To the contrary, some marriages are toxic, and divorce is a lifesaving measure. The learning opportunity is this: if we view marriage as a context for mutual growth and self-discovery, then we can look at the strife of an uncelebrated marriage or divorce as a context for learning, too. We can use the opportunity to identify patterns of character and history that are destructive, or which fail to nurture the inner life of one or both partners, or their shared life as a couple.

I have actually seen simple divorces we might describe as good ones—divorces where the mistake of marriage was clearly seen and agreed upon and the legal contract ended with "no-fault" and no children. That is a rarity and actually suggests there was never a genuine marriage of emotional intimacy. Divorce of this kind cannot teach much except to note that a swift realization and resolution of mistakes affirms our capacity to learn from them. We sometimes take a few steps on the wrong path of life. That is not a problem if we recognize it, identify the mistake, settle up with integrity, and move on.

But most divorces—the vast majority of what now is the majority of outcomes of most marriages—are painful to excruciating. And when children are part of the equation, the pain level is exponentially greater. Divorce like this is a context of hurt and of loss; the lessons to be gained there are painful ones, but no less valuable as opportunities for self-discovery and growth. Just as in marriage, those lessons are available to us if we move beyond blaming, look below the evidence, the rubble of the relationship, and ask: how did I get here?

When Irene heard the words "I want a divorce" from her husband, Ben, she honestly thought he was joking. But he wasn't. He had waited until the last child was off to college to free himself from a passionless marriage. They had never known passion. He had not minded at first, because he was afraid of passion. But as the years went on, Ben found that he felt passion for other women. He had never cheated; maybe that was his problem, he said to himself, but now he wanted to know and share passion before he died, and while he was still young enough to grow in the glow of it. He also knew that passion was impossible with Irene. In fact, her absence of passion had been what attracted him to her initially; she was safe, predictable—emotionally undemanding. It was as if all passion had been removed from her in infancy, and she had replaced it with loyalty—dogged loyalty—and efficiency. She wasn't even a particularly kind person. They had used each other, and their marriage, as a place to contain their fears and conflicts without working to resolve them. Now he wanted to be done with that; he felt it was his time to enjoy the rest of his life. He avoided thinking too much about the consequences for Irene; he believed that this would be the end of joy for her, whatever joy she could ever feel, but that should not trap him. He couldn't allow it to—it was her problem.

For Irene, the dawning awareness of what this meant was beyond devastating. She had found her purpose in this life of devoted marriage. They were a good-enough team. Ben had never been a very passionate man; he was very obsessive. She provided the home life, the plans for play, the family, the child care, the connections to his miserable family, the nursing care for his fragile ego, and even some of the earnings. Because she alone was responsible for the care of their children, she had never pursued a career, limiting her outside involvement to a part-time job to supplement Ben's income. She had sacrificed her own higher education and career development for his, and to care for their children. She had left herself completely dependent upon him, a feat of loyalty and faith, she had always thought, in light of the fact that she and her mother were abandoned by her father when she was five years old, and she didn't really trust men too much. She had always envisioned this as a sign of their commitment; she depended on him to be the provider for the family, and he had depended on her to be the caregiver. Now, the terms had changed. Now, this betrayal; Ben was going to seek his happiness, without any thought of hers! He wasn't even interested in talking about it. His mind was made up. He was through with her and already focused on the future he desired.

She wondered if there was another woman. He denied it, but she was never sure if he was protecting her, himself, or his assets.

So they went down that dead-end road. She remained in a state of shock for the entire time, two long years of legal process. It felt surreal to her. It was happening all over again—that vaguely nauseating feeling she only faintly remembered from the earliest memories of her father's abandonment of her and her mother.

She got a good-enough lawyer, but Ben was dictating the terms of the financial settlement, and they ignored the sweat equity of her years of homemaking, child rearing, and supporting his career advancements. Each time she challenged the terms, her lawyer shrugged, sympathetic, but blunt in his conclusion: "You're getting screwed, but there is nothing you can do about it." Ben agreed to pay child support for their two school-age children, to the extent of financing their education, but not beyond—because, after all, this was *his time in life*. She would have to support herself. She got the home but had insufficient income for its upkeep. She would not get a share of his pension; she had never thought about the fact that he had chosen not to place it in joint ownership. Had he always been thinking about this—all those years?

The answer was yes, on some level he *had always been thinking about this,* not in this exact form, but as a man emerging from the inhibitions of his own childhood. She had not thought about parting at all, because she had latched onto this marriage to repair her own childhood. She made her compromises up front with this rather plain man who offered security and no romance, in order to heal the scars of those uncertain years spent holding her mother together and running interference between her estranged parents. At least she would not have to worry about that with this man, or so she had thought.

As for Ben, he hadn't married with an idea of compromise in mind. He married to complete the picture of his life without challenging the fears of intimacy that haunted him from his own childhood in the shadow of an oppressively possessive mother and censuring father. He had been the child to succeed for each of them, for their reasons, not for his. He had done so for them, not for him. He had never been able to live *his own life for himself.*

For both Ben and Irene, the echoes of their respective childhoods had never been silent, only hard to hear in the commotion of living life. Now those echoes were ringing as loudly as bells inside a church tower. They couldn't hear themselves think for all the noise of these hurts—these *old hurts*—made anew.

What failed here? This was a marriage that had celebrated one thing, and only one thing, that was mutual for both partners: safety. With hindsight, you could say that the marriage had been insufficient from the beginning. For this shelter of safety in marriage, they both sacrificed their dreams: his of passion and hers of professional achievement and attainment. Nothing else could be celebrated after that because the requirement for staying in the shelter of safety was that she sacrifice her future as a productive, accomplished professional, and he sacrifice his passions.

To truly celebrate this marriage would have been to address that which was too painful for them to address: the sacrifices they had made for the cold reward of safety. Instead, he lived more out in the world in his career, and eventually found himself ready for passion. She lived a more constricted life in the original agreed-upon shelter. When he was ready to move on, she was not. The incapacity of this marriage to celebrate itself beyond the singular element of safety assured its doom from the outset. It takes more than safety to make a marriage. It takes safety first, but from that safe place there must be some kind of celebrated evolution, the effort by each partner to grow, and to grow the marriage—mutually change and evolve the marriage contract.

Contemporary marriages don't do well if they are obligated to maintain the original contract. The contract must change, it must evolve. In the old days when a man and woman had to accept their lots in life, it was easy to maintain the original contract and maintain a marriage even if it was miserable. But we no longer hold that men and women must accept their lot in life; the contract exists to be renegotiated, amended, or evolved. For Ben and Irene, the essential nature of their personalities made them seek refuge in a limited contract, but those very qualities pointed to its end, as well.

(121

• CELEBRATION DEEPENS REWARDS OF COMMITMENT •

No couple is without old hurts, either individually or in their shared relationship. Legal vows of marriage cannot heal those hurts, erase them, or prevent them. That is inside work, the work of defining and redefining ourselves in the way we celebrate ourselves and our commitment to a shared life.

We have few chances in life to capture all the echoes of our life together in one moment. In loving intimacy to a committed partner or spouse we have such an opportunity. It is the same continuing journey of everyday intimacy that creates the celebrated marriage.

(Work: An Expression of Life)

The greatness of work is inside man.

KAROL WOJTYLA (POPE JOHN PAUL II)

Marvin was in his late sixties or early seventies when I met him in a pottery class at a craft school in Maine. A retired merchant, he had spent the past few years of his life studying to be a potter—he wanted to be a good one. Marvin had long collected the pottery of the young and undiscovered potters of New York City. He filled his home with his treasures. Sometimes the potters whose work he collected became famous, and he moved the piece he had bought when they were young to a more prominent place in his collection. He still loved the others as he would have loved his less spectacular children, if he had had any. Each piece of pottery represented a person whose destiny or fate was important to Marvin.

Now, in his retirement, Marvin had decided it was time to learn to throw a pot himself; he wanted to be an artist. He had the shapes of his pots clearly in his head; all he had to do was make them—throw them, glaze them, and fire them. He started with classes at the local YMCA, then moved up to the summertime craft school, on the coast of Maine, where I met him. Marvin was the oldest in our class, with other students ranging in age from middle-agers to young college students, almost all of whom were reasonably skilled and headed into careers as potters, woodworkers, sculptors, printmakers, and painters. Marvin, too, wanted to achieve something with his art. He wanted, before he died, to create something beautiful, matching the images that crowded his mind.

Marvin's problem was this: his heart and soul were in his work, but he could not get his fingers, palms, and wrists to create the images that were in his mind. Marvin's pots became a source of humor—painful humor—in the school. He was a terrific sport. Each of his pots he judged on its merits, and by his own reckoning they had very few merits. "Now there's a real *tup!*" he would say of a little pot that, as the Yiddish word implied, was functional but without a trace of artistry. Sometimes he clearly felt disappointed with the outcome of his efforts, but Marvin was a patient man. He potted on, trying one form after another and one glaze after another.

One day I passed the pottery studio and heard what sounded like a small celebration. Marvin excitedly invited me to enter and step over to see the pot he had just finished shaping on the potting wheel. Still damp, this clay creation was beautiful indeed, and he gazed at it with such pride that his joy was contagious. Everyone in the studio felt a few degrees happier that day. Marvin's pot was the center of attention. There was a great deal of talk about the type of glaze he should use after the first firing.

Marvin's pot came through the first firing in fine form. He could now handle it and pass it around for another round of admiration and comment. A few days later, there were enough pieces done by

WORK: AN EXPRESSION OF LIFE

the students in the studio to load the kiln and fire it up for the final glaze firing, an overnight process. The next morning, we arrived to a disaster. Air bubbles trapped in the clay of one piece being fired had caused it to explode in the kiln. The explosion had destroyed every other pot in the kiln, and Marvin's piece was among the casualties. Everyone was upset by their losses, but as Marvin sifted through the rubble, collecting the pieces of his pot from the heap of ceramic shards in the kiln, we all felt his pain.

At dinner that evening, we mourned our losses and talked philosophically about art and craft and perfectionism. Suddenly, I realized that Marvin was not among us. After dinner, I wandered over to the pottery studio. There sat Marvin, alone, assembling the pieces of a classmate's pot with glue, into a near perfect semblance of its original form. I was uncertain whether I should interrupt him, but finally I walked in.

"What's up, Marvin?" I asked.

"You know," he said, keeping his focus on the clay pieces as he ever so carefully joined them together, "I'm not sure my destiny is to make pots. I think my destiny is to save pots."

I didn't understand at first until I looked at his handiwork. He was doing an amazing job of assembling those pieces.

From that day forward, Marvin completely shifted the focus of his work. He turned his full attention to the art of restoration. His work was so skillful that often you couldn't even discern the original fracture lines. Marvin became a devotee of ceramic repair and the joy of bringing success from disaster for others. He became an aficionado of material, form, function, and glaze. He became accomplished and respected in his work.

Marvin died several years ago. When I think of him, I see him sitting on a stool at his worktable with pieces of broken pottery in front of him as he quietly and precisely mended one piece to an-

In the
moment

other, re-creating the form that once was, and filled with a sense of impending pleasure when the owner of that piece would see it intact again. In Marvin's search for a way to express his creativity through pottery, he had wrestled first with the clay, but later, he also had wrestled with his inner artistic dream. He was forced to compromise his dreams, but not his inspiration. In his work as a restoration craftsman, he found a way to bring who he was to his new work, and find himself, as well, in this new endeavor.

Marvin's search, his self-discovery, and his joy, represent the challenge and reward accessible to each of us in the realm of work. Each of us yearns for self-expression and meaning in our work, whether we work in a studio, an office, a factory, a restaurant, a hospital, or a home. To the extent that our work allows us to experience this essential part of ourselves we feel affirmed and celebrated in it. To the extent that our individuality and self-expression are discouraged, discounted, exploited, or unappreciated, celebration is lost and our efforts leave us deprived, drained, and ultimately desolate in our work lives. Marvin found what was essentially to be celebrated in himself, his gift. He had a great aesthetic sense and a generous spirit. In the recovery of the beauty of others' art, he satisfied both.

• WORK AS A MEASURE AND A MARK OF SELF •

Our experience of celebration through work includes exploration, discovery, and sharing, basic elements of the celebratory process, but there is more. Every living thing seeks to leave its mark in the world, to be effective, whether that is expressed in a salmon's struggle upstream to spawn or a toddler stacking blocks to make a tower. We marvel at the works of nature: the spider's web, the beehive, the beaver's dam, even the work of cells and organisms invisible to the eye. It is all part of the amazing complexity of a living ecological system. As humans we invest our work with meaning beyond its function in our ecosystem. It is part of human nature to want to know ourselves as effective or to see our work as having an impact on our surroundings and those that inhabit it. The more highly developed a culture, the more complicated and difficult this task becomes because we are more removed from our basic place in nature and in the ecological system or food chain of everyday life. The industrial revolution, now echoed by the technological revolution, has lifted humankind from the basics to a place where we can be both more effective in, and more removed from, our natural place in life and the work that goes along with it.

Celebration offers both a way to know our effectiveness and a way to transport it from one venue to another. Working is like painting ourselves on the tableau of life. So much of the satisfaction and disappointment in our work life comes from the presence or absence of being able to celebrate ourselves in this manner. So much of the conflict between our work and personal lives emanates from the disparity of feeling celebrated in one venue but not another.

Using the process of celebration we can identify what is essential in ourselves and take those essentials into any venue in which we find ourselves, be it work, love, parenting, friendship, even adversity. It creates a type of transportability of what is essentially us while providing a means of relocating that essential in another venue by recelebrating it in that context. It lifts us above the obstacle of any one venue or any one moment by allowing us to reconstitute ourselves beyond the obstacle.

If celebrating means taking note of and naming, sharing, and arriving at a place of awe and mystery, then in our work we have the potential to do just that. If we can find and feel our impact on life in our work, we can recognize it and name it and either do it in partnership with others or share it with our friends and intimate partners. We can step back and say, "Look at what I've done—what I have created in this life." This is something that can be done by farmers, assembly line workers, secretaries, artists, housewives, househusbands, doctors, and even lawyers and politicians. It really doesn't matter what we do as our work; it is in feeling the effect of our doing that work that it becomes an expression of our inner selves.

• ORIGINS AND ECHOES IN OUR WORK LIFE •

There are only a few ways we can truly get to know ourselves in life. It is through work that we have one of the clearest senses of ourselves in action as effective people. How we do that, how we perceive that, how we understand that, is shaped, as always, by the origins and echoes of celebration in our lives. It is no coincidence that certain professions "run in the family," when the family culture celebrates that work and those who succeed at it.

Our work life might feel like a coincidence or the result of happenstance, but it seldom is. It takes some time for our work to shape us and for us to shape our work to see and hear the echoes of our life's celebrations, but most of us in our middle years smile and laugh at the seeming coincidence of our chosen work and our history. My mother was a great listener; I'm a psychoanalyst. My wife's mother was absorbed with proper dress and social custom; my wife works in women's fashion. My friend was born to parents who each needed his help to define a sense of self; my friend is an image consultant. Social fairness was of the utmost value in another friend's home; that friend is a judge. Freedom to be individuals was valued in my cousin's offbeat family; my cousin is a weaver living on a wool farm in Maine. This does not mean we do not have real freedom to choose our work; it means that the echoes of work celebrated in our family of origin resonate in a special, and often inviting, way for us.

However, as in friendship and marriage, we can choose to use this arena of work as an opportunity to be open to new ways to see and understand ourselves, new ways to grow, to mend, to heal.

MARGE: WORK TENSIONS AND ECHOES FROM CHILDHOOD

Marge was successful and unhappy. "I am not good working with other people," she concluded.

She had risen high in her field but had had to move from one place to another to do so. This, in and of itself, was not atypical for her line of work, but she knew that the moves were also prompted, each time, by tensions at work.

It was hard for Marge to see at first, but once she looked more closely it was apparent that these tensions were the result of echoes of old relationships, which now "infected" her work life. She was brilliant and talented; that was well recognized. However, when another person got an assignment or promotion that she felt she merited, she dove down into a black pout. She couldn't pull herself out of it.

These were echoes, indeed, of feeling cheated as the second child of parents who had only enough love for one. Her mother and father had wanted one child, and their firstborn daughter was the love of their life, the celebrated child. Then came Marge. Despite her many accomplishments, the prevailing family climate was that she was a burden, too labor intensive. All problems that came their way were somehow referred back to Marge's presence. It was not spoken; but it was communicated. It was known.

That was the dark place to which Marge descended any time her superiors gave her work "siblings" those benefits she felt should be hers. She saw work not as a place to paint her tableau but as a marketplace for love and recognition. There was no precedent in her life for celebrating her sense of herself in her work, and any potential for such self-discovery was either ignored or subordinated to this desperate attempt to get *love* from her work. As a result, she missed the most affirming experience she might have gained from her work, in her hunger to rectify what was missing in her past.

MARTY: LEARNING TO TAKE THE RIGHT RISKS

Marty looked a bit like a wet gerbil when he first came to see me. He was working in a federal program for recent college graduates. He was definitely not challenged in his work. In truth he avoided challenge. He was dating a girl who shared his cautious aversion for life, and the two of them lived mutually sheltered lives.

"I think I'm depressed," he said. I asked him to elaborate on this sense of depression, and he noted how few highlights he could recall in his life. He had excelled at school but had only vague and generic ambitions. His whole family appeared to share this cautious lifestyle. His parents had not expanded their horizons beyond the place in which they had landed after finishing their career training. His brother held a job far below his qualifications. The family seemed to share a dim view of life. They felt Marty lucky to have found a girl at all, let alone one who didn't challenge his "fragile capacities."

"What is fragile about your capacities?" I asked.

"Well you know, I get anxious—very anxious—if overwhelmed," he said matter-of-factly.

"Getting anxious is part of extending oneself into the world," I said. "It is not necessarily a sign of fragility."

Marty laughed and reflected further on his family's style of responding to anxiety. In their midst, anxiety was a red flag, an alarm, a call for help, and help came from everyone. There was little differentiation between anxiety over school tests or over medical diagnoses; anxiety was a threat, and the first and foremost goal was ending the anxiety.

Once Marty began to understand that in some circumstances anxiety was a normal, healthy part of life, it didn't take long for him to begin to take a few risks and flourish at the discovery of his ability to withstand the anxiety inherent in this kind of risk and change. After a time, he decided he had to part company with his girlfriend, who remained steadfast in her aversion to ideas or decisions that carried an element of risk or change.

We also needed to address the fact that he had a limited vocabulary for expressing his own interests and ambitions in life. Every time we would talk about these, he would frame his answers in terms of his family culture and wanting to satisfy family expectations. He had not developed the syntax of self-expression. His was subordinate expression; his life had become the subordinated expression of his parents' approach to life. So we began the process of celebrating self-expression, self-ambition, self-inspiration, and learning to stay that course even when it contradicted the family culture and put him at odds with those whose approval he had sought all his life.

Marty began to step out of the shadow of his history. He signed on for some sports activities in the local community center and began to date other women. The change in his outlook and even his appearance was dramatic. This wet gerbil began to fill his skin. He grew into an increasingly fit, smiling young man. Even if I could see the insecurity in this new demeanor, his smile was genuine and his eagerness for the next new discovery was evident. Then he set about to look for a "real" job.

One day he arrived with news: two fine job offers. With an interest in politics and government, Marty had applied at a politician's office as an entry-level staff person. Knowing that such jobs are hard to get, he had also explored a teaching position in a middle school. To his amazement, he received offers from both.

He described both positions as well as he could. Both sounded good. I asked what he was looking for in his work. This question took him by surprise. He thought quietly, then said he didn't really know what he was looking for. He hadn't thought about it in those terms.

"Well, what do you have to offer those two respective worlds of your work?" I asked.

"I love literature, and I know I can teach it," he said. "I don't know if I connect with the kids, though. I wasn't exactly in the cool group at that age—or any age for that matter." He laughed. "I do know that I have a real wish to do something with my work life."

"It sounds like you need to feel your effectiveness in whatever choice you make," I said as we parted.

The next time, Marty came in with a renewed confidence. "I took the teaching job," he said. He seemed pleased.

"What was the determining factor?" I asked.

"I thought about what it means to feel effective, and I decided I would feel more effective working with thirty kids; I could teach them something about the wisdom to be derived from literature. I'm not afraid of connecting with them. I know I'll find a way. I didn't think I would feel the same kind of effectiveness in an entry-level job in politics. Anyway, after a year of two in the classroom I think I'll be better at any other job."

Marty had found a place to start developing the skill of painting the tableau of his life with his own efforts and ideas. He needed to feel that heady feeling of accomplishment that seemed to be inhibited in the family that had raised him. Marty needed—and was ready now—to learn how to place himself in the context of his own ambitions and take steps along that path, wherever it would lead.

WORK: AN EXPRESSION OF LIFE

ALEX: LOSING A JOB, FINDING A SOLID CENTER

If we can learn to celebrate fully who we are, we also become more resilient in our work lives. Change becomes less threatening, and we're better able to tap into our strengths and hold ourselves until a new venue is found.

For Alex, the injustice was palpable. This fine man discovered in his fifties that he was not a person; he was a fungible component of the company he had served with love and loyalty. He was out of a job. Alex was more than devastated; he felt destroyed. He had always defined himself by his work, his job—this job—and now this job was gone. He had tried to use outplacement services to find another job, but there seemed to be no demand for a person with his extensive experience and high salary history. When he lowered his salary requirement, prospective employers seemed suspicious; he was overqualified, and why would someone so qualified settle for a low-paying position? Time wore on; his confidence and self-esteem plummeted. His wife and family tried to be supportive, but over time that felt even worse.

"Pep talks don't help," he said. "I have to face the facts. I'm used up. That's what it comes down to—I'm like some commodity in the global marketplace that no one has any need for anymore."

"It is possible that you are used up in that particular field," I said, "but that does not mean that the person who you are is used up." I hadn't heard him make that distinction. His personhood had seemed to end with the job.

Some of Alex's history was traumatic, however the traumas of his life had not limited his talents and skills. He was a good-enough father, an excellent worker, a creative man, and a good friend to many. With the loss of his job, however, Alex had been dealt a blow he hadn't expected in life. It had knocked him down, and he was having trouble finding a new place to plant his feet in his world and feel his value.

We spent some time trying to understand who he was apart from work. He had never done this. He simply *was* a friend, a lover, a husband, a father, a member of the community. Alex had never noticed *what* it was about him that could be noticed and named and known in all these contexts. As he thought about that, some patterns began to emerge. He noticed that in all these contexts he was loyal; he was responsible; he was caring; he was the consummate communicator. Alex began to *know* some core truths about himself. He also began to feel a sense of his creativity, his capacity to contribute to any situation in which he found himself. Then, once named—once known—Alex had to take that celebrated self into the new world—his new world, in which he was not a fungible commodity but a person with a strong core sense of his self that he could articulate. Now his challenge was to find a new context, a new place, to put himself. All previous assumptions—his earning potential, his lifestyle—all were going to have to be open to change. The one thing that didn't have to change was who he was at the core. That had been discovered and named and shared and now could be transplanted into a new venue.

Soon Alex's job interviews began to feel different, he said, adding that he felt "more adventurous and less defensive." He was not a commodity looking to be consumed by another company. He had a real sense of who he was, what he could offer, and what he wanted to offer a potential employer. He even walked away from some interviews saying that the companies or positions were not a fit for him.

The capacity to celebrate himself and thus know himself led to a stability that was palpable and that shone through. Interviews felt a bit more mutual. He felt the force of personal substance—emotional ballast if you will—in his continuing search. He would ride the waves, not be rolled by them.

Opportunity came from an unusual place. One of his interviewers, who could not offer him a job, instead called a colleague and recommended Alex to him.

"You have got to meet this man," the interviewer told his colleague as Alex listened. "There is a levelheadedness about him that you need in the chaos of your organization."

Alex met the interviewer's colleague and was offered a job. He felt it was a great fit, and they cinched the deal. Alex's comfort level with himself and his capabilities was infectious. There is nothing more infectious than celebration. A person who can celebrate himself or herself in a manner that is not a defensive show of force can transform those around them and draw others into the celebrated moment, which resonates back and forth with echoes of their respective pasts and new sounds of their shared experience.

The human soul wants to celebrate; that is how we know we are alive. Many people get lost in the drone of their workday. When we can find ourselves in our work or even in the search for work, we find resonance in the world.

Will all respond? No, of course not. Many are not able to do so. However, there is not a better natural selection process for us, as job seekers, than finding a place that receives, in a positive way, our celebration of ourselves and our work. That is an indicator, better than the best benefit package, that we have found the right workplace—our blank canvas—on which to make our impression.

SIX-FIGURE SLAVES: SUCCESS AND COLD COMFORT

The long-term damage of the uncelebrated childhood emerges clearly in the work life of adults I call six-figure slaves. They are usually bright and talented people who have moved easily into their chosen careers and moved up their career ladders with agility. Work is not a conflicted area of their life. Work is natural and easy. They value their work, and they are valued at work.

Among my patients, the six-figure slaves are usually attractive people. They seem powerful and dynamic and interesting, and they live in a style befitting the rewards of their work. They frequently find themselves in so-called committed relationships and easily place their spouses or life partners in the designated slot in their life, just under those slots occupied by work. The only problem is that work occupies many slots before we get to that place marked "love of another person." Money and the perquisites of power can hold a relationship together for a long time; that is, for a long time until the other person asks for a bit more, such as devotion to themselves or family. At this point, the six-figure slave stares blankly, not comprehending the request.

It is inconceivable to ask a six-figure slave to arrest his or her pace and development at work. The slavishness behind the success begins to show:

"I can't just stop my work!"
"All I've accomplished will fall apart."
"I could lose my job."
"I would lose the very essence of who I am!"

It quickly becomes apparent that the love for a significant other—no matter how significant—is a distant second to love of work. At home, they are bored in a short time. They must distract themselves with the accoutrements of their success—their toys, lovers, spouses, and children.

Their attempts to comply with the request to turn their attention away from work makes the slavishness of their connection to work even more painfully apparent. The moment they stop the pace of work, they become depressed—this is usually experienced as boredom—and if not allowed to return to work, they become despondent and do something rash outside the marriage or with their financial life to alleviate and break the hidden feeling entrapping them. As with someone addicted to drugs, there is a withdrawal state. A workaholic cannot "just quit."

JUDD: SCRIPTED FOR SUCCESS AT WORK ONLY

Judd was a really nice guy. He was tops in his field. He was shocked when his wife said she wanted a divorce. The shock was not just the news, for which he had no warning, but that this was the second wife to say and do the same thing.

"It's like they owned the same script!" he exclaimed.

"No," I said. "They each had the same husband."

Judd couldn't figure it out. He saw himself as a truly loving and nice person. Yes, he worked too much, but he had to, and then there was the retirement. In two more years, maybe three, he would be set up. Then he would relax. He was sure he could relax then.

But a second failed marriage? Judd felt forced to look at himself this time. His answers didn't work. He was truly anguished. He sincerely wanted happiness and love. He was a good man, but two women—two fine women—had found him not good enough. He loved his children and felt they loved him but at times didn't feel that he was an essential part of their lives, except for his financial support. When honest with himself he could see that the previous marriage had been based on factors other than love—timing and business. He felt like a man in a bad dream, moving toward a goal with desperate haste but constantly beset by obstacles and detours. For once, Judd could not fix it.

As we worked together in therapy to examine the pieces for a more insightful picture, Judd came to see that he was a practical man, one who didn't express emotions openly very well. Interestingly, though, that was not the complaint he had heard about himself. The complaint from both wives had been that he was unable to move very far from his work. Work came home with him, sat at the dinner table with the family, went to bed with his wife, and was indeed an integral part of their sex life—any spontaneity was gone, and sex was timed around his work demands and schedules.

Work took priority over all the events of his children's lives, went on vacation with the family, via cell phone, and determined all planning for the future. Work was always on his mind. Work and the exigencies of work defined his life. All others had to surrender to that priority.

His current wife finally gave up when she realized that any time she mentioned a family plan that involved Judd, he would quickly refer to his work commitments and give them top priority. She realized that she and their family would always be second, and she wasn't willing to continue in that kind of marriage.

Exploring the history of this character pattern was made more difficult by Judd's seemingly shallow emotional life. He simply didn't feel much, except occasional anger at work and frustration with loved ones, and he literally didn't remember much of his childhood before age fourteen or fifteen. While such memory gaps are not unheard of, they are also not routine.

Judd was the child of an honest, hardworking, mainstream, middle-class family. His mother had been kind, loving, and attentive. She had been an at-home mom and seemed content. However, a more telling picture of his mother evolved a bit over time. She also had been depressed at the time of his birth. He found this out by inquiring, not by memory. She had been depressed by her loneliness; her husband was away at war. She needed the help of her parents to care for Judd after his birth. When his father returned, she was better, but times were hard. Money wasn't the issue. The real problem was that her husband's work demanded his being on the road a great deal—several days each week.

In time, Dad drank when he was home. And then there was the hint of a brief affair. It was never discussed. It ended, if it ever existed, and that was all. Growing up in the shadow of his parents' silent, strained marriage, there was little celebration of Judd or anything else, for that matter. Judd was truly an uncelebrated child. He had very little sense of his value or talent. In fact, as an adult, nothing about his bearing reflected his high position in his profession. There was no hint of success about his demeanor.

Then, in a therapy session one day, Judd finally mentioned an accident that had occurred when he was sixteen years old. He had been driving a friend home when a truck swung in his path, forcing him to swerve off the road. The car overturned and his best friend was killed. In our session, he spoke of this in a detached way. He had very little memory of it, and no memory of dealing with any feelings about losing his best friend and having been the driver of the car. At the time, it had been quickly put to rest at home. His friend's family understood the accidental nature of the incident and didn't blame Judd. Judd's parents indicated it was "over and done with" and preferred not to talk about it. So it was, but his memory of that time and much before that closed as well, because memory requires access to the feelings that go along with them in order to be tacked down and integrated into our life story. If access to feelings is denied, then the memories themselves become inaccessible, and the loss of them both stunts emotional growth and development.

Judd's work had given him a refuge from the complexity of relationships and other aspects of family life. At work, he could excel, and at work he was appreciated. In fact, the harder he worked, the more he was appreciated. So it was in work that Judd first found himself rewarded—celebrated.

And it was at home, with his wife and children, that Judd did not permit himself to be a real enough person to be celebrated. Judd the professional took over for Judd the man. This was all right as long as everyone accepted the substitution and was content. The problem arose when his wife or family asked for the presence of the man. He then felt inadequate and felt blamed for being so.

Judd blunted the pain of the raw sense of blame and inadequacy by further achievement at work. He felt this proved that he was a competent and beloved person, and a good provider. Wasn't that good enough? he wondered. The answer was yes, for a moment, but it needed another dose of success medication to continue to dull the pain of his sense of his uncelebrated self.

In fairness to Judd, he had married women who were content with who he was and with the fruits of his success; they were proud of him. It was over time, with the new dimensions and demands of children, that they began to ask for more of the man that they "knew was there," but he wouldn't show himself. Judd was bewildered and felt a bit betrayed, though unable to name the feeling, let alone express it.

Unable to express himself and feeling quite inadequate, Judd doubled the only efforts that he knew how to manage—his work. He spent more money on the family, buying wonderful things and arranging for wonderful vacations, but he was unable to engage in any deeper way with his family.

Judd's wife withdrew into her own interests. She cared for the children and busied herself with her hobbies. She asked for less and less and finally for nothing. It was no surprise that, one day, she asked for a divorce.

In therapy, Judd had to revisit all the painful feelings and memories from the shambles of his second marriage. He would flare with anger—rage—when he thought I was recommending he cut back on work. I had only seen that kind of rage when I removed the drugs from an addict whose life had been equally wrecked by his addiction. In this case, there was no physiological withdrawal state that required management, as there is with alcohol, tobacco, or drugs, but it was a withdrawal state all the same.

Judd suffered sleeplessness, irritability, paranoid thoughts about what would happen at work should he not attend to everything, and an impending sense of doom. He mistrusted me and barely held on to the alliance in our therapeutic task. He sought endless support from his friends and children, calling them to talk when he felt lonely or anxious. He would seek support for his rationalizations—that his work habits were understandable and "normal." He tried, sometimes in vain, to leave work in a timely manner, but he could not always pull himself away.

For Judd, work was a defensive strategy. Work was a place where he didn't have to deal with the pain of attachment. He had built a wall around those feelings back in adolescence, at the time he lost his friend in the car accident. In terms of emotional awareness, he didn't know about himself before that time, and afterward he didn't want to know. Work was the only conflict-free place where he could celebrate himself. In the world of attachments, love, and devotion to people, Judd risked meeting and penetrating the wall he had built around his emotional life, and entering the pain of loss from the death of his childhood friend.

In some ways, it was helpful to show Judd the similarity of his suffering to that of a withdrawing addict. That made sense to him. Like all addicted people, Judd didn't have a very well-developed emotional vocabulary. He didn't know if what he was feeling was fear or sadness. He just felt some uncomfortable inner state that said, "Work harder, and that will make you feel better." With the realization that he was inclined to use work as a narcotic, he also learned that he, like other recovering addicts, could become more attuned to his inner feelings, even name them and respond to them, in ways other than diverting himself by working harder.

Our work in analysis provided Judd with his first experience at a noncareer relationship in which he could explore and express his feelings, safely peel back the layers of life experience to search for patterns and self-discovery, and in common parlance "get a life." Judd's life had been composed of moments of action—action that brought pain or pleasure or a sense of accomplishment. But without an emotional vocabulary, Judd was little more than a worker bee with a genetic encoded mission and no sense of himself being built in the context of his work. In short, through the celebratory process of psychotherapy, Judd was becoming a "self"—a person who continually developed before his own eyes and senses. The idea of expressing himself ceased being a mocking platitude and became a reality in time and place and in relation to other people in his world.

Judd was learning how to see and think and feel about his life in the context of other lives and events. His experience of himself took on more dimension because he was able to sense himself—appreciate himself—in many more everyday ways. Judd began to understand why some moments felt affirming and others not. Some moments did not resonate for him at all. Other moments echoed the sounds of Judd's history, and whether painful or pleasurable, they affirmed his existence by defining his past and illuminating the present as an opportunity to grow.

Not all hardworking people are workaholics. There is a great difference between a person who is motivated by healthy ambition and the desire for a creative outlet in his or her work, and a person who is driven to work, unconsciously seeking to repair the losses of an uncelebrated life. The person who was celebrated in childhood and has internalized this capacity, is able to enjoy the fruits of ambition.

For the workaholic, excess is the symptom, whether it shows up in the chase for money, promotions, prestige, or perfection, and whether it plays out in an office or at home. The excessive drive for external experiences of success reflects the depth of the absence of it in our inner life, and our hunger for it. The celebration of oneself in work can be corrupted, just as it can be corrupted or distorted in any other context, for defensive or manipulative purposes.

The person who is obsessively driven to achieve may be desperately trying to obtain the experience of celebration that was missing or insufficient in childhood, or in important adult relationships, hoping that one more achievement will win the affirmation that is missing.

• BETRAYAL IN OUR WORK LIVES: WHEN CONTRIBUTION IS DISTANCED OR DENIED •

If Judd was overinvested in his work, there is an equal and opposite problem that wounds others in the world of work. It is work that does not allow us the satisfaction of investing our creative energy, and breaks our connection with the process or the outcome of our work—the fruits of our labor. Technology has facilitated work and revolutionized work, but it has, in some cases, also broken the connections that make work rewarding in basic human terms.

If we are too far distanced from any affirmation of ourselves as contributors, then we're also not able to access the personal and spiritual nurturance that work can provide. Then, work becomes a one-way energy flow: it draws on our creativity, energy, and inspiration but sends little nourishment back. We grow tired. Our spirits sink. We lose motivation and perform automatically, like some lower form of trained animal life or some high-tech robotic arm. We are dehumanized, and that makes us angry. That anger can take many forms, from the crazed loner who vents his rage with a gun, to widespread social unrest, when a dehumanizing work environment affects large numbers of people. Most of us encounter some aspect of our work life that makes us feel diminished. Most of us feel disappointed or angry at times. Our mistake is in believing "that's just the way it is," and there's nothing we can do about it. Helplessness only adds to hopelessness.

It doesn't take a lot to feel celebrated at work. A boss can do it with a smile and a comment. A coworker can do it with a generous comment. An appreciative spouse or family member can do it. We can do it for ourselves, if we know how; we can set a goal or a rhythm for our work, and smile, congratulating ourselves when we accomplish it. As disarmingly simple as it may sound, it is that easy to initiate. Simple acts of recognition, appreciation, encouragement, or empathy create a space, an experience of celebration, that enlarges with time and attention. Whatever we do, if we acknowledge that we spend a large amount of our life at work, then we must make the effort to bring celebration into that realm, or we risk the erosion of our humanity, and invite personal, and sometimes social, instability as well.

In a former Communist Eastern European country recently, I had the chance to look at a culture after a hard war. They were on their way to recovery. The scars would take years to heal in some cases, as with victims of torture or land mines, but some were disappearing quickly. As I contemplated the major impediments to the nation's recovery, I realized that it was not torture victims or land mines, but the legacy of a depersonalized work life under communism. These people had worked for fifty years for the glory of the state, deliberately forsaking personal satisfaction and the celebration of their individual contribution. These fine people, with a rich cultural history, had lost their sense of self in their work. Work was celebrated for the state, not the individual. They had lost a sense of motivation, personal motivation, to succeed.

We talked about their life under communism, "the old days," which some found preferable to the present struggle to redefine themselves.

"Where did you seek your individual and personal identity in the old days?" I asked. They didn't, I was told. "To do so was to take away from others, and that was not right," was the answer. As one man told me: "I knew my value as a worker for the collective good. I didn't have to seek my identity in my work."

This might look good on the surface, but the cost of such thinking was debilitating. These people had lost pride in themselves as contributing individuals, and they lost individual motivation. Over time, they had almost lost their individual cultural identity, subsuming it to the new collective identity. Productivity fell and quality was abandoned. There were no motivations for either. Not that the state didn't try to reward work with money and privileges, but that didn't work very well, because the individual had lost a sense of self and pride in the process.

I have never been very doctrinaire about capitalism versus communism. However, I now know that the spiritual cost to the human psyche has to be a serious consideration in social planning. This is evident in all socioeconomic systems. In our capitalist culture, inequities or exploitation in the workplace, or corporate or governmental downsizing, carry this same potential cost—the loss of the sense of the celebrated individual as worker and significant participant in the social fabric.

• WORK AS A CELEBRATION OF WHO WE ARE •

It is this inner work we do that gives meaning to the other work we do out in the world. Innocent of malice, life betrays us; our work is not always the work we once dreamed about for ourselves. Sometimes it isn't even work that we would have imagined possible for ourselves. It may be better. It may be worse. Or it may simply be different. What we make of it defines its value and meaning to us.

My mother had a dream, and it was not motherhood. We never knew that, my sister and I, in all the years our mother was alive. Rose was a loving and masterly mother. She was a natural, and the same qualities she brought to her life's work as a mother, she also extended in her marriage and to family and friends, creating the home that welcomed them all, and a relationship that enriched each one. She was a girl in the 1920s, in an era when women had fewer choices for careers and faced formidable barriers to work outside the home. Her old-world parents were modern enough to venture to this new land, but not so modern that they would allow their daughter to throw gender traditions to the wind. They preempted any talk of careers as unladylike. "Women's work is in the home" was the operative phrase of her culture, and in that culture, she was a celebrated woman.

It was only after my mother's death at age sixty-four that we learned of her youthful career dream. A bright, enthusiastic high school student, in her senior year she secretly applied to a university and was accepted. In her high school yearbook, which we found after her death, was a picture of Rose, along with her classmates. Under her photo, as with all the others, was written where she was headed next and what her ambitions were. Under Rose's photo was written "Columbia University" and "Surgeon."

It was a path she never followed, nor even spoke of to us. I imagine now how she must have mourned this life unlived—the life in which her passion for knowledge and caring would have taken her through medical school and on to a career as a surgeon. At the same time, I know as a witness, the way in which she expressed her individuality and passion in her career as a mother, a volunteer, and as a respected and beloved elder in her extended family. This is the lesson she taught, replacing a sense of oppression and external definition with an internal sense of herself, which she could bring to any work and any circumstance.

Times have changed, and the oppression of tradition and discrimination has eased, and yet, even engaged in work we choose, we still face a similar universal dilemma: do we allow our work to define us, allow external voices and events to define who we are and our deepest sense of worth? Or do we purposefully define ourselves from within, celebrating ourselves in our work without defining ourselves by our work? Whether we work for money, for love, or for a combination of the two, it is vital that we express ourselves in our work. When we open our minds to the process and accomplishments of work, to its place in the natural order of life, and the possibilities it presents to us, work becomes a celebration and a key piece of the celebrated life.

• WORK AS A CONTEXT FOR SELF-DISCOVERY •

Work is many things to us: it is about making our mark on the world. It is one of the major activities in life that allows us to place ourselves out in the world and in relationship to others. It is a financial and social necessity. Yet it is also an arena in which we learn about ourselves and develop our deepest selves.

In our work experience, every job—not just the perfect job—teaches us important things about ourselves. It is a bit hit-and-miss at first. We work. We find earning satisfying; we find tedium dissatisfying. We may find creativity exciting and find following set patterns boring. We may find personal conversations over work enriching, and find working in isolation draining. It is a process of discovery against different backgrounds. Some people find isolation at work a welcome relief. Some find the demand for personal initiative overwhelming and just want to be told what to do.

Interacting with work is different from interacting with loved ones or friends. The mutual context of friendship or a loving other person, which contributes and changes our very selves, is less so at work. While not without a sense of being affected by our work, we for the most part apply ourselves to our work. Work is a medium upon which we make many marks. They are different marks at different times and with different tasks, however the many small marks begin to define ourselves, much as the childhood connect-the-dots drawings made a picture.

(147

Deep within each of us is a dynamic core that resonates to some activities and not to others. Different activities feel different to us. Some activities feel exciting and satisfying; others feel dreadful and painful. We tend to move from one activity to another based on how it feels inside to us.

We humans do not have a personal core in the geological sense, as in the core of the earth. Poets have used the idea of the heart or brain metaphorically to describe something they see as our core. In reality, our core is not a place; it is a dynamic. It is the relationship between our inner lives and our outer lives. We discover our core self by the interactions we have with all the elements of our outer world—which includes people, places, situations, tasks, rituals, religions—and work. In our celebration of ourselves in the context of work, every work experience becomes a valuable step in the process of discovering ourselves.

My son Aaron, as a teenager, worked in food service for three years. "Never again!" he concluded one day as we talked with his friend Kate about their respective job searches.

"Why not?" I asked.

"I hate the smell, the feel of food on my hands, and having to be nice to obnoxious people," he said.

Kate felt differently. "Oh, I just love serving a meal to people," she said. "It's a bit like conducting an orchestra for an audience that's already excited to hear the music. I love the connection you feel as you help people decide their meal choices and watch them enjoy the food."

"No, I prefer art handling," said Aaron. "It's cleaner, and almost magical. Just think of it. Someone, maybe hundreds of years ago, actually painted or sculpted or crafted this same piece with their own hands. They held it and formed it, and now I'm holding it and forming a new experience of it. It's as if the time between us has collapsed into a moment. The artist and I are each holding the piece of art together, the artist's thoughts and mine are speaking to each other over time."

"Too intellectual," muttered Kate. "Too many abstractions. I can't get *my* hands around that idea, and I don't feel the artist's inspiration. It's just a painting."

Aaron and Kate were each forming their sense of their respective selves. They each felt a natural connection with one kind of work and not another. Job satisfaction is about being able to feel that connection, feel we are capable, competent, and making a mark in the world with our work, whatever it is.

• DEFINING OUR WORK IN OUR OWN TERMS •

Mary was an older Irish woman, maybe sixty-five, who still had that lilt of an accent in her voice. To my fourteen years, she seemed very old. We met as riders on the bus each day, very early in the morning as I headed to high school. We rode together for four years and we talked about everything. I got to know her family and she, mine. I listened to her, as I had become accustomed to listening to the other old people in my life.

Mary worked as a soldering person on an assembly line in a pinball machine factory. She soldered twenty-three different wires to twenty-three different points in the pinball machine's "brain." The wired board would then move on, and another would take its place, and Mary would meld twenty-three more wire tips to twenty-three more points. She had done this for more years than I had been alive—many more. Mary took enormous pride in her work. She did it well and seldom had a rejected board. She would worry if the bus were delayed because her boss would dock her fifteen minutes if she was even a minute late punching in.

Mary's work would have been another person's nightmare. But for her it was rhythm and satisfaction. "They changed the wiring and now I have only nineteen solder points on each board," she said one day. "It's elegant, much more elegant, but I miss the other four solders; it's broken my rhythm. I need to think of a new Irish ditty that will work."

Mary was making her mark on her work and finding herself in her work at the same time. She admitted that it was boring work, but she liked it, and she liked her sense of proficiency. She also felt it was a "bit macho," she said sheepishly, giggling. "How many people can you say you have met who are solderers?" she boasted and laughed, inviting me to share this celebration of herself as a working woman—as a solderer.

If we have become spoiled in today's work life, it is because we expect the work to form us and not the other way around. We demand that work be stimulating and challenging and fun. The idea that we can find pleasure and a way to mark our presence in life from within, and apply it to our work, is a bit scorned. Yet that is exactly what we must do. If we cannot, there will be no job that will capture our attention for long. Work cannot make us, but it can help us discover ourselves. It is only in the voluntary dynamic of

WORK: AN EXPRESSION OF LIFE

celebrating ourselves in our work that we begin to reach that center—that core—of our being in work.

That's what Marvin did when he discovered a surprising satisfaction in applying his skills to the reconstruction of pottery rather than the construction of it. He discovered that his love of humanity was rewarded by taking a pot that was another person's loss and giving it new life.

That's what Marty felt when he realized that he would have a better chance of "making a difference" as a teacher in a classroom with children who needed him, rather than as a staff assistant in a more prestigious political office.

That's what Alex, between jobs, did as first he developed a language for expressing his inner self, and then used it to think about what he had learned about himself during his long working life and what he wanted to express next. This new sense that he had something to contribute to work, rather than work contributing to him, placed Alex in a very different position as he moved out into the job market.

Judd had let work become both definition and refuge from feelings of inadequacy in family and other more intimate relationships. He had to break his habit of using work as a lover—a safe place to go when he didn't feel up to the task of being in a genuine relationship with another person. Judd had used work defensively, detracting from the joy and celebration of work as well as from the joy and celebration of personal love—it was a lose-lose situation. If we use work to self-medicate for emotional pain, we cannot discover ourselves in work any more than we can discover ourselves through alcohol or drug abuse.

There are implications to looking at work as a contributing piece of the celebrated life. They are no longer new ideas. Industry found out long ago that workers who have a sense of participation in their work will be more productive, have less sick time, and stay at their work for many years more than workers who simply punch the clock and are extensions of the industrial machinery. Industry may have known this, but much of industry has not used this knowledge in the workplace. People know that they will spend a great part of their life at work and must seek some sort of job satisfaction, but many have forgotten the notion that this means that a dynamic between them and their work requires activity, not passivity, in achieving such satisfaction.

Celebration in the context of work starts with imagination about ourselves and how we can see those translucent images of ourselves in work. It moves on from there to testing the fit of the work to ourselves, molding ourselves as we go, and trying to mold our work in ways that express who we are. Over time, it is not the work experience on our résumé, but our experience of ourselves in our work, that enriches us the most and prepares us for success wherever we go, and whatever the nature of our work.

(Spirituality: The Ultimate Mystery Story)

Faith is the subtle chain
Which binds us to the infinite.
ELIZABETH OAKES SMITH (1806–1893), "FAITH"

There was a time in my study of medicine when I felt that I held in my mind all that there was to know about the human body and all its myriad anatomical, physiological, and neurological processes. It was an amazing feeling, not of power, but of humility. Saint Thomas Aquinas said that if you contemplate all the orders of life, the sheer magnificence of that complexity proves the existence of God. For me, that complexity is a humbling magnificence—a mystery. It speaks to me of our small but important place in the order of life.

However we access it—through our work, love, religion, or a walk in the park—to feel connected to that mystery is to feel the grandeur of life and our evolution. When we seek that connection, we are expressing a basic human desire to feel one with the universe. It allows us to know ourselves a bit better and to feel that we have a place in the grand scheme of things. It feels safe, and from that place of safety we can venture forth and take the physical and intellectual risks necessary to progress, not only in our private lives, but also in the larger life of family and community. It is important to acknowledge that mystery and celebrate it regularly.

The acknowledgment of mystery is one of the essential elements of celebration. I have spoken of it earlier in this book but not really defined it. For me, the definition comes down to this: the spiritual and the vast mystery of life are one. The mystery of life provides the legitimate basis for awe—for sensing one's place in the universe. And awe is the final element in celebration. Mystery and awe are the aphrodisiacs of life. You can see it in the faces of babies and small children, before rationality and life itself have put a limit on mystery and awe. They delight in the smallest things. Their faces light up in the face of life and living phenomena; they revel in sensing themselves to be part of this fresh new universe. Our faces light up at the sight of theirs, reflecting their awe with our own. There is no need to provide the rational too soon. It is good to languish in awe for a while each day. Awe and mystery—these essential parts of the spiritual and essential elements in celebration—are both inspiring and humbling at the same time.

It is in the search for knowing our place in the universe, the search for that connection, that we actually experience *being known*. It is a bit like a baby who, cradled in our arms, searches our face and the contour of our body to feel connected, to feel known and safe in our arms. The search and the experience are one.

• MYSTERY VERSUS THE YET-TO-BE-DISCOVERED •

We live in a highly scientific and technologic age. The answers to questions about our bodies and the diseases that plague us, our environment, and our astrophysical history come at us with incredible frequency. Our passion for knowledge, our belief in science and technology, is absolute. It is interesting that in this fast-paced, high-tech, information-rich culture, there is growing interest in the spiritual. What is missing from the flood of scientific and technological answers available to us? I believe that often what is missing is the wonderful humility of sensing our place in life's milieu, and feeling connected to and known by the spiritual forces of the universe.

There are some skeptics who suggest that our desire for spiritual connection springs from our fear of the unknown. Freud was a man of science in the tradition of the nineteenth-century Darwinian revolution. He firmly believed that all effects had distinct causes; that there was a rational explanation for everything, however difficult it might be to discern. In the end, the scientific mind of his day was rooted in hyper-rationality, where all was considered eventually discoverable and predictable. The unknown was simply that—not *yet* known, but knowable—and a mystery was simply knowledge waiting to be discovered. Little was left to spirit, except to be viewed as the common man's defense against fear.

To the contrary, I believe that the pursuit of what we call the spiritual, in whatever form, can be a search for our own completion. This is not a search motivated by fear, though sometimes we may be afraid; it is a positive search for our place and our meaning in the universe. In that search we must admit the mystery of life itself; not the factual origins of life, which can be ultimately known and seen, but our evolution as living beings uniquely capable of contemplating our own existence.

Mystery is different from the "yet-to-be-discovered." The greater our power to observe the universe, the more we can discover and know of those facets of life that previously were simply yet-to-be-discovered. But this is not the true mystery of creation and spirit! When one contemplates the myriad coincidences required to create life in any form, let alone the level of our humanity, we are forced to admit that we live *within* the matrix of that mystery we seek to know, and therefore cannot ever fully know it.

As impressive as are the achievements of science and technology, they are about the elements of life—the information about life. But information is anonymous and indifferent to our being. Those achievements of science and technology "know" us as data, but not as thinking, feeling beings. Our relationship to the scientific and the technological is limited to the rational aspects of life, the known and yet-to-be-discovered, but not the mystery.

We are threatened today by disconnection and constant change resulting, ironically, from the very discoveries that connect us electronically and technologically. We are threatened by anonymity in a world of incredible data. Our interest in the spiritual reflects a basic human need to stay connected to our roots in the universe amid disconnection and change. This need is rooted not in fear but in our humanity. It is, by nature, a positive force in our lives. Today, scientific advancement notwithstanding, we search all the more urgently for our place in the greater mystery of the complexity and coincidences of the universe.

At first glance, our dedication to science and technology, and our fervor for spiritual expression and the search for spiritual answers, would seem to be contradictory, but I see the twin passions as a natural expression of human nature in its fullness, the pairing of intellect and spirit. What is essential in our time is that we acknowledge what is greater than ourselves and our scientific and technologic discoveries; that we name our sense that there is something greater, a mystery we cannot solve but can celebrate, and that we not shy away from calling it spiritual. The celebratory process, in which we embrace the moment and surrender to meaning and mystery in it, helps open the spaces in our mind that are narrowed by logic. That process permits a dialogue between our inner inspirations, which fill our unconscious life, and the enlightenment and expanse of the spiritual. This dialogue between our inner inspirations and the spiritual exists on a plane above logic and science, but not above celebration. In celebration we find a place for us that is both grand and humble. The celebratory process holds us up to the background of life itself—to be part of life and the mystery of life. Here we find the surety and comfort to rise above good fortune and adversity.

SISTER THELMA'S LESSONS IN CONNECTION

Sister Thelma was an unlikely role model for a fifteen-year-old Jewish boy. Nevertheless, there she was, standing *very tall* in her full white habit of the Order of the Poor Sisters of St. Francis Seraph of the Perpetual Adoration. She would have been tall anyway, but the extra height added by the crown of her veil made her presence seem even bigger.

I was already a veteran of two years' part-time employment, first as a short-order cook in a neighborhood delicatessen and then as an offset pressman at our neighborhood newspaper. Now it was time to get serious. I needed a full-time job and I thought it wise to see how medicine looked from the inside, since I was getting a good deal of pressure from the outside to become a doctor.

There was no full-time work at the hospital for someone my age, but if I volunteered, I would be considered as soon as something opened up. I asked to work in the emergency room. It was both dramatic and offered a chance to see a great deal of medicine in vivo— in real life. Sister Thelma greeted me with a serenity that was unfamiliar to me. She smiled, and her eyes were gleaming with quiet joy and a great deal of playfulness.

"So you're our new volunteer," she declared. She then interviewed me about my motivations to work in the ER, and she learned of my wish for paid, full-time employment. "We'll see in time," she finally concluded.

Her first lessons were about our major mission, which was to heal whatever came through our doors. Sister Thelma's caveat: care must be guided by the principle that we must never neglect the dignity of our patients.

"This neglect of our patients' dignity can take place by word or deed," Sister Thelma went on to say. "I will forgive mistakes, we all make them, but it is hard to reckon with such disrespect that preys upon the already compromised dignity of the sick." She spoke in a very serious and still serene manner. She spoke as if she were reciting a basic truth of humanity—a law of nature. It would take a long while for me to realize that she spoke with the certainty of one who was devoted to the basic laws of the human *spirit* more than nature. Dignity, for Sister Thelma, was a matter of human spirit and soul in the face of the indignities of nature. Sister Thelma was demonstrating by word and deed the celebration of the spiritual dimension of humankind.

It seemed to me a strange lesson on that first day in the emergency room, yet it is a lesson that was echoed many years later by other mentors in my life, and now by me. I cannot always tell where the nature of men and women ends and their spirit begins. However, this lesson of respect for the spiritual dimension has proved to be a vital part of my understanding of people, my celebration of their life dilemmas, and their healing.

It wasn't long before I was working full-time as a surgical technician in the emergency room for Sister Thelma. The lessons of anatomy and medicine were not hard to learn. The lessons of the spiritual were subtler and more difficult. "Sister," as we called her, was an enigma. She was a woman of devotion and nursing, but she was also a woman who had deeper layers to her personality. Clearly, she had chosen the "religious" life of a nun, but she lived it her way, which included a freedom to be playful, or even a bit sacrilegious, most often with her humor. But a thread of connection between her and the spiritual in life was always there. I came to know her well and saw that she "touched" that thread not so much by being religious, but by being *real*—playful, candid, honest, and open. She moved around this way freely, tethered to God.

One day, Sister Thelma asked if she could attend our family's Sabbath dinner on some Friday evening. She knew that was the only evening she couldn't schedule me for work, and she was intrigued. My mom was delighted, so the arrangements were made. Sister Thelma and Sister James Marie (the nuns always traveled in pairs) came to dinner. As my mother was laying out our regular Sabbath feast of chicken and beef, I was suddenly mortified to remember that, in these pre–Vatican II days, Catholics were supposed to eat fish on Friday.

"Sister!" I exclaimed. "I forgot to tell you—we don't have fish on Friday."

"No problem," she said with a bemused smile. With that, she dipped her fork into the glass of water by her plate, cast a few drops upon the beef and chicken, and said, "Swim, fish, swim!" She was teaching me a lesson I would hear again from wise mentors in my life: that it is more important to respect the spirit of a person than the forms of any rule or observance.

The lessons from Sister Thelma were many. I came to know her history. It was a hard life that preceded her entry into the convent. There was poverty and prolonged physical pain from an almost fatal accident. She struggled with her devotion to the order, but not in her devotion to God. She found her footing in that. Her spiritual grounding centered us all, especially when events threatened chaos in the emergency room. She would hold us all together by her sense of perspective in the face of disaster. This was *mere disaster*, but in the scope of all we were and in our connection to the larger, spiritual realm, it was no more than that. Her sense of her place in the realm of the spiritual gave strength to her patients and her staff.

"Completion" and "connection," or being in a state of "connectedness" are very closely and deeply linked. Our original separation from the womb is repeated in a series of developmental steps that take us on into the world. With each separation from that original connection we gain and we lose. At some subliminal, or unconscious, level we carry with us this sense of "disconnection" or live in a chronic, nagging state of "disconnectedness." It carries a cost; it is a bit debilitating. The search for the spiritual is a search for a higher level of connection or state of connectedness that can only be achieved if we accept the losses of early separation and venture forth as searchers for the next. The serenity and peace that surround a spiritual person can make them seem as if they have carried that same serenity of the womb with them into the world. Seeing it, as my coworkers and I did in Sister Thelma, we recognize that a person is reconnected to this higher level of what we call the spiritual. Each of us, in our own search, can learn from others on the same journey, but the actual connection is something we have to discover and cultivate for ourselves. The architecture of that connection varies dramatically from person to person, culture to culture, but the commonality is in the power of celebrating the connection to the mystery of spirit.

• CONVERSATION WITH GOD: THE SYNERGY OF RITUAL, MYSTERY, AND AWE •

Connections and connectedness are what form us, sustain us, mature us, and create grief and illness when severed. Spiritual life is the life of connection to the greater theater of the universe around us. There is power in this connection. There is power in sharing the search for this connection. That is why humankind has sought collective forms of spiritual worship or searching.

Celebration is the way we mark and process and search for the spiritual in our lives, whether it be God or the greater natural forces, or the deepest reservoirs of our minds. By definition, celebration marks the moments that span interior life, exterior life, and time. Celebration is how we know the spiritual, because the spiritual has no other real vocabulary. We give it vocabulary through the assemblage of celebratory processes in our lives.

I was once fortunate enough to be invited to a friend's ordination as a Roman Catholic bishop in Chicago. He knew of my interest in the Church liturgy, even though I was not Catholic. In several past conversations, I had told him of my interest in attending the highest of masses, one that would not spare a moment of ceremony. At the time, my only thought was that I was curious. It was an old interest stemming back to the formative years of my life when I had attended Roman Catholic liturgy with my Catholic friends. I now can see that what attracted me was my interest in the deeper qualities of celebration.

My friend saw to it that I met and sat near Cardinal Bernardin, someone whom I believe to have been overflowing with humility and genuineness. At the time, I was aware that his cancer, while arrested for the moment, would eventually take his life. After our meal, we all adjourned to the cathedral for the ordination of my friend. The ordination was filled with all the pomp and ceremony and glory I could ever hope to see. During one part of the ceremony all the attending bishops placed their hands on the heads of the three men being ordained. It was a symbol of the passing of the Holy Spirit through the sacrament of Apostolic Succession.

There were many bishops in attendance, and that part of the ordination took some time. I was seated in the congregation only twenty feet from Cardinal Bernardin and facing him. During that prolonged part of the ceremony, our eyes met. His were filled with a simple joy and pride in those being ordained, and a heightened sense of the moment as one filled with the mystery of the Holy Spirit. His eyes were so alive and expressive that I can still see them today, long after he is gone. I have to close mine to see his, but when I do, I see his eyes sparkling and beckoning me to share the joy he had found in his life, his flock, his faith, and his God.

At its best, organized religion is an attempt to help people comprehend and have this dialogue with God, the spiritual. For many of us, religious tradition and ritual are a source of strength, courage, and resilience. Regardless of the name we use for God, all religions share the common language of celebration. We see in religious tradition perhaps the most elaborate use of the elements of celebration to shape human experience and expectations. Every ritual is designed to set a moment apart, recognize it, and name it. We share the moment when we gather as members of a congregation for prayer or community service, or alone, in our private conversations with God. We use biblical stories, sermons, and commentary to celebrate the ancestors, origins, and echoes of our particular faith heritage. We create holidays to celebrate our stories, and in so doing, we create a context for our lives and give meaning to our existence. Liturgy and prayer speak forthrightly of divine mystery and awe, and invite us to engage ourselves in that language, open ourselves to those thoughts and that experience.

It is not by coincidence that throughout every culture, music and art have always been central to religious expression, bypassing the limitations of language and logic to create an experience that reverberates in our conscious and unconscious celebration of ourselves. So it is in church or synagogue or mosque or temple or tribal gathering that we immerse ourselves in these experiences that speak past word and story to the deeper experiences of our mental life.

As evidenced throughout history, the deep, unifying power of celebration in the name of religion can be used to bring people together or to separate them; to cultivate trust or suspicion; to generate love or hate, peace or war. The destructive side of religious celebration shows itself in barbaric acts of historic magnitude— the Crusades and the Inquisition in centuries past, and the more recent terrorism by religious fundamentalist extremists—but also in everyday ways we use or allow religion to create division in our communities or personal relationships. In contrast, we see the life-affirming power of religious celebration when it facilitates connection, peace, and healing, as so many did in interfaith gatherings following the September 11, 2001, terrorist attacks. These were community expressions of the desire to speak to the higher moral goal of all our moral faiths in the face of these divisive forces.

• THE HEALING SPIRIT: CONTEMPORARY, TRADITIONAL, AND ANCIENT CONNECTIONS •

Formal religion isn't for everyone; but spirituality is. In many ways, we are a more sophisticated audience, and our world is a more complex, interwoven one than that in which our ancient religions were born; at times the old answers seem inadequate to new questions. The language of religion itself can feel confining. It's a bit like all the words that are used to describe the character of wine. Wine is a taste. Our minds do not know wine by words. However, we search for words to describe our experience of wine. In a similar fashion, our minds do not know the spiritual by words, but we must use words to communicate and describe it if we are to share our experience with others.

Today, we enjoy a great freedom to seek or create new connections, individually satisfying connections with God or the spiritual. We are free to draw what we need from different faith traditions, different languages of faith, and pursue our own sacred conversation through meditation, community service, social action, creative expression, or in the other ways we live our lives.

I became friends with Lisby, a fellow psychoanalyst, by chance, over dinner at a health care conference. Our backgrounds were as different as could be, but they seemed to overlay as if by some computerized digital trick in which two very different images can be made to merge. I think the common link was that we both had charismatic, "spiritual" mothers. Hers came from a long line of mainline Episcopalians, devoted to a profoundly spiritual sense of nature, as well as to the church, devoted to God and all that was spiritual in life. Mine was an old-world Jew who was devoted to God and found spirit in her connections to the mysteries of our lives and our survivals. My friend Lisby's mother advanced her spiritual sense with walks in the woods and a profound belief in the power of spiritual healing and a sacramental view of life, while my mother steeped her spirituality in tradition; we didn't "keep kosher," but she "koshered" our meats (including pork, when it graced our table) in salty brine because, she said, it connected her to five thousand years of Jewish women who had cooked dinner before her.

Lisby and I talked about our families, and then our discussion drifted to the subject of spirituality and healing.

"You know," I confessed to Lisby, "I do believe in the spiritual aspects of healing." At the time, it was a radical statement for a physician to make openly.

She looked at me with surprise—quickly replaced with eager pleasure. When she spoke, she did so with the quality of a fellow conspirator. She had several experiences she wanted to share with me, ones that she rarely discussed with colleagues. "We're of course not alone in thinking about these things," she said. "And there's a marvelous amount of learning from the people who've been here before." That marked the beginning of our long friendship.

Lisby *knew* the spiritual. She lived in the spiritual world not only as a searcher but also, I came to learn, as a sufferer. She had been diagnosed some years earlier with a serious, potentially fatal, disease. She had survived much longer than medical textbooks would have suggested possible, and she finally had been told by her doctors that she appeared in no danger of dying from her disease. She was an accomplished woman, holding several undergraduate and graduate degrees in diverse subjects from music, to economics, to psychology. She probably would have been drawn toward a spiritual search regardless, but her illness made her search for relief and healing more urgent. Lisby never ignored the aid afforded her by modern medicine, but she did not depend solely upon it. She adopted her mother's faith in the spiritual, but she did so as the social, psychological scientist she had become. It was not just a matter of faith for her; it was, in Lisby's view, equally a matter of science, but science with a spiritual component.

Lisby observed and collected many reports of phenomena in her own life and the lives of others to help map out the forces of life that we call the spiritual. She worked with healers, dowsers, physicians, theologians, physicists, and others who were living, working, and searching into the realm of the spiritual. In time, Lisby drew on her strength of character to speak out about her experiences and what she was learning.

Although her condition remained erratic in strictly medical terms, Lisby was healing. Every day, everyone else's personal tragedies afforded her a healing insight. Some felt put off by her otherworldly healing process. She talked about her healing, and to do that she sometimes had to talk about her pain. She did not complain at all about her pain, quite the opposite. She was almost stoic about it, but she was ready to describe it when she felt it might help direct the spiritual forces to aid the healing process. Lisby even had a healer with her in surgery, a major surgery that she had done only under moderate sedation. Her three surgeons, whatever they privately thought of this, noted nonetheless that her postoperative healing process was remarkable: she was released from the hospital after thirty-six hours, having been told to anticipate a stay of anywhere from five to ten days.

Lisby was a phenomenon to be experienced. A fragile, brilliant, lovely woman, she was this beacon of connection to the spiritual world. One day when I commented on living with chronic disability, she rebuked me.

"Harvey, I have no intention of 'just living with this.' It simply doesn't have to be like that. If you give it the chance, it makes life not less, but more meaningful—not less, but more worth living!" she said. I then began to understand that I had to change my vocabulary. She was in the process of overcoming her illness, spiritually, if not medically—but she clearly believed a spiritual cure and medical cure were inseparable.

By celebrating the spiritual forces in life and calling them into her life in various active and deliberate ways, Lisby was overcoming her debility. Her body was becoming one with the spiritual forces she celebrated. Her suffering was simply one manifestation of her being. Her remarkable recovery from surgeries, the lack of expected progression of her illness, her adjustments to bodily limitations, and her healing were all part of the celebration of her connectedness to spirit and energy beyond what we are yet able to measure.

The persistence of humankind's hold on the spiritual is based in our intuitively knowing something that science has not yet demonstrated. It has something to do with connections, in this case connections that are real forces between points of matter and energy and people. I believe these forces link us to one another and to the universe of matter and energy. Can I prove it? Well, yes, in a way. The data is in on many of what we call anecdotal evidence of the importance of connections. Married people are healthier and live longer than single people. A dog or cat can prolong the life of an older person. Some people believe they have demonstrated that talking to plants makes the plants grow better. We know that talking can bring a person out from under deep suicidal despair. In one African community, I witnessed a community use the celebratory process to bring healing to a postpartum psychotic woman. In a swirl of healing chants, drumming, movement, and dance around her, her husband, and their infant, they called upon spiritual forces to deliver her from her delirium. I saw her transformation and watched her return to hold her baby tenderly.

I find proof, too, in the striking serendipity that so many of us witness at one time or another. We have seen things happen. A mother or father who senses that their child is in need from a great distance. A person with a terminal disease who lives well beyond medical expectations, only to say farewell to a loved one who is on the way. A phone call that comes when it is so desired and needed. The power of a group of people to heal or alleviate someone's pain and suffering. Coincidences? Yes, in one sense, but when taken together—when all that I have seen and of which I have heard is taken together—the sum is greater than the total of mere coincidences. It is about connections between people and forces of energy and matter—mysterious forces—that can effect change.

I don't think we have fully appreciated yet the power of conversancy and connection with the spiritual forces of our lives. Jung proposed that human experience, repeated and repeated generation after generation, could eventually become genetically encoded. The great Jesuit anthropologist Teilhard de Chardin proposed an evolution toward a common human mentality, and even Melville in *Moby Dick* proffered great import to premonition. In science fiction, there have been some marvelous depictions of this power. In *Childhood's End* by Arthur C. Clarke such power is evolved; the evolution is to one universal mentality, the combined powers of all minds. These are not flaky people. So many times these powers are first depicted in fiction or spiritual writing because someone has a glimpse into the mystery of the spiritual.

What have they sought to explore and explain? They have seen something that needed to be addressed: people are connected beyond language and bloodlines. They have looked over humanity and generations and they have seen that there is a force and power to be harnessed in understanding these connections. So, for me, the spirit is about forces of connection. This unseen, intangible dimension of human life can feel odd and even a bit scary. It is easily abused and overestimated as much as it can be underestimated or trivialized. I believe that celebration is a way to experience and know these forces, harness them, and use them in our lives.

The celebration of the spiritual is like all other celebrations. It is not the ritual that any particular religion might place on the story of God or God's works. It is, rather, the recognition of amazing complexity and coincidence in our lives and the life of our universe, naming it as spiritual, sharing our sense of our own histories as we contribute to this search, and finally, in the sharing of the mystery of the spiritual and in the awe it inspires.

We need celebration of the spiritual *in* our lives to provide context and perspective *on* our lives. We tend to be egocentric by nature. Our worldview is limited—even with all its new technology—to what we can conceive, and we cannot go very far beyond. The perspective of the spiritual is one that says there is much more to discover and further to go. It says that we are only human beings and that we *are* human beings. Yes, we might be the result of random growth of hydrocarbon chains, but is it conceivable that such randomness occurred? That fact in and of itself must speak of so much more to which we are connected. It does not give us a goal in life, but it does give us a context in which to live. Those who do not have a context in which to live do not live long. The troubled young people who affiliate with gangs and criminal activity do not value their lives or the lives of those in their community because their context does not affirm the spiritual within them and to which they are connected. Others among us who choose hate or violence as a way of life have missed the essential link with a life-affirming spiritual force.

Sacredness is an important backdrop for our lives. We must have some point from which to measure our place and our direction and our progress. That point is the sacred. I really don't care what name is assigned to that point; it is always the same point. It is the point at which humankind said that there needs to be meaning to existence. If it is not inherent in existence, then we must invent it. Our entire mentality demands meaning. The truth of the meaning of our existence—of all existence—rests in the point of sacredness, and the fact that in totally different places, totally different cultures, from the most primitive to the most sophisticated, each and every one invented the point of sacredness—the point of meaning. This is called a hermeneutic proof, and it carries an entire philosophy and credibility behind it. It says that if we keep arriving at the same point from many different places and times, then that is an affirmation of truth.

Different people call the sacred by different names, from God to nature to science, but regardless, it still establishes a point that gives meaning to our existence. This point, this sacredness, should not be trivialized. If we hold the sacred as such, then we can hold the measure of our place and direction in time. Much as there is an actual place where definitive measures of the inch, foot, yard, centimeter, and meter are kept in safe holding, so the definitive measure of humankind is in the sacred.

If we had taken out that measure and applied it to what was happening in 1932 in Germany, we would have known that humankind was going awry. If we take it out and hold it up to the refusal of the United States to sign a humanitarian land mine treaty for military strategic reasons, we would know that it is a wrong-minded decision. If we hold it up to the barbaric acts of terrorism inflicted by extremists here and around the world in the name of God, we can see their lie. They are hypocrites, and we know it when we hold their actions up to the universal measure of the sacred. Across cultures, religions, races, and ethnic identities, we all can and should participate in honoring the sacred, the life-affirming celebration of spiritual connection.

The spiritual is in us, and it is limited only by our own fears, and the constrictions we place on ourselves from letting it infiltrate all the moments of inspired connection throughout our lives. What we call the spirit is as vast as our capacity to connect with it inside ourselves, outside ourselves, beyond ourselves. Celebration affirms and expands those connections, and through celebration we discover the presence of spirit in our lives and the knowledge that it is infinite.

(Adversity and Healing)

Sweet are the uses of adversity,
Which, like the toad, ugly and venomous,
Wears yet a precious jewel in his head.
SHAKESPEARE, *AS YOU LIKE IT* (ACT 2, SCENE 1)

About a hundred years ago, a Russian-Jewish peasant boy of eighteen fled persecution and forced service in the Russian Army and, with his family's blessing, escaped to Vienna. There he struggled to survive. One day, he chanced to meet an engaging Viennese girl about his age. She sewed lace and served tea at home, as did all girls from fine Jewish families in Vienna around 1905, and although we know nothing of what brought the two together, we know that they fell in love and married in that gracious city.

A short time later this peasant-dreamer-son-in-law announced that he and his bride were moving to New York—the land of opportunity. The Austrian bride's family was devastated. They thought that America was a crude, violent place. However, faced with this nonnegotiable situation, they sent another daughter as chaperon. That was my grandmother.

In New York, opportunity proved to be another word for struggle. Life was hard. Both women worked long hours, sewing garments in a sweatshop. My grandmother met and married a man who was a cabinetmaker and a socialist labor organizer from Eastern Europe. She was not in love, but she had it on good authority that he was not married "back home," and they shared a desire to raise a family and establish themselves in their new homeland, America. Life was difficult, but they survived and thrived.

Forty years later, the family story was now rooted in America with two generations American-born. I was five years old, and home was a one-bedroom apartment in a predominantly German/Irish/Italian Catholic neighborhood on the north side of Chicago. Everyone was poor, but we didn't know it. In our apartment, the kitchen was tiny, with a small table, which would sit four, wedged between the stove and the sink. There was a dining room and a living room, one bathroom and one bedroom. My mother and father slept on a fold-out sofa in the living room. My sister and I slept in separate beds in the bedroom. There was a "divan" in the dining room for those who came and slept over.

In the years just following World War II, the Nazis were banished from Europe, but their American counterparts were unrepentant in our neighborhood. Some neighbors routinely dumped garbage on our back porch and watched, laughing, as my mother would clean it up. I would ask, "Momma, why do these people do that to us?"

"Shh," she would say, "don't tell your father." That was all.

We would sit in the kitchen, the four of us, or in the dining room if my mother's brothers had shown up for dinner, and she would comment on her search for relatives from the Holocaust. I would hear them talk about "showers" and "ovens" and hear frag-ments of stories about life and death and concentration camps, and I would be frightened of these otherwise everyday words. Showers, ovens, and death? Children, camps, and death? The dark images scared me.

But there was more to the scene. My mother laughed about many things. They all joked and laughed. They were alive, after all. (**173** Their parents had immigrated years earlier. They were born Ameri-cans. They were grateful for their destinies. In comparison, they could laugh about their own fates—the ordinary trials and tribula-tions of everyday life.

If that one Russian peasant hadn't run off with my great-aunt to America, we would all be ashes, they would joke, with a touch of sobriety. If my grandmother hadn't been sent with her sister for the sake of propriety to that crude, rude America, our bodies would be among the six million—as were those relatives who had stayed "back home" in Vienna.

They moved smoothly from talk of those who were missing, to reflection on the unknowable qualities of fate and destiny. They moved seamlessly from terror to triumph. They spoke of those whose lives were lost, as if they had been here only yesterday, and of those whose choices had led first here and then there, as if that, too, had been only yesterday, and finally to this group of us, the el-ders with their coffee, gathered around a dinner table on a tree-lined street of brownstones and apartment buildings in Chicago. Even as my mother cleared the bigot's garbage from our porch, we celebrated our lives as Americans. For me, young as I was, the im-agery of past, present, and future lives blended like the swirls of milk in their dark coffee, until those missing from the table and those gathered around it shared the same place in my mind.

I watched and listened through these family meals and remembrances but would not know the full worth of what I was learning until years later as I faced adversity in my own life and in the lives of my patients. In those moments, I have been struck by the return of my childhood lessons, the unknowable qualities of fate and destiny, and the evidence from my own family story that adversity is an impartial catalyst for change. If there is meaning to be made of illness or adversity, it is in the relationship we make with it. If we can accept it as an integral part of life—if we can celebrate life *with* adversity—then celebration transforms adversity into a vehicle for healing, for discovery, and even for opportunity.

The basic human desire to rise above adversity requires first that we come to terms with it. The defining elements of celebration create the blueprint, the mental strategy that enables us to seek and embrace meaning in the experience. Through celebration we pay purposeful attention to our adversity. We identify it and give it a name. We open our senses fully to the experience, drawing from our conscious and unconscious mind; we open ourselves to the presence of mystery and awe, and the potential for discovery. We share it, perhaps different aspects of it with different people, or memories of people, close to us. Some aspects of our experience we might choose to share only in a spiritual sense, with God.

Most of us are ill prepared to bring celebration, and therefore meaning, to adversity. Very little in the tenor of contemporary life prepares us to do this. We invest little, if any, time in practicing the slower, reflective art of *being,* or the process of living. It is the remedy, the *doing,* to which we more often devote ourselves. We pride ourselves on being problem solvers, and, of course, problem solving is a good thing. But adversity is a problem on a large, complex scale resistant to a quick fix. Adversity isn't something we can solve or fix; it is a human experience. We might be able to solve or fix some aspect of the cause, but we cannot solve or fix the experience of adversity. And to ignore it or deny it only creates additional complications, whether they are practical, physical, or emotional. If we ignore a disease, it grows harder to treat. If we ignore a social problem, it leads to revolt. If we ignore emotional pain, it surfaces eventually in destructive, or self-destructive, behaviors.

When we are unprepared to actively engage in it, adversity not only upsets our finely tuned schedule of commitments, but our emotional and spiritual equilibrium as well. This is true whether the adversity is our own or we are reacting to someone else's troubles. But if we use celebration as our architect, we can draw from lessons long forgotten and from sources close at hand, to transform adversity into a meaningful, valuable passage.

The meaning of adversity might not be high and noble. It might not lead us to spiritual heights or higher moral comprehension. It might only say to us that adversity is, that adversity cannot be avoided in our lives, that part of living is embracing adversity, but in that we have sought and recognized and named the meaning of a particular adversity. At other times adversity might indeed lead us to some deeper insight in our life, or toward our goals.

I experienced this for myself just a few years ago when I began to lose my sight.

• My Journey: Trading One Kind of Vision for Another •

It started with what appeared to be a trail of smoke in my field of vision. Nearing the end of a patient's therapy session, it drifted by, like the smoke that rises from a cigarette sitting in an ashtray, a gentle, beautiful trail of smoke that undulates its way up and spreads its reach wider as it rises. But there was no cigarette and this was not smoke. As a physician, I knew immediately that it was a hemorrhage inside one of my eyes. Peacefully listening to my patient, I remained calm as we concluded the session and I called my doctor.

Within a few hours it was confirmed that my retina was detached and torn in two places. My doctor explained my options. I had a 50 percent chance of repair with a laser procedure. If that failed, I had an 80 percent chance of repair with immediate intraocular surgery in the operating room. Those odds sounded encouraging. We tried both. Over the next several months we tried again and again—six times in all. Along the way, as I lay recovering from the third or fourth operation, I realized that it was not going well.

The healthy human eye must maintain a certain internal pressure to function. My eye was losing pressure and would soon collapse forever. Also, the doctor was already seeing signs of trouble in the "good" eye. Again, my doctor laid out my options. We decided upon a two-step laser surgery process for that eye—the "good" eye—to prevent its following the same course as the first. I asked and was told that I had about a 30 percent chance for total blindness. This simple problem was gaining some gravity.

I was dealing, for the first time in my life, with real physical loss and disfigurement. This was no textbook, no published study. It wasn't happening in someone else's life; it was happening to *me*. It was a sober moment. I had never thought about being blind. I had to ask myself: What does this mean to me?

As a physician, I was naturally intrigued by the pathology of my eyes and the technology of the curative attempts. This intellectual engagement would prove to be my handle on what would become a roller coaster of medical efforts and dimming hopes. It helped me focus on the medical detail, without becoming emotionally overwhelmed by it. Being a physician also gave me a perspective on illness in general that helped. I knew that I would survive this illness, but that for everyone, survival itself holds two possible outcomes. Our lives can be unchanged or changed by the consequences of the illness. If it were a head cold, the consequences would suggest no significant change in my life. But blindness made significant change inevitable. What remained to be seen was the extent of that change—and how I would respond to it.

With that solid perspective in mind, I was free to move into what was happening to me; to seek its meaning. I don't use "meaning" as in reading tea leaves, but rather in the way we can explore and listen to our inner selves to discern the significance of what is happening to us. It is natural for me, a psychoanalyst, to seek meaning in everyday life. It is also natural for me, as the child of my mother and my history, to seek meaning in my life. I have not always taken the time to know it, but I am aware in some constant drone of my soul that there is meaning to every part of living.

So, as I lay in my bed at home that morning after surgery, I thought, What will you do if you are a blind man? There was no wait for the first image. It was of Sister Thelma, Order of St. Francis, Seraph of the Perpetual Adoration, my boss in the emergency room of St. Francis Hospital, during my adolescence. Sister Thelma had died years before, but now here she was in spirit, standing just behind my right shoulder, with her hands folded under her white wimple and her Franciscan knotted ropes hanging from her waist in her white habit, showing me how to type.

"These are the home positions, and these are the fingers you use on the other keys. Now just type and keep your discipline about which fingers you use. You can do it!" came her voice, as clear in my mind as the moment she'd first said those words some forty years before. In one week of typing admission forms for patients coming into the emergency room, I had become a touch typist, thanks to Sister Thelma.

So: I could type! I would be a blind man who could type. This was a start. But what did I want to type? Again I didn't have to wait. I would write about celebration. Not about parties but about the deeper role of celebration in our lives, celebration as a source of suffering and a source of healing. This thought had been percolating in my mind since I had returned from a consulting trip to Angola. I wanted to write about those people in Angola, who struggled in their war-ravaged land to revive traditions that celebrated their humanity and their possibility, to wrest one moral victory from the landscape of defeat. I wanted to write about other casualties—people here in the relative safety and comfort of American life—people who suffered uncelebrated lives and struggled with the emotional wounds and disconnection of that experience.

I sat down at the computer and began to type. Twenty pages later, I opened my one good eye to view the damage. It was not bad. With the help of the spell check I could get those thoughts down on paper; I could do what I had intended to do for more than a year since returning from my Angola experience. Other commitments had kept me from it before. Now my illness left me no choice. It removed me from all that was busily occupying my life and gave me the uninterrupted time to sit and think about this.

From then on, each day I wrote a little. The thoughts poured out of me. I realized that, although my life had been busy and satisfying, I also felt that this celebration concept was something important, and that to write about it would require a change in my life. Previously, I had been unable to tailor my life to accommodate that change. Now change was the order of the day. I had no choice. I knew that eventually my eye disease was going to result in at least some permanent vision loss. Now was the time to write.

As I reflected on my deteriorating vision and the inevitable change in my life, the nature of my illness held a further message for me. I needed to recognize the difference between sight and vision. My sight was impaired and would become more limited over time. But my *vision*—my ideas and my desire to live life fully and to contribute—was anything but impaired. I needed to start respecting my vision.

The truth was that I had limited my creative vision through the years as a response to the demands and expectations of the professional hierarchy of my field. I remembered my younger days as an art student, a time I had cherished, when I had felt inspired by vision. I recalled my days as an idealistic medical student, when I had been motivated by an exhilarating vision of curing the sick. My vision of relieving suffering and bringing healing to lives had come with me to the study of psychoanalysis, and eventually into my practice. But the responsibilities of being a leader in our professional organization and maintaining a medical practice had stunted the scope of my vision. Now it was time to rediscover and develop that vision of possibility. I could choose to make meaning of my illness, as a symptom of my soul's needs, not just the symptom of my ailing eyes.

These were the first steps toward developing a relationship with my illness, accepting it as part of my life and learning to live fully with it. Other aspects of this challenge were more practical but required an emotional adjustment, as my experience of myself changed from a very independent person to one who was clearly dependent on others in new and basic ways.

The simplest things loomed as practical and emotional challenges. For instance, I hate being clumsy. I had to get used to being clumsy. I discovered my vain side. I was clear in my mind that I wanted to *look normal* even if I couldn't *see normally*. If blind, I would need someone to make sure my attire was presentable each day.

I could no longer drive. I hated being a passenger. I was going to have to learn to be silent in the face of my wife's driving skills—not a bad lesson. Eventually I found that not driving created a very different day. It was a comfortable day at a very different pace. Walking was wonderful. So, being somewhat clumsy and unable to drive, I began to learn about myself as a dependent person. I had to look at myself as the object of my family's concern and my friends' comments.

When I turned to those around me, I found that most of my friends were awash in their own fears, which they churned into palpable anxiety. They wanted to "fix it," but of course they could not. So they focused their comments instead on the need to find someone who *could* fix it. They would ask routinely if I had confidence in my doctor. I received endless recommendations to go to *"the"* doctor in various places all over the world. I did not find this helpful. It actually hurt a bit. I understood their fear, but I had already made it clear that I respected and trusted my doctor. A doctor myself, I had chosen him for good reasons. I knew it was not in my best interest to let their anxiety erode my alliance with my doctor and my relationship with my illness.

Their concern was also a reflection of their own fears of adversity and their own discomfort in the presence of mine. Some even began to stay away and stopped calling. This disappearing act was not because they were not caring friends, but because they kept hearing that the last surgery had failed and the outcome was not good. It was clear that I was going to be blind in one or both eyes. They feared my adversity and helplessness because they feared adversity and helplessness in their own lives. I appreciated those friends who were courageous enough to say they were concerned and sorry and leave it at that. I wanted interest and concern and empathy, but not the burden of others' fears.

I turned to my wife, Jane, and my grown sons, Aaron and Josh, more than ever before. Despite their own sense of calamity, they stood firmly by. They expressed confidence in my alliance with my doctor and respect for my relationship with my illness.

I turned to my illness. It became a new part of me to explore and "play" with. One night at dinner, while I still had two eyes, each aimed in a different direction due to all the surgeries, I commented to my family that in order to get only one image I had to keep moving my head around, weaving side to side, to find the position that allowed the two eyes to focus on the same point. At that moment, I was also wearing dark glasses because I was so light sensitive. One of my sons congratulated me on my impressive imitation of Stevie Wonder. We all laughed—and what a relief it was to be able to laugh! We were all beginning to get to know this new part of me and "play" with it—with me. I gained new respect for "just being there" with illness, whether mine or somebody else's illness.

I was sad—and feel it still at times—with the growing realization that at some point in the future I might be blind. One day at dinner with my two sons, I looked across the table and saw one son, but not the other, who was sitting to my blind right side. I realized the day could come when I would see neither. The sadness came in a trip to Paris when I sat at a sidewalk café, people-watching while having lunch—my idea of a perfect moment. I thought of the future, when I might sit in the same place but be blind to the joyful parade of humanity. The sadness came when I first visited an art museum following the unsuccessful surgeries. I love art museums. This time, I was unable to take in the visual scope of the exhibit in the same panoramic manner as before. That made me very sad.

All that said, I have felt sad, but not endlessly so, because I also feel a genuine sense of opportunity and adventure. Not a happy adventure, but adventure nonetheless. This is the emotional juncture that leads me back in memory to the days of my childhood in a family that celebrated life in its fullness—adversity and adventure alike—and I can see where and how I first learned the lessons that are so valuable to me now.

My patients have different personal histories. Some struggle with recent complications in their health, work, or family life. Others are engaged in continuing struggles with adversity originating years, even decades, before. Many are survivors of painful childhood experiences and carry deep emotional wounds from those formative years. Interestingly, for some, even when family has failed to provide celebration's lessons in resilience, a similar education of the spirit had occurred with others in school or their religious community, during an adventure experience, or in seemingly mundane moments of life. However different the details, we all face a similar challenge in learning to engage adversity, develop a relationship with it, and through that process discover new facets of ourselves and new opportunities.

• AT THE HEART OF HEALING •

All healing begins with the exploration of our relationship with our adversity and our celebration of the gains. Healing is a mysterious process. Oh, we know a lot about how tissue heals, but we don't know a lot about why it sometimes should and doesn't, or why it sometimes does when we would not expect it to do so. We know little about healing the soul, spirit, and psyche. But there is a great deal of agreement that a person's motivation to heal contributes significantly to healing. The incidence of sickness and death is very high among people who feel life is of little value to them.

The process of claiming adversity as part of ourselves and celebrating it in the fullest sense initiates healing, whether it is emotional healing or physical healing. Sometimes it is both.

SHARON: NOTHING TO LIVE FOR
BUT A DAY AT A TIME

Before I became a psychoanalyst, I was serving as the consultation psychiatrist to a large hospital, and one day I was paged to come "stat"—quickly—to the cancer treatment unit, where a patient had just attempted to kill herself with an overdose of pain medication.

Sharon was in her thirties, a woman who had been fit and suc-
cessful, at the top of her game in her career and her home life as a wife and mother. Now she was a hunched jumble of skeletal limbs in a hospital robe. Her skin was pale and dull, and she looked at me with sunken eyes that flashed with anger, resignation, and still some fear. She wanted to die. She was a gifted biochemist and head of a research team, attuned to the smallest aspects of life, and was devastated by the diagnosis of a vicious cancer that would undoubtedly kill her soon. She had undergone elaborate surgery that basically took out and rearranged a lot of her insides. She was married and had three very young children. The day she felt so weak and so despairing that she didn't want to see her children anymore was the day she decided she was ready to die.

"I can't put them through this. I should just disappear and not let them see me waste away. I don't want them to remember this," she said, pointing in disgust to her mutilated body.

"That is one choice," I said. "But, have you really considered what you *would* be leaving them with if you killed yourself?"

After a silence, I suggested that she could always keep suicide as a backup plan, but a bit more reflection wouldn't be a bad idea.

We talked a bit and agreed over the next hour that I would see her at least twice weekly or as often as she wanted until she died. I would be with her through her death. I would help her children and husband to whatever extent I could and to whatever extent she wanted.

The work began the next day. She was weary and demoralized. Her dreams of a future were gone. Her life was wretched; she was taken from test to treatment to test to treatment. She was in pain. She was rapidly losing weight and energy. The radiation was only making matters worse. She didn't even see the point in the radiation and chemotherapy. Why not just cease the torture? For her and for everyone involved, she said, it would be such a relief if she just died.

Over the course of a few sessions, as she described her feelings, it became clear that she had lost all sense of her value on this earth. She was "being done to . . ." and not "doing" anything. I was a fairly young psychiatrist at the time, not highly experienced, but intuition guided me to make an observation and a suggestion, first that she had lost a sense of her value, and second, that she was surrendering too much to the treatment. She needed to remind herself of her scientific knowledge and her personal power of decision. The easy decision was to die, because that ended her need to use her personal power and capacity to plan her future, limited as it was.

Sharon was intrigued. The fact that she was an accomplished scientist had been forgotten, abandoned as irrelevant in the context of life as a patient, a victim of disease. As a matter of fact, she was a rather precocious young scientist, already recognized for her leadership capacities. Why had she so surrendered? We continued to explore this idea while she would sit and suck on ice chips and vomit into a bedside basin.

This treatment went on. Mostly, I listened. Then one day, she wanted to hear no more of my suggestions or observations. "I've been too invaded upon already," she said, defiantly. That was the first flickering sign of her old spirit. She began to insist that she receive her radiation treatments on time and not wait for an hour or more in the waiting room, where her now very thin frame couldn't take the hard seats. She refused experimentation. She had submitted to the surgery, which was experimental, but no more.

Then one day when Sharon came into my office, there was a different look in her face. She was more animated.

"Sharon," I said. "You're breaking our contract. You and I agreed that I would see you until you died. You're not dying."

Sharon smiled.

"I've begun to notice that myself," she said. "I guess now I'm going to have to do it the hard way. I'll have to live like everybody else, push on one day at a time."

Soon after, Sharon stopped coming for therapy. I faded into the backdrop of the life that now lay ahead of her. But for me, it was a first lesson in the healing power of celebration. Her value as a woman—not as a diseased or dying woman—had been forgotten in all the commotion of her illness. Our work in therapy had reminded her of it, reconstructed that frame of reference. It was aided by the fact that she had been a celebrated child and student, professional, mother and wife. I didn't have to do those lessons. She didn't need me for that.

In therapy, Sharon had learned to celebrate adversity, though we never put it in those terms. I don't mean that Sharon left therapy a "happy" woman. She did not discover a lucky lesson in her death sentence. She didn't suddenly find that her terrible struggle with cancer was opening new vistas of opportunity. No, Sharon's condition was grave, but in these weeks of reflection and reconnection with the woman she was at a deeper level than disease, Sharon had cracked her suicidal despair and developed a relationship with this adversity. In therapy, through the process of consciously identifying the moment, opening up to discovery, and sharing the experience—the celebratory process—Sharon was able to make a conscious choice. She might be dying, but she was going to live it. She was going to rejoin her life in progress as an active participant.

Remarkably, Sharon didn't die, and it makes her particularly memorable in this context. But the lesson Sharon offers is not in her not dying. It is in her decision to fully live what life she might have left. That was her greatest accomplishment, and that success is something any one of us can choose for ourselves.

There are times for surrender and times to fight. It is a bit like jujitsu. It is a question of balance and leverage. Part of developing the relationship with our illness or adversity is in knowing when to press the advantage and when to retreat or succumb to the moment. The idea is not to be one way or the other only, but to be part of a dance with adversity. You cannot develop a strategy until you explore your relationship with the adversity or illness. If we can't do this for ourselves, we must turn elsewhere. We must have our pain lessened so that we can think clearly. We must seek the patient support of our friends and family—sometimes we must seek therapy. The goal of therapy is to provide us with an emotionally safe place and supportive environment for this process of exploration and discovery. This is how hospice provides a healing affirmation of life amid death. This is how a traditional healer in Angola mends lives torn by violence, and how friends, family, or faith help any of us survive loss. This is how each of us can develop a strategy to engage life, whatever it deals us, and invite healing to begin.

TAD: OVERCOMING HELPLESSNESS, ENGAGING IN PROCESS

Tad was a brilliant man and an excellent business manager. No one would have suspected that he had survived a hellish childhood, a kaleidoscope of poverty, neglect, hardships, and uncertainties, or that he was still held captive by the emotional experiences of those early years. His intelligence was his cover.

Tad had always been saved by his intelligence. Early on, his teachers had recognized his exceptional mind and helped him gain access to the best high school in the area. From there, he had received a scholarship that enabled him to attend college and, in turn, graduate school. Tad excelled at all intellectual pursuits. When he left his home community, he "left behind" his past and became a sophisticated man. He married a very smart and sophisticated woman, whom he loved, and he went to work for a Fortune 500 corporation.

Tad's mind seemed to know no limits. When, as an adult, he approached music, as a lark, for the first time, his teachers sat in amazement at his ability. He was encouraged to learn more, and soon he was writing and performing original works in small venues to appreciative audiences.

For all his brilliance, Tad was brittle. The slightest adversity, the slightest bump in the road—a bad flu, criticism at work, an argument with his wife—threw Tad into a downward spiral of uncertainty and obsessive ruminations about his health, about whether or not his job was secure, whether his performance was up to par, or whether his marriage could survive. He was unable to focus on anything or anyone else. When his wife finally threatened to leave him because she could no longer live with his terrible, aching uncertainties and his combustible emotions, Tad became depressed and agitated, and sought treatment.

The process of psychoanalysis enabled Tad to reconstruct his mostly forgotten history, to find the sources of the inner conflict that undermined his life now. Tad had memories—too many memories for his own good. He had had to suppress them if he were to remain sane. In the safety of our therapy setting, he was able to let the memories come forward; he recalled far earlier memories than most people, things that had happened when he was only about two years old.

His parents had been worse than unloving; they had taunted him cruelly as sport, taking sadistic pleasure in making him feel worthless. He could remember being placed outside to give his mother "privacy" while his father was away. He could remember the physical violence and frightening scenes of jealous rage and demeaning shouts between his mother and his father. He could remember his mother's contempt, her undisguised anger that she had ever married his father, and then given birth to a boy she felt destined to be "nothing but trouble." He could remember, vividly, his father's death when he was six years old. He was left with adult questions about whether someone could have helped his father, who lay gasping for breath for what seemed like a very long time. He could remember how helpless he felt to affect any of this, yet feeling drawn into all of it.

Tad could also remember the refuge of school—it was warm and rewarding, and good food was served there. He could remember taking his excellent report cards to his mother, who scoffed at what a waste it was to be a "bookish" boy. Tad felt humiliated at home, yet he would panic if his mother were not there when he came home from school.

The very process of psychoanalysis was the celebration that Tad needed. The process of my listening to him, asking him questions, learning about him, and ultimately knowing him was reparative in itself. His suspiciousness, guardedness, and tentativeness were accepted and understood between us in the context of his unfolding history. In his therapy, Tad was able to celebrate his existence and his talents, and ultimately his life itself.

He came to see that adversity felt overwhelming to him, as he had first learned it—as a helpless child faced with hostility and disregard for his existence. He could see now that adversity was not only a challenge to his talents and skills but also had always contained the echoes of that helplessness, which he never wanted to revisit. He was now also able to see that he was no longer helpless— he could bring his powerful intellect and his capacity for emotional expression to bear upon the moments of his life and cope.

He soon learned to recognize when he was experiencing this helplessness response; now he knew what was happening to him and knew how to "walk himself through" his history and into my office and out of my office again. As time went on, this little mental meandering happened less and less.

As these lessons were put in place in his psychic structure, he was able to remember good things, the people who had helped him, some happy moments with his mother and father. Eventually he became interested in the music and rich traditions of his rural culture. When he combined that with the musical talents he was already quickly developing, he shifted from a successful career in business to a successful career as a musician.

Fully celebrated, the rich tapestry of Tad's history, including the thread of adversity, became the fabric of success in his work, his art, and his life.

• ORIGINS AND ECHOES IN ADVERSITY •

In adversity, we see again the power of celebration's origins and echoes to shape our lives. The echoes of Tad's life resonated deeply in his everyday adversities. It was the echoes of an uncelebrated childhood that made this capable man feel helpless and threatened. It was the echoes that made him freeze in fear—fear of the past adversities in which he was truly helpless to lend his power to the moment, rather than the current adversities he suffered.

For each of us, the echoes of our life—the lessons and words and looks and feelings of our origins—influence how we react to every moment, including moments of adversity.

Why is a certain kind of moment an adverse one for one person and not for another? Life's echoes define the moment. Our fears are both rational and not rational. We must respect both, but in celebrating the adversities of our life, we can separate out the rational fears of the moment from the irrational fears of the resounding sounds of the echoes of our history. I find the sounds of spoken German disquieting, even though some of the sweetest people I have met are German. I cannot ignore the images of terror that filled my childhood accompanied by the background music of the German language. My mentor, Lucie, had a doctorate in German literature. She was a refugee from Nazi Germany. However, she said that there was no more pleasing sound to her ears than that of Schiller poems being spoken or sung in German. Her echoes were different from mine.

We all eventually face adversities in our lives. Some will surprise us because we weren't expecting them. Some will surprise us because we are *not* shaken by them as we would have expected. We cannot predict the nature of our adversities, but we can prepare ourselves for them by developing the capacity to celebrate all different kinds of moments in our lives. The process is the same; it is only the text and the feelings that change.

We can name the adversity—but be careful to name it accurately. It is not enough to simply name the circumstance: "I lost my job" or "I have a serious illness." When we peel back the layer of circumstance, we reach the more meaningful fears or concerns that haunt us. For instance, "Will I be demeaned in my children's eyes?" Or "Will I fail those I love?" We must share. This is when we must share because we cannot do all for ourselves, and because we will cheat ourselves of the power of another individual's echoes in that moment. We must recognize, in time, the mystery of the adversity and stand in awe at the meaning of that adversity in our lives. All adversity has meaning, not necessarily divinely assigned, but generated in the way we come to terms with it. Not all meanings are welcome, but they beckon to be understood and used.

ELEANOR: NAMING AND CONQUERING FEAR

Eleanor was suddenly—shockingly—divorced. Her husband made his intentions of becoming a deadbeat dad quite clear. This was not really a surprise, but she had practiced denial for a long time. Eleanor was scared to death. She had not worked at her chosen career for fifteen years. It had been a mutual decision, one that she now regretted. We talked about her quandary.

"Searching for a job is a humbling experience," I said.

"Thanks, but I've been humbled enough, thank you," she said.

"You are going to have to move into your fears," I said.

"What does *that* mean?" she asked.

"It means first of all naming all of them and then moving into those names of fears one at a time, as if they are stage settings," I said. "It means living in those settings and speaking the lines of each place that you inhabit."

She paused, then began:

"I fear I cannot support my children financially or emotionally. I fear I cannot keep my home—their home. I fear that I will embarrass myself trying. I fear that my friends will judge me as flawed because I couldn't keep my marriage together and then couldn't support my family. I fear loneliness. I fear becoming a dried-up, sexless hag with neurotic kids. I fear the judgment of my family."

Eleanor suddenly looked up, and with fire in her eyes she said, "Yes, I fear the judgment of my family, specifically my father more than anything. Everything I mentioned was what he said I had to prepare myself to avoid. He said I had to marry well in order to avoid those catastrophes. I fear the predictions of my destiny, given to me by my father, will come true."

As she reflected on her father's grim countenance, a new insight emerged. His focus on potential failure and her need to avoid it reflected his own fears, the failed person *he feared becoming himself.* "I will not do that," she said. "I can do this." Eleanor sat back, visibly more relaxed.

Her fears would visit at night. Her fears would visit in certain alone moments when another blow came her way from a prospective employer or her husband's lawyer. She had to rename and revisit her fears in order to reorient herself. It became a full-time job, just living in her adversity and moving through it. She began to feel it to be a sort of blood sport. She was determined to walk out of the ring and onward.

Eleanor had to use her friends—the same ones she had felt would judge her. She did so with a boldness and candor that encouraged them to help and disagree and even fight with her at times. She strengthened some of her friendships and lost others; she held on to her home and kept her children together and got a job. She eventually felt that this adversity had been a valuable misery in her life. She was far more "actualized"—real to herself and others—now than she had ever been during her marriage. At times she almost wanted to thank her ex-husband—that bastard.

In the end, adversity is just another moment. It is not greater or lesser than the moment of falling in love, or the birth of a child, or the accomplishment of a life dream. It just has other feelings and texts and echoes attached to it. We can move into adversity as we move into any other moment: engage it, draw from it, and create meaning in it that enlarges and enriches our experience of life—celebrate it as a part of life.

SAM: SUCCESS ON BORROWED CONFIDENCE

Sam was terror stricken when he lost his job at age forty-seven. Sam's wife became the instant stabilizer of his life. She assured him that he would be all right. She assured him that they would be okay, that his children would understand. Sam, whose childhood was clouded by his father's chronic underemployment, was not sure. However, theirs was a good marriage and he could let himself borrow from her confidence to stabilize himself. Sam could use her confidence, based on different sounds of *her* childhood, from which to launch his search. His search—within himself and in the job market—took this moment—the adverse moment—to reshape the direction of his career.

Open to his wife's encouragement and the possibility of success, Sam was able to make bold steps instead of timid frightened steps. He was able to embrace the echoes of his youth and use his insights about them to guide himself away from his irrational fears and face the rational challenges ahead. His creativity and confidence impressed people during his interviews, and someone finally took a risk on him and employed him in the direction of his newly chosen path.

In our complex Western mentality, we have lulled ourselves into believing that adversity and celebration do not belong in the same sentence, but other peoples at other times have taught us that celebration and adversity are comfortable mates on the spiritual and human plane of existence. In addressing the wretchedness of people, Jesus spoke of adversity as the path to both enlightenment and salvation, and of using the adversity to know one's place and learn one's place in the universe. Jesus was not the only mentor who spoke of adversity as a path for personal and social discovery. Part of Gandhi's truth was that an adversity imposed upon a people or a person could be diligently examined and then be turned into a strength to be used against those who imposed the adversity. More recently, the United States has found its cohesion and strength in

embracing the challenge of terrorism.

Our job is not to avoid adversity, be it personal or social. Our job is to remind ourselves of the capacity of the human spirit to embrace it, and move into it as part of our lives. Leadership and inspiration emerge out of adversity, not because they offer a solution for it, but because adversity guides us inward to discover the depth and greatness of our own humanity.

(Death and Dying: Connections, Closure, and Continuation)

As a well-spent day brings happy sleep, so life well used brings happy death.

LEONARDO DA VINCI

In a fantastical Japanese rock musical I once saw, a group of contemporary teenagers in Tokyo travel through a time warp back centuries to the age of the great samurai warriors. They meet a samurai and confront him about his devotion to samurai practice. "Why do you go through all these rituals and customs?" they ask derisively.

The samurai answers, "You seem to live to avoid death—to deny it. I live to honor it—to be ready for it." The samurai was telling these youth that the reality of death gave meaning and context to his life and that theirs was empty because they did not have that context.

In studying life, I have never been far away from death. None of us is. We each have a relationship with death and we live in that context, whether we consciously acknowledge it or not. Beyond whatever religious beliefs we might hold that link a righteous life with a rewarding hereafter, most of us prefer to avoid thinking about death, even to the point of avoiding being around people who are gravely ill or dying. Occasionally we can't escape the confrontation. War and violence, accidents, illness, or old age confront us with the physical reality of death. But death is more than just a biological end point in life. It is the backdrop against which we see and experience life. If only unconsciously, our own death sits in the back of our mind from the moment we are born. For each of us, there is a moment between every breath and between every heartbeat when we are confronted with death. If we seek to live a celebrated life, then we must acknowledge the context of death, and open ourselves to the lessons it offers.

As a young man, I always found it a bit implausible when someone said they did not fear death. How was it possible to approach something as completely unknown and final as death—something that had no explorers or maps or outlines—without some fear and trepidation? Then, as a physician, I was privileged at various times to witness someone die with equanimity, even in the face of fear. I came to realize that it was not an absence of fear in the face of death that differentiated people as they faced this daunting final life experience. It was their equanimity that gave them courage. Where did it come from?

In the company of the dying, I have made an effort to be as close as possible, and to learn from them. Their insights, when so close to death, time and again reflect the power of celebration and the celebrated life to transform even this most challenging final passage into a meaningful experience for the dying and survivors alike.

• CONNECTIONS: FRIENDSHIP, KINSHIP, AND FAITH •

Mary Sullivan was seventy-eight years old. Her kidneys had stopped functioning, and she was a patient in the kidney dialysis unit at my hospital, when, as a young psychiatric resident, I was asked to give her a psychiatric evaluation. I had been called by her doctors to declare her mentally incompetent because she had asked to stop the dialysis, which would mean her certain death in a short time. If I declared her mentally incompetent, then her family and her doctors could continue the treatment until, as they put it, "her mind cleared."

It was routine. I would check her mental status, and if I found either organic or functional impairment, I would declare her incompetent, and then her civil rights would be taken from her until a mental health hearing could take place. In the meantime, her family and doctors would be in charge of her life.

As I entered her room, she looked up at me with expectant eyes. "Are you the doctor—the psychiatrist?" she asked.

"Yes, ma'am," I answered.

"Thank God!" she said with great relief. "Maybe you can help these poor young doctors. They think I'm crazy to want to stop this kidney machine stuff, but I think they are crazy to continue it."

Mary spoke with a slight Irish accent. She had a wonderful smile as she declared the "young" doctors to be crazy.

"Well, crazy is my specialty," I declared. "So let's see just who is crazy and who is not." She laughed, and I proceeded to ask a few formal questions like the date and place and about current events.

Mary humored me. Finally, she couldn't take any more of my silly questions and said, "Look, Doctor, I didn't ask for this. A year ago I went into a coma from kidney failure, and while I was out of it, my children couldn't let me go. They agreed to put me on the dialysis program. I woke up feeling fine, thank you, and they were very proud of themselves.

"They hadn't thought about how this would be for me and the family, though. For one year, I have had to come here and be connected to this machine for four or six hours, twice a week. It completely controls the lives of my entire family—all my children—and do you know who I live with, and who cares for me? My older sister! No one complains—of course they wouldn't! But the damn thing hasn't worked. My veins and arteries are too old. The shunts keep breaking down and clogging. They have to dig deeper and deeper to find a good vein and artery. It's simply not working for anyone. It's time to stop!"

"I can see what you mean, Mrs. Sullivan. But aren't you a good Catholic?" I asked, having seen her parish priest with her previously.

"Yes, I have tried to be, all my life," she replied.

"Well, have you thought of the suicidal implications of your decision?" I asked. Mary was relieved because she knew her answer would trump any objections.

"Doctor, we took this out of God's hands a year ago. I just want to put it back in his hands," she said plaintively.

We sat silently for a while. "What will you do, Doctor?" she softly asked.

"I will tell them they must respect your wishes," I said.

Mary grabbed my hand. She held it to her cheek as a tear came down. "Thank you. You know, I don't want to die. I'd like to live and enjoy my life, but it simply is the time. There is a right time," she said. We both cried.

"May I call you Mary?" I asked.

"Yes, of course," she said.

"Mary, I want to ask you a favor that you can refuse without any guilt. It is a selfish favor. I want you to let me come visit with you each day. I want to listen to your thoughts as the next few days proceed toward your death."

"I don't know, Doc," she said. "This is awfully private. Let me think about it."

I left Mary and went to my office and sat in heavy silence. The phone rang about an hour later. "Doc, it's Mary. I'd like to have you visit. If it helps you to help others, I'd like to do that," was all she said.

Mary lived for ten days; she was able to speak to me for eight of them. She was sad, but relieved. She was, above all, content.

"Why are you content, do you think?" I asked.

"Well," she said, "my faith helps. I feel connected to God and all his creatures. I believe in heaven, but I know that it is probably a silly idea. Either way, whether there is a heaven or not, I believe in God and his hand in all life—all creatures and creations. If I feel connected to God, then I am connected to everything he created, and that is like heaven. On earth I am connected to my children and my children's children. I am connected to my sister and my friends. How can I feel insecure? I am content that I have served them all and I have been served by them. I am part of them and they are part of me—not just by blood, but by friendship and kinship. I guess it's about connections."

It is about connections. It is the celebration of connections that can calm our fear and make us content in the face of death. Celebration is, in its essence, about connections—recognizing them, naming them, feeling their effect, sharing them, even mourning their loss—and bringing those connections into our conscious experience of the moment. If we can do that for all the various important and even small moments of our life, then it can serve the same useful purpose in these very final, most important, moments.

We all fear death. This fear is natural—unavoidable—yet it varies greatly from one person to another. I believe it is the breaking of connections that makes us fear death, whether we express that fear in trepidation or sadness, or, as some do, in anger and defiance. What we fear is this ultimate loss of connection. The thought that our connections, which have been so completely part of our being, can be finally and forever broken is a terrifying thought. It is a terrifying thought because these connections feel like essential parts of our being. Their loss, particularly if the loss is abrupt, threatens our very being, the way we know ourselves in the context of this other person.

If you amputate a limb, it is common for the amputee to "feel" the limb, as if it were still there. We call that experience a "phantom limb" sensation. It is the same with connections to important parts or people in our life. If we lose a loved one, it is a common experience to fleetingly "see" the person in a crowd or reach for the phone to share a piece of news or gossip with that person as if they were still alive. We may purposefully listen to a piece of music, visit a place, or make a special recipe we once shared with them. We are trying to keep the connections.

When we offer comfort by saying that a loved one who has died is "in a better place" or "we will see them in eternity," the comfort lies in the thought of them in a place where we will meet them again. We pretend that the connection is not broken, but it is. We feel a physical hurt and pain in the center of our body and our being. The French don't say "I miss you," they say *"tu me manqué"* which translates as "there is something missing from me, and it is you." That says better how we miss the person who has died—something is missing from us, and it is the deceased. If we celebrate connections during our life, we will be able to celebrate them in dying and death. The capacity to celebrate our connections places us in the center of all life and spirit. It allows us to feel connected far beyond our mere selves. We can call it heaven or nature, but at the heart of it, it is connection.

Mary celebrated her connection to her children and her God, and through them, her connection to life on earth, as she knew it, and life in heaven, as she believed it would be.

• DEATH IN THE CONTEXT OF LIFE •

Emotionally we all seek to be important, to feel that our lives matter. It is much easier to consider death if we are able to see and understand ourselves as part of a system of life, a community, that preceded us and will continue after our death. If we are born to be part of a historical system—a family and a culture—then we carry that history with us. It reduces the existential terror of "that is all there is." Such terror, which grows from the loss of a historical context, motivates all sorts of behavior, including greater tendency toward violence, sexual promiscuity, and delinquency. If we can behold and appreciate the historical context into which we are born, then it is easier to see merit in being an honorable part of a long tradition, and easier to find comfort in that.

LUCIE

Lucie was my friend and mentor. She was the mentor to literally thousands of people who were privileged to know her in one way or another. She was a physician, psychoanalyst, child psychoanalyst, and she also had her doctoral degree in German literature. She was respected as a true Renaissance woman. Lucie didn't have children of her own, but she had stepchildren who lived far away; she had these many students and friends; and she had her beloved literature.

We invited Lucie out to dinner to celebrate her eighty-fourth birthday, along with a couple of other mutual friends. She used a wheelchair routinely by that time, but her physical infirmities rarely dampened her pleasure in conversation. As talk around the table warmed up, I noticed that Lucie was not quite with us. This was very unusual for this woman, who was usually the vibrant center of any exchange of ideas.

Then, suddenly, Lucie interrupted our conversation.

"I had a dream the other day," she said. We fell silent.

"I dreamt that I was sitting at a dinner, like the many wonderful dinners I have enjoyed at your home, and that I was eating and enjoying the food without any problem from my emphysema. I could eat all I wanted and not be short of breath. I was taking food off of other people's plates and tasting everything. It was delicious! Suddenly a waiter arrived and took my plate away. But I wasn't finished! I started to object, but then I realized that I had had enough. I was finished. I appreciated the meal and the sharing, but I had had enough. And then I awoke.

"I realized that I dreamt of my death," she said gently. "I have enjoyed, so much, sharing your table and your life. I would like to do so much more. But—I have had enough."

We sat with tears in our eyes. We lifted glasses to the past, and she toasted our future. Her dream now informed all of us. Enough: Lucie had enjoyed enough of her life. It begged the question of whether she would have wanted more—I think she probably did—but she was satisfied that she had had enough. She wanted to bring closure to her great life. This capacity to accept enough and bring closure is the attainment of real peace, a celebration of life and death.

Lucie lived on for a few months more, and drew on all these connections to come to the conclusion of her life, to come to closure. She wanted to die at home, and as the end grew near, one day she retreated to her study, tended by her housekeeper and companion of many years, accepting notes from friends, but declining all visits. She wanted no lifesaving measures taken, and didn't want this final episode of her life complicated by any interventions by well-meaning friends.

When Lucie finally died a few days later, we all gathered at her home after the memorial service. The shawl that I had crocheted for her was draped over her chair in her study. Her books were open. We looked and realized that she had spent her last hours reading the German poets regarding their wisdom about death. She had been studying—preparing—for her own death. Lucie had been determined to die as she had lived her whole life: in her own way, connected to her friends, her family, and her literature, and bringing all these pieces to a thoughtful, deliberate, and meticulous conclusion.

• CLOSURE: BRINGING PEACE TO CONNECTIONS •

Closure is a celebration of connections, too. It is both the living and the dying who need to bring closure at the time of death. Why is closure so important to us? What does it accomplish?

In all my years of work with people and with populations, I have witnessed that the unfinished business of life exerts a far greater negative influence on us, even as we are dying, than business that is finished, resolved, and wrapped up. It almost doesn't matter what the business is—how wonderful and thankful we are for our connections or how horrible or painful the relationship was. If closure can be brought to those issues, then with it comes peace of mind. Connections can be remembered in context, and celebrated.

Closure means feeling satisfied that what needs to be acknowledged has been. Closure means that we feel heard—listened to. Closure means we say what needs to be said, that we have said it all about our issue with that person, and we feel that there is nothing to be gained from lamenting loss or in carrying the grudge or the hurt anymore. That means we must speak about love and about loss. We must speak about regret and remorse. We must speak of gratitude and resentment. We must speak of dying. We must all speak—those who will die and those who will live. We must find a way to say it all and feel listened to. We must name, we must share, and we must bring ourselves to this last moment to celebrate the connections that were and the connections that will remain.

With love this is less difficult. However, the unexpressed feelings of love, while they can be a burden, are lighter than the unexpressed feelings of hurt and resentment. The negative feelings weigh heavier on our souls. Negative feelings stand firmer in the way of a good death. We must speak of our souls and from our souls. We must admit the truths and care enough for the living and the dying to grant the dignity of truth to the moments of death. Even hard truths will lighten the burden of this moment of mystery and awe.

I remember sitting at the funeral of a very prominent colleague, a woman who was a pioneer in her field, a powerful, and often difficult, personality. The eulogist was a lifelong friend and colleague. She stood before us and began with an anecdote about our departed colleague that clearly depicted her very difficult character. The eulogy proceeded to mention, in great detail, the many hard edges to our departed colleague's character, and the pain she inflicted on her students and friends. I leaned over to a friend beside me and asked, "Is this a eulogy or a character assassination?"

She whispered back: "I don't know, but it is the truth that needs to be told."

We dishonor the dead when we polish their story to our liking, and we diminish the healing power of the truth when we turn away from it.

LEO: CLOSURE AND NEW BEGINNINGS

Leo was afraid that he couldn't deal with his father's death. His father was old, but not in immediate danger of dying; he had time.

The man was a true patriarch. His life had been the big life, the one celebrated in the family. Father was a prominent banker; in younger days he had survived the Holocaust. As a survivor and a leader, he was highly respected in the community, and was greeted everywhere he went. To be the son of this father was a privilege in itself, but also a burden. The greatest burden was the relative unimportance of Leo's own life. His life, his character, seemed only a reflection, good or bad, upon his father's life.

Leo's solution was to escape. He established his life elsewhere. He entered therapy to begin to come to terms with his own uncelebrated life. And now, the time was approaching when he had to come to terms with his feelings about his father, and represent the family appropriately in the rituals that would accompany the patriarch's death. He worried: how could he carry this off with love and integrity?

Much of our work in therapy centered on Leo's sense that he was, in an "honored" way, the victim of his father's life. Yes, his father had survived a great deal of misery, only to come back and live a life of honor and glory. Sadly, though, his prominence, and Leo's feeling of being inconsequential, made Leo the second victim of his father's history; but he had to accept that his father was the first. That was his history as much as it was his father's. His father had not chosen his life as it played out, but he did embrace it and make something of it. If honor came of it, that was just another part of his history. The fact that his father did not share the honor by honoring the life of his son for his own value was a fact of Leo's history, just as the Holocaust had been for his father. Leo would have to make something of his life himself.

Looked at this way, Leo began to understand his father's death as an opportunity to accept and embrace his own history, which unavoidably included his father's. To celebrate his father's life was

DEATH AND DYING

not the continuation of a loss, but the celebration of a part of his own life.

His father's death was drawing near. The occasional hospitalizations were increasing in frequency. His father's heart was failing. Leo visited his father in the hospital. He brought some kosher herring—his father's favorite and strictly forbidden by the doctors. They conspired, with mutual glee, at overcoming the oppression of these "guards" of his father's well-being. It was, on so many levels, a minienactment of the horrible years of confinement, and overcoming, together this time, oppression in a life-threatening circumstance.

One day Leo's father spoke to him in a way he had never done before.

"The world brightens when you visit," he said. "I don't fear death knowing you are here."

They kissed for the first time. They cried together. His father died in Leo's arms. And following his death, Leo led the community in preparing his father's body. He washed his dead father's body. He dressed it in simple cloth, as was the custom of the Orthodox community. He followed the coffin to the grave and helped bury it. In the year following, Leo would go to his father's grave and sing the songs of the Sabbath that his father so loved. Both had overcome their oppression and liberated each other in the process of living the old man's dying. They had been able to celebrate each other's lives and what they brought to each other by existing for each other.

Leo was undeniably born into a long and complex history. He was born into a legacy that had overshadowed his own life. He had to claim the legacy for himself and pick up the reins of that legacy and guide it where he wanted it to go. In the process of bringing closure to the hurts of his undervalued life, Leo found the means to continue. It was not just an irony that those means were the same as those that served his father and his father's legacy. Leo was his father's son. He was the heir to his father's legacy; he needed to claim it—celebrate it—as his own before he could create one of his own.

• SHOCK, GRIEF, AND RECOVERY AS A NATIONAL EXPERIENCE •

So much was summed up in the terrorist attack of September 11, 2001. We were, as a nation and as individuals, forced instantly to see life in the context of violent death, massive death. We saw the material icons of our society horribly—unbelievably—disappear before our eyes. We saw the symbols and our sense of peace of mind and security evaporate in moments. We heard the stories—the endless stories—of the last phone calls from those trapped in the hijacked planes or the buildings, to loved ones, even to telephone operators, to anyone with whom the dying could connect one last time. And the words were "I love you" to family or friends. "Tell the kids I love them and always will." "Tell my wife that I loved her." They were the words of love and connection and even closure. They were the words that took us into these horrible moments, but also provided the way to continue and commemorate and convey to the generations to come, the meaning of life and our duties to civilization. It was in these last words before death that we saw connection, closure, and continuation captured in just a few moments and just a few words.

Initially, the visual images of the attack, the survivors, the rescue operations at the death sites, and the photos and names of those thousands of people missing filled our consciousness. Then, beyond the unimaginable loss of lives that day, came the realization of those other kinds of casualties. Our peace of mind was gone. Our assumption of safety, always an illusion, was gone. Denial was no longer an option. The ever present death threat from global terrorism, which we had largely ignored, became a conscious backdrop for everyday life.

How do the elements of celebration aid us when we are confronted with death in this and other disturbing contexts—children's deaths, accidents, terrorism, and other violence?

Some search for divine meaning in the capricious, senseless deaths that surround our lives and fill the news. I don't subscribe to the notion that God seeks vengeance by guiding the hands of terrorists who would kill children on the way home from school, or other innocents in the course of daily living. Nor do I believe God deals out disease that grabs our loved ones at a woefully premature age. Whatever we think about a God-force, it is not lent weight by such happenings. No, the meaning we seek in the face of those deaths does not lie in the capriciousness of nature or the perversion of the human mind.

Meaning can be found in the way we deal with the irrational and the capricious nature of life. Can the abrupt and unjust end of life tell us anything about life itself? Yes, but the message is hard. Life is a fragile construct. It depends on the amazing cooperation of myriad physical, mental, and environmental forces. When those forces cannot cooperate to sustain life, does that mean that life loses its meaning? No, it means that we must seek greater meaning to life than even the amazing cooperation of those myriad forces. Meaning is something we seek—and gain—by placing ourselves fully in the moment, asking ourselves the questions that come to mind, offering the answers that are inspired from within or aided from others. This is the celebratory process.

It is in this internal and external dialogue that meaning, our personal meaning, can be found. Is this God's meaning? If by fully witnessing this moment of painful and seeming senseless death, we are drawn to a deeper understanding of life—even the capriciousness of life—then we have experienced God's meaning.

In the days that followed that September attack, we saw on a massive scale the power of the shared experience, this time one of loss, grief, anger, resolve, and the beginnings of recovery. Although many victims used their cell phones to assure loved ones or say a final good-bye to them, in essence the thousands who died were denied the luxury of process, the opportunity to die in the care of loving family and friends. It was left to the survivors, individually and collectively, to make meaning of the losses and integrate this new and terrible experience into our lives.

At first, there was the national gasp, echoed around the world, which seemed as if it would never end. How long could we take in our breath and wait, and wait, and wait for something rational to make sense of the overwhelming irrationality of the images and the facts we were seeing and hearing? The answer is that we could not hold our breath forever and passively wait for sense to be made of such a sinister, violent act. We had to exhale, accept that these thousands were inexcusably killed and gone forever, and find a way to reassemble our lives.

Within a few days the universal gasp gave way to a universal sigh and a universal sadness, expressed openly. "I feel like crying," "I cry all the time at simple things," "I cannot shake the sadness," "I cannot focus on anything else," were the comments I heard from so many here and abroad. We still watched, but the images of the crash sites, the planes penetrating the towers, and people waving desperately, or falling, from those towers gave way to the scenes from the heroic rescue operation. All too soon, as it became clear there were to be no more rescues, we were then immersed in sights and sounds of bagpipes and funerals. Eventually the bagpipes fell silent, too. Throughout it all, we heard the stories of ordinary lives interrupted by death or loss, and then the stories began to tell of the victims' lives, the way they lived and loved and worked up to the end. We began to celebrate the gift of their lives in the context of their deaths.

We were having a national funeral that spoke of many different types of loss at the same time. We told the people's stories so that they would not pass silently. We spoke of rebuilding the same towers. "We have the plans; we will rebuild exactly as they were before," a leader said. Then other voices said, "We can't build exactly as they were before, because it will never be exactly as it was before." Some said a huge memorial should replace the destruction. Others said that was too much; we could not devote so much to memorial. We were entering a national grieving process.

Grief is a very individual thing; it is not done by committee. No matter who scripts the funeral, the grief is left to each of us individually. But grief is not done alone. We sit together and we speak of who and what was lost with them. We allow all the rest of the feelings to emerge and be given voice. We feel helplessness and try to deal with loose ends, and the loss of direction or purpose. Creativity begins to return slowly, and we begin to think about how to incorporate the memories and meaning into our life.

Time sometimes must be allowed to stand still, and we must hold the moment. Then we must allow the rest of our sentiment to come forth and awaken creativity. We are not all going to create "the" memorial, but we are all going to create "our" memorial. We are going to integrate this new state of being, this state of being without what and who we had before. In the reassembly of our lives, we will find in the infrastructure of the new life we will create a place for that and those who were lost, which will help us be able to move on. This is grief at its best.

And if you look back at what we have gone through and are still doing, we are in a full embrace of this experience. We have recognized the moment of loss. We have named it in its many forms. We have told the stories and we have brought forth our own unconscious inspiration to bear upon this moment. We have held time, slowed it in our minds, and we have been awestruck not only by loss but also by our creative power to grow out of the integration of this moment. We have stood back in awe at the mystery of this massive loss, the outpouring of compassion that first filled the void, and the massive gain that will follow.

• AFTER LIFE: A CONTINUATION OF LIFE AND LOVE •

We must continue to celebrate connections after a life is over. However death occurred, whatever the tenor of the relationship, we must not disown our connections. We must take note of those moments when we feel the pull to connect with thoughts of a deceased friend or family member. We can stop and ask, "Why do I want to speak to this person now? Why do I wish I could turn to them now?" The answer will be a celebration of some part of our connection to them.

We must name those moments and share them, with the memory of the departed or with God, if we wish, and with others around us. This is the way we weave those who are absent into the lives of those present. This is how we continue the connections, and make the experience, insight, and inspiration of those past available to us again. This is the only afterlife we know about.

• REMEMBERING ROSIE: A TIME FOR HOT DOGS •

My mother didn't think she would make a very good old lady. She didn't want to be an old lady. It wasn't about vanity; it was about her idea of living. If I sit back and let my mind try to capture the one motif of her life, it was action. I can remember being a small boy, grabbing her hand and racing to keep up as she rushed from one place to another, going about her daily chores and rounds of visits and caring. People would joke that I was like a flag flapping in the wind behind my mother as she went about her day.

When I went off to college, her pace only increased in daily variety, now that she didn't have to tend her children. She tended everyone else, as a friend or helper. Her rounds were legend. She mused, more than once, "I don't think I want to be a very old lady. I want to die putting my coat on, going out the front door to meet someone I look forward to seeing."

She called it exactly. She was only sixty-four—hardly an "old lady"—when she died of a heart attack on her way out the door to meet my father, who was waiting for her to join him for a lunch out. It was as she would have wanted it. For us, it was a shocking loss.

As our long-distance family began to assemble later that evening at my sister's house in Chicago, we initially sat in stunned conversation and silence. Then my eyes met my cousin's, and we both smiled.

"We're hungry," he said. "We want hot dogs, Chicago hot dogs."

Let me explain. In the early days, in our small one-bedroom apartment, in the summers we would sit after dinner on the back porch to cool off. The dinner was over and the dishes were done. We would sit and visit with one another and with our neighbors.

Mom loved "chasing" one flavor with another. Sweet desserts were chased by salty snacks. Throughout my childhood, in the relaxing after-dinner time on the back porch, we heard the bells heralding the arrival of the hot dog vendor and his cart three stories down and on the corner of the two busy streets next to our building. Mom would ignore the bells for a while, and then she would say, "How about a hot dog as a chaser?" We would scamper down the wooden back-porch stairs to the inner courtyard, cross the alley and the gas station lot, and begin to smell the hot dogs before we arrived at the corner. We would have our chaser and go back and go to bed. It was being a bit bad together.

In school, before the day of school lunches, I would walk to a little restaurant near our elementary school, where Mom would wait to have lunch with me. There was no time to go home; it was too far. She would order my hot dog and have it waiting with a paper napkin over it to keep it warm.

Or if, during an afternoon visit, someone said, "I'm hungry," Mom was up and out, going down the back-porch stairway three stories to the ground, leading us to the corner hot dog stand for that chaser. We did a lot of "chasers" all day, but they never stopped being special. So when my children were old enough to cheat and be bad together in this family conspiracy, and we visited my mother or our cousin Rolla, we had hot dogs. When we went to Chicago for weddings and funerals and bar mitzvahs and Passover and Thanksgiving, we had hot dogs

So now, at home for the first time without Mom in charge of the kitchen, we dispatched my local cousin to the hot dog stand nearby. He came in with two large bags of hot dogs with all the fixings. We ate; we remembered. We reordered. We ate some more. We ate through our tears. We remembered some more.

In the mourners' car, coming home from the burial, I said to my sister, "Can we bring in hot dogs?"

"Hot dogs?" she said. "We have platters of fish and delicatessen cold cuts; that's the traditional food."

"No, hot dogs are our traditional food," I said. "I will eat the fish and cold cuts, if I can also have hot dogs." We sent poor cousin Eddie out for many more hot dogs. It was a feast. No, it was a Eucharist! We ate the hot dogs in memory of my mom, but more than memory, it was in connection to her.

It became a family story. It was, and continues to be, repeated at all family gatherings. After my nephew's wedding, we went out to eat hot dogs. After my brother-in-law's funeral, we brought in hot dogs. When we gathered at Rolla's table for a visit, we brought in hot dogs. And we always remembered Mom. It's about connections and celebration.

So it was that when I mentioned to my twenty-one-year-old son, Aaron, that I was writing a chapter about death and dying, and the significance of remembrance around death, his first response was, "You're going to talk about hot dogs, aren't you?" This is how it happens. He had come into the family tradition through celebration and connection to people and generations he didn't know—but could remember.

As a nation, we formalize this sacred act of continuation with memorial holidays. We clear the space on our busy calendars and create the opportunity to reflect, remember, share stories, and find new meaning in the lives of those now gone. Whether we remember as one, or one of many, and whether we remember through intimate traditions of food, music, a favorite phrase, or a sunrise, celebration continues the discovery process of life—the revelations of life.

For Leo, closure with his dying father brought healing after years of emotional struggle. Sometimes, as survivors, our struggle for closure lasts years after death and loss. Nothing about human nature is linear. We are really somewhat random beings that respond to the stimuli and needs of our bodies, minds, environment, and souls. We do not grieve our own mortality or the deaths of others in a programmed manner, one feeling after another, as some have suggested. We do it at our own pace, in our own way, experiencing feelings that at times conflict or overlap, leaving out some steps that have been suggested and lingering on others. Closure and continuation are not achieved in a neat order. The connections pervade all our efforts to grieve. These connections pull and push and block our efforts to grieve. Yet, in time, unforced and celebrated, those connections bring us to closure.

• WE DIE AS WE LIVE •

It is said that the ceremonies of death are for the living. Obviously, the person who has died is beyond the effect of our ceremony marking his or her death. So it is true, eulogies are for the living. We give eulogies and find that which captures the particularity, the specialness, of the person, and we praise the person. We tell each other what it is about the deccased that we found praiseworthy. The eulogy is a form of lesson to remind us of our time and the summation of our lives. The way we mark the part of life we call death determines much of how we see and craft the rest of our lives. What shall we stand for? What will be said about us? In other words, how shall we live our lives? Will it be said that our lives added to the celebration of life itself?

The ceremony of death is really a celebration of life. Whether we rejoice in the life beyond mortality, or see ourselves return to the human spiritual source, or see the life of the individual as only a mark on the record of life for all people, our ceremony of death informs us once again of the sources of our humanity. Funerals rise to praise that source and tell us of our need to remain an inspired part of humankind. We must contribute, the ceremony tells us, if we are to be enriched by the source of humanity. The elements of praise, the recognition of our humble place in the source of our humanity, and the recognition of the mystery of life itself all bring us to a point of celebration.

I was disappointed at an earlier age when I discovered that the mourner's Kaddish prayer at Jewish funerals is actually a communal and individual affirmation of faith. I had always thought that those untranslated Hebrew words were some sanctification of the life we were noting in its passing, but the prayer had nothing to do with the deceased or even with death. I was mystified as to why this was the holy prayer at the time of death. Now I know. It is that prayer which constitutes the Jewish celebration of life itself and of our appreciation and gratitude for life. To acknowledge the power of a spirit beyond ourselves, a source of our humanity with which we carry out a much larger plan of human evolution, is to celebrate. The Kaddish celebrates life and devotion to the mystery of life in the face of the mystery of its end.

How each of us faces our own death is based on how we view our lives to that point. I have been blessed to be part of the deaths of several people to whom I was close. As a physician, I have witnessed the deaths of people I don't know. Even before that, when I was an adolescent and worked in a hospital emergency room and as a surgical technician, I witnessed the last moments of many lives. I can say that there are good deaths, bad deaths, and inspired deaths.

The British author Evelyn Waugh, in his novel *Brideshead Revisited*, has a passage about death in which he briefly alludes to the quality of dying. Lord Brideshead lies dying. He is attended by his physician. After finishing a bedside visit, the physician is escorted to his car by a close and intimate family friend and former son-in-law of the dying Lord Brideshead. "You must admire his will to live," he says to the doctor. "Oh, you think so," replies the doctor. "I think we are seeing a fear of death, instead of the will to live."

The physician, who knows his dying patient, points out that his death recapitulates his life. This selfish man, who couldn't celebrate anyone or anything, but just selfishly enjoyed his inherited privilege, is dying still frightened of the mystery of life and its conclusion. And while his death is taking place in the grandeur of his castle, in a historic, canopied bed, attended by his family, it is a bad death. It is a death of fear and anguish, devoid of celebration for the dying aristocrat or those who surround him. In the end, it is an empty life, which leaves his children with an empty space in their souls.

From my own days with Sister Thelma in the domain of the hospital emergency room, I remember one elderly man who came in to die. His neck, badly eaten away by cancer, was wrapped in dressings. He was slowly bleeding to death, as the cancer was attacking his arteries and veins. He was not in great pain. He was appreciative of our care. He stayed in the ER while his grown children gathered around. He slowly slipped into unconsciousness. I remember sitting beside him, stroking his arm, and occasionally taking his blood pressure and pulse, marking his progress toward death. At some moment, his children asked if he could still hear them. I said yes, I thought so. They stood around and said the rosary together. I saw him draw his last breath during the rosary but said nothing. Then they were done and he was gone, leaving his children with hearts sad but full.

Freud suggested that there is an instinct in humans to gather and grow and connect and live, and there is an instinct to separate and waste and disconnect and die. We are unconscious of both. It is this instinct to disconnect, to die, that causes us to turn away from love or opportunity or challenge. It is the instinct to gather and grow and connect, even in the context of death, that allows us to truly celebrate life.

(Living with **10** Celebration)

To affect the quality of the day is no small achieve-ment.

The Eurostar train between Paris and London travels through a tunnel 150 feet under the surface of the English Channel, then across the miles of historic fields, farmland, and villages of southern England and northern France. I boarded it one fall day in Paris and couldn't help but feel a part of history as I rode the path of this centuries-old dream of a connection between England and continental Europe. Napoleon first thought of doing it. It only took two hundred years to accomplish one of the great feats of technology and architecture.

The Eurostar travels very fast, and I mean *very* fast. Sitting in the train, you don't really feel the speed. It is quiet and smooth. But looking out, particularly when you are traveling alongside the highways, it is impressive. The cars on the highway are traveling at seventy to ninety miles an hour, and the train speeds past them as if they were standing still. I have driven that route to the north of France; it takes a lot of time. On the Eurostar it melts away into minutes.

As I sat there that day, on my way to a conference, I was taking in the technological marvel of it all. Why couldn't the United States invest in such trains? Airplanes are wonderful, too, and they have their place; but train travel offers a completely different, richer ex- perience. Train travel makes getting from one place to another drawn out enough in time that the word *voyage* has meaning. You "participate" in train travel. As I sat thinking, impressed by the feat of technology and public policy that created this supertrain, suddenly I felt that something was missing from the experience. It pulled me from my reverie.

At first I couldn't put my finger on it, but then, as I looked out upon the passing landscape, it came to me. It was nearly impossible to see what passed before my eyes—it was passing so fast that I couldn't take it in. That last thought about participating in train travel didn't work. It was going too fast. My eyes could take it in, but my brain couldn't process what I saw. *There is a lovely country church, but, oh, there is a ruined château, but, oh, there is a farmer plowing the remains of harvested crops into the ground.* Each scene flicked quickly to the next, faster than the blink of an eye.

The train remained a technological marvel, but now I could see there was a cost—a sad cost. The speed of travel was enhanced, but the more deliberate joy of train travel was diminished. The participation of traveler with the landscape was seriously impaired. As I sat with this thought and watched the blur through the window, I realized that, in every aspect of our lives, this is the challenge we face in finding meaning in contemporary times. Our lives are filled with technological marvels, opportunities, and experiences that were unheard of in generations past. I wouldn't give any of them up. But there is a price. In the fast pace of our days we easily lose a sense of participation in the landscape of our lives. We can see it all pass, but so quickly that it doesn't really—cannot really—register in our minds.

For our children, particularly our young children, this blurring view of life denies them the deeper experience of themselves in the moment. They need this to develop a richer sense of the inner landscape of the mind and soul, and the outer landscape of family and community that surrounds them. As we grow older, this loss is felt in different ways, showing itself in a sense of isolation, uselessness, sadness, and sometimes depression. The unexamined, uncelebrated life is, to borrow from Thoreau, a life of "quiet desperation." The complexity and pace of life today have the potential to deliver us into desperation ever faster, and younger.

The celebrated life is a life lived to its greatest depth and texture. We find it in our relationships with others, in our relationship with ourselves, and in a feeling of connectedness to the greater mystery and awe of life. This is celebration, and whether we are conscious of our need for it or not, intuitively we seek it.

My mother made it look easy. Everyday life was a slow, intricate, and often difficult experience for my mother and her generation, but celebration was built-in for us; with lots of time and little money, we mined each moment for all it was worth. Over the years, the colorful thread of life stories that wove through the conversation in our home became the fabric of our family life, and the backdrop for another generation.

Today, our lives are defined by speed, technology, and affluence that typically disconnect us from that fuller experience of the moment, and of each other. We don't have to get off the train, but we do have to rediscover a way to capture the moments and process them. We have to find a way to fully experience everyday moments and integrate them into our larger experience of life, or the hasty blur itself becomes all we know and feel, a desolate inner landscape.

We have the tools to reclaim and revive celebration in our lives, but we have to make a conscious effort to use them. Even when we're motivated to try, moving from talk to action can feel awkward. We think of expressing our appreciation to someone, yet we don't quite get around to sending the note or making the call. We excuse ourselves from a meaningful gathering, or from speaking up about something important to us, telling ourselves that we won't be missed or that our comments are unimportant or unnecessary. Beyond the hurry imposed by our overscheduled lives, this procrastination, or sometimes reluctance, is a way of avoiding risk. When we invest ourselves in the moment, express our feelings, and invite others to join us, even in the most mundane moment there's a chance we'll feel foolish, get our feelings hurt, or be misunderstood. There is little we can do that makes us feel more vulnerable than dipping down into the depths of our mind and soul and speaking from that place. It takes some amount of courage to do all that, however simple the moment may seem. We would be naive not to be reluctant, but we cheat ourselves and the moment if we let reluctance define our lives.

How to begin, then?

In a sense, celebrating anything, anyone, anytime, at any moment in time is like creating a small piece of theater. As in any theater production there are elements that, in some way, must be included for the piece to work. Each one adds an important dimension to our experience. When I go to the gym to work out, I frequently skip the abdominal exercises. They are hard for me and a bit humiliating. And the fact that I skip them is clear in the results

I get—and don't get—from my workout. You cannot cheat the elements of the exercise. It's the same with celebration. We must practice those elements that don't come easily.

In previous chapters, we explored celebration as the process through which we interact with a moment in ways that create meaning, whether it is meaning of our own making, or meaning created by those around us. We examined the elements of celebration that invest a moment with lasting resonance:

Recognizing and naming the moment

Opening ourselves, mind and body, to the full sensory experience of the moment

Sharing the moment with others, with the memory of those absent, with God, or simply with ourselves, creating feelings of connection

Recognizing mystery and awe in the moment

Understanding these elements is an intellectual exercise, a deliberate search for celebration's origins, echoes, and new sounds in your life. Living with celebration is a simple practice, a way of tapping into the energy and possibility of the moment, no matter what the circumstances. The next chapter discussion is devoted to parents and a strategy to keep celebration at the heart of your relationship and responses with your children. For any of us, however—children or no children—the following five principles take you straight into the celebrated life, and make it easy for you to create the celebrated life for yourself and those around you.

Principle One: Openness

Be open to the possibility of the moment.

Sometimes a patient who has been seeing me for many months or even years enters my office and says, "When did you get that picture over there?" I point out that the picture has been there since I (223 moved into the office years earlier, and all the time I have been seeing them. We then have a bit of fun trying to understand why they are "seeing" it for the first time.

We see things when we're ready. We see things when we're looking, when we're open to the world around us. When we are overwhelmed by any aspect of life, we easily miss what else is going on around us. However justified our concerns about money, health, family, or work, when we are preoccupied our experience of the world is narrowed and we miss many of the moments—the everyday mundane moments—worth noting.

To be open is to be alert, available, and prepared to embrace the moment as it unfolds. Openness leads to an experience of connection, both inwardly and outwardly. We connect to the mystery and to the deepest sense of ourselves, and we connect to those with whom we share the moment.

Openness also feels vulnerable, but that *is* what we really are; that is what it means to be human. We cannot be open without being vulnerable. Vulnerability in the celebration of life is not a deficit; it is a strength. It may even call for courage.

Openness allows us to appreciate the essential mystery of our lives and to experience the wonderful, humbling, yet empowering sense of awe about our life and the lives of others. Only by being open can we access our deeper inspirations and bring our creativity, ourselves, to bear upon the moment or occasion.

Fear is the greatest obstacle to living with celebration, and modern life is rife with fears. Some are obvious—fear of physical harm, fear of losing a job, losing a lover, or losing our health or financial stability. Others are silent nagging fears, like the loss of our dignity, individuality, or independence. We lessen fear when we feel effective in the moments of our life. Openness, contrary to the "wisdom" of those who are afraid, helps calm our fears. Being open to recognizing and naming and embracing moments is the only way to be personally effective—to calm our fears and feel confident.

We think about being open to new experiences, but it is just as powerful to be open to new understandings of people, relationships, and episodes from our past. The past sometimes holds pain and confusion, and reopening these moments can be difficult. However, if we fully engage all the elements of celebration, we make the experience less overwhelming and learn new things about ourselves and our past. Openness is about turning on our senses and tuning them to a moment in time, a message, a person, a scene or a thought, for instance.

How do you practice being open?

Be available to the moment. Resist the rushed life. Take time for reflection, by yourself or with others. Refuse to be hurried. Linger in the moment.

Engage fully in the moment, whether it is a moment of conversation, observation, reflection, or action.

Be open to a full sensory experience. Consciously peruse your surroundings, as you might study a still-life painting or a movie clip. Close your eyes and listen for the background sound that surrounds you, and the other sounds that drift in and out of your space. Pause to savor a bite of food. Drink in an aroma. Feel the sun or the cold or the breeze on your skin.

Be open to a new idea or another point of view. Listen fully. Resist an impulse to respond with an opinion or a suggestion. Invite elaboration.

Don't be afraid to create ceremony. Look for ways to make traditions and rituals more meaningful by making them more personal and affirming.

Think of yourself as a work in progress, and be open to the idea of every experience as an opportunity to discover something new about yourself, to learn and grow.

Principle Two: Sharing

Share the moment to enrich and enlarge life.

As children we are told to share our toys and games with others. These onerous instructions have a purpose. That purpose is not only to establish a common social order, but it is also to show a child, firsthand, that the experience of sharing can be uniquely and surprisingly fulfilling. A shared moment opens possibility. It invites collaboration and creativity. It cultivates connection.

Sharing is a dynamic exchange. To let someone use your implements or ideas is not the deepest sense of sharing. But to exchange ideas or experiences and let the other influence our thinking or participation, *that* is sharing in a deeper sense.

We first learn sharing by the participation of family in our discovery of life and the world around us. To put your child in front of a television set to watch Mr. Rogers or *Sesame Street* is not the way to teach sharing. Sit with your child and share the experience of those same programs together, and you have a beginning. Use that experience as a springboard for sharing your own thoughts and stories, and inviting your child to do the same, and you create a new experience of sharing your *selves*.

We must learn to *be with* one another. It sounds ordinary, but time must pass as we sit, walk, play, even sleep together. Sharing and time are very integral. It takes time to share a life; there is a pace to sharing. On the surface it can be a hectic and exciting adventure, but below the surface of our being, the pace of being together is slow and attenuated. To share at this deeper level we must have a palpable sense of the other person's presence. That takes time.

Conversation is a form of sharing. Talking was invented by humankind to communicate, to allow us to make sense of life and to find our place in nature and time. The human capacity for speech works to strengthen connections, to calm anxiety about what is happening in and around us, and to organize and make sense of our world and our lives. Talking has taken on many forms: communication, ritual language, prayer, song, but most of all conversation. The process of listening, reflecting, and responding creates a new experience and a new dimension of understanding between us, or among us.

Sharing is an energizing experience. It is why so many people come away from a shared celebration feeling renewed. Contrary to appearances, sharing can also be a conscious part of many solitary experiences. The solitary experience is really an experience "shared" by different levels of our minds. The conscious level of our minds can speak and listen to the unconscious level through dreams, daydreams, fantasies, memories, meditation, and prayer. Those who came before us, those who participated in forming our history, and our family history are in us. Our spiritual selves can be contained in religious faith—our faith in God—or other less formed ideas of the greater dimensions of life. If we are open to them, these elements can transform a solitary moment into one in which we do not really feel alone.

In the deepest part of our conscious and unconscious experience of being human in the vast cosmos, sharing speaks to our fundamental humanity. It says that, by the sheer fact of being able to share the moment, we are participating in an experience that has a universal human dimension. We are part of humanity. It is the thread of mystery and the feeling of awe that actually make us feel safer rather than fearful.

How do we practice sharing?

Push the pause button on multitasking and focus completely on the shared moment, whether it is in a casual conversation, around a meal, in the car, or watching a television program.

Share time in active doing. Take a walk with someone, go for a bike ride, build a bird feeder, plant some flowers, cook a meal, bake some cookies together. Be a partner, not a critic.

Share time that is quiet or contemplative: Watch a sunset, listen to music, sit and read, or engage in some other quiet-time activity with someone you enjoy.

Talk to strangers. Look for the opportunity to transform routine encounters into something richer. Share adversity without trying to fix it. Be an empathetic listener. Ask if you can help. Recognize that pain and suffering, whether it is physical or emotional, can be obstacles to sharing; be patient and supportive.

Savor solitude. Daydream. Take undisturbed time for yourself, by yourself, to think your own thoughts, refresh yourself, and reflect on this time and place in your life. Fantasy is good for you! When you create fantasy, you share one part of your mind with another. One is the author, one the audience.

Principle Three: Recalling and Recounting

Tell the stories; share the secrets.

Beyond our anatomy and physiology, what makes us human is story. We are a great collection of stories, some of them archived deep within the storehouses of our unconscious and some at our fingertips. Some of our stories are easily retrievable, and some are so deeply buried that it takes a great deal of investigation, and sometimes help, to uncover them. But when all the psychological and physical and physiological science is said and done, we are who we are in the way we define ourselves through story.

In everyday life, story enables us to recognize a moment in time and create meaning around it. Again, the steps in storytelling mirror those of celebration: recognition of a moment, naming the moment, bringing forth history as a context for the story, and recognizing, with awe, the mystery of the moment. Story *is* celebration; it is hard to imagine celebration without a story as an integral part of that moment.

Imagine an Easter vigil mass without the story of the last days of

Jesus' life and his agony and words on the cross. How could one wait for the anticipated resurrection and share in the mystery and awe of this evidence of his divinity without the story that leads up to the moment and is contained in the moment?

The Jewish Passover seder is much more than a meal at which food is enjoyed and a few glasses are lifted to freedom. The enduring power of the seder tradition is in the story of the passage from slavery to freedom and the way it is told and retold each season, integrating history with new meanings from present-day life. A recent immigrant might share a story of oppression and the road to liberation and freedom, or we might share a personal story of recovery—liberation—from disease or disaster.

More personal or intimate stories help us celebrate one another's lives, from the love story of an elderly couple to a child's excitement over her first soccer goal, or grief at the death of the family dog.

We are flooded with stories. Our lives are overstocked with fictionalized dramatizations in film, books, television, and computer games, in the form of sitcoms, biographies, histories, newsmagazines, and "reality" TV. It is sadly ironic that we live in a time where, through the media, we witness hundreds of stories a week, or even in a day, but we rarely tell our own; we may not even be aware of our own story. We are so able to fill all our time with other people's stories that we are in danger of losing our own stories. The characters and stories portrayed in the media may resonate for us; we may "find ourselves" in the dramas and sitcoms that flow past us all day, but we can keep "finding ourselves" like this and never *know* ourselves. It is seductive to watch the stories that come scripted and packaged for us, but we need to tune in to the real stories that are *our* lives and the lives of those around us. Like them or not, our stories are our reality. If we wish to be "real" to our children and our loved ones, we must tell our stories and seek theirs.

Family folklore and tradition are the stories a family chooses to capture and remember. It is what people in the family develop as a "code" for important points, markers of life. Celebration calls upon parents, grandparents, aunts and uncles, and distant relatives to take the time to tell the stories of the family, of the culture, of their respective epochs. Generations must tell their stories. We must learn to sit and listen, to be fully present for the telling, the sharing, and the reflection. Why? Telling the stories provides much of the text of celebration. Telling the stories sets the stage for recognizing the important moments of our lives. Telling the stories contributes to our sense of participating in time itself and therefore lays the groundwork for our personal immortality.

Stories untold carry a different power. Secrets are like cancers in a family or social group. From a single event, the damage grows as the secret-keeper struggles to hide it. Fear feeds it; the fear is that revealing the secret will damage our lives or those of others in some bad way. But over time, the secrets themselves and the efforts to keep them hidden shape lives and destinies. Secrets can obscure the meaning of our lives. A large secret can literally obliterate the essential stories of our existence. Spoken secrets are liberating. Shared, they become stories that can open us to new understanding. As stories, they affirm our existence. Even if they are painful, the story of a secret enables us to find new meaning in our lives. To tell the secrets allows us to fully acknowledge the truth of life, to celebrate the truth and the consequences, and be enriched by it all.

Being a good listener is one of the most important parts of sharing. But first we must listen to ourselves. We must respect our own deeper thoughts and reflections. We must be willing to speak to ourselves the stories of our past and the past that preceded us. Once we have listened to our own stories we are ready to listen to others from other people and then to bring ours to share. We must all become storytellers.

Telling the stories and telling the secrets does not require great amounts of wisdom or education. We all have stories, memories of family, or simply of fact, without interpretation or judgment. The telling itself is more important than an explanation. Like a landscape that changes color, depending on the light of the day, a story's meaning is created not in the telling alone, but in the telling *and* listening. A story shared resonates, creating echoes and reflections of infinite effect.

We can use story to make meaning of our wounds and losses. Wounds and hurts and losses cannot be made to feel like fun and joy and games. They are what they are meant to be. They are not events beyond our lives, outside our lives, but they *are* our lives. Wound, pain, and loss herald our separation from our maternal womb. In some ways, life requires wound and hurt and loss to move forward. Adversity isn't necessary in life, but it is a natural part of life. The problem with wound and hurt and loss and adversity is not the sadness and pain, but the fact that we seldom try to make sense of these parts of our lives. We don't often look for meaning in pain or loss. In ignoring the meaning of loss and hurt and wound, we lose a large part of the meaning of our lives.

We can teach one another the meaning of loss. If we become ill, or we lose our privileged position in the family constellation, or at work, or in our social group, there is not necessarily a "higher" reason for these losses. They simply happen. The meaning is not to be found by looking upward to "the gods," but by looking inward. We can make meaning. It is truth, because we have made it from within ourselves in response to our experience of pain or loss.

LIVING WITH CELEBRATION

Too often we allow the rush of everyday life to crowd out the time for recalling and recounting. Don't wait for a funeral to reflect on the continuing journey of life.

Use simple occasions to mark a milestone and place the present moment in the context of personal and family history.

Ask to hear the stories. Too often, adults assume "everyone already knows" or nobody wants to. Children get the message that their stories aren't important, or experience tells them that if they share a story from the day, some adult will overreact.

Develop a vocabulary for celebration. Give names to feelings that define the moment. *Proud, happy, sad, angry, excited, disappointed—*these are the words that describe feelings and lend color to what would otherwise be the pallid moments of life just passing by.

Be an appreciative listener. Welcome detail. Listen for feelings. Ask for more. Reflect on the story and share your thoughts. Don't interrupt. Don't correct. Don't judge.

Defuse a secret by sharing it, with sensitivity and thoughtful timing. Trust your intuition about timing. Timing signals itself—the feeling that you need to tell or it needs to be told.

Principle Four: Play

*Think outside the box, color outside the lines, play
outside the moment.*

Play and celebration share the common element of opening us to an infusion of unconsciously inspired experience. To a great extent, the capacity to play enhances the capacity to celebrate, and the inhibitions to being playful likewise inhibit celebrating any moment in life.

D. W. Winnicott, the great British child psychoanalyst, spoke about how one person helps another in a therapeutic setting. He said it was about play. He said that therapy takes place in the play between two people. He went on to say that if the person seeking help did not know how to play, the first order of business was to teach him. And if the person providing help didn't know how to play, he went on to say, then that person should get out of the business.

You might say he was thinking of children when he spoke. I would say his insight applies to us all—you and me, adults, important people, educated people, responsible people—and not just to the therapy setting, but to the setting that, for each of us, is everyday life. We can help one another through play. We can know one another through play. We can know ourselves through play. Play offers a unique venue in which we can express parts of ourselves that cannot easily find expression in everyday life. As folk wisdom tells us, all work, no play, makes us dull to the core. There is more to play than running around a field, shuffling cards, or hitting a ball back and forth. What is it about play that people, from kitchen philosophers to great psychoanalytic thinkers, are trying to say?

There are a few things we can agree upon for starters. At play we let go of the constraints and formalities of daily life. There is a certain abandon to play. But what is abandoned? I believe that we abandon the barriers to joy that daily life demands. It's not that we can't have joy in daily life without play, but it is a more modulated joy. It is a joy that unconsciously takes social constraints and necessities into account. This constraint is both emotional and physical. It is a necessary convention for the smooth functioning of society. It also inhibits, by intention, impulse, and instinct from bursting forth. In so doing, it constrains the pure joy of early life before we learned how to be "good" children.

There are those who cannot play. They approach even sports or card playing or board games with a seriousness that prevents play. They might claim to be playing, and they might be doing something called sport or recreation, but they are not playing at it. They are afraid, I think, to "let go" and give free rein to impulse and instinct, lest there be some unhappy consequence. Somewhere, sometime long ago, they feared the consequence of their own natures and how the people around them would react to their honest expression of themselves. There is fear of risk and fear of failure. In a sport they have to win the game; in an art class they have to produce the perfect piece; in a conversation they have to be right. There is no room for the risk of play.

The beauty of play, the importance of play is just that—it is about giving rein to our natures. Play permits us to refuel our civilized selves with our instinctive selves. *Play* is a word with a double meaning. It also means flexibility, as in the play that makes a rope line a little looser. Play makes our natures flexible. Play encourages those with whom we play to be flexible also. Play requires that we accept one another's natures and move around those natures in a wonderful dance of instinct and impulse. Play becomes a form of social intercourse, akin to the role of sex in the intimate relationship, where we each must surrender and enable the other to do the same, both enriched by the experience.

Have you ever watched someone play and have no fun? Have you ever watched a parent at the sidelines of young children's games screaming and angry with their child or others for some error in the course of the game? There is no play here. There is no infusion of spirit or wisdom. There is only the violence and rigidity of a person who is afraid to play—to share deeper psychic and physical energy— in order to bring about growth and flexibility. They cannot even stand in a relaxed manner. They are stiff, and their shields are up.

Play sometimes has some structure, some rules. However, overly structured play defeats itself. There is a real difference between play and competitive sport. One should be clear what one is trying to do. Play should be play without regard for the victory or the defeat. Is there room for overlap? Yes. There is a time for play and a time when the skill level and the mission of the enterprise changes and victory and defeat *do* matter. We can develop skill at play. We can learn the finer points of the sport at play. However, to confuse the two can bring sadness and grief to play that can seriously limit skill. If that happens early in life, play and competitive sport impede each other, and all players become losers, no matter who wins the game.

To play, let go of outcomes. Practice not needing a light moment to go one way or another, but engaging with whatever way it goes.

Play for fun. If it isn't fun, it isn't play. If you can't engage in an activity without feeling pressured to win or do well, then find another activity to try *just* for fun.

Learn from children, puppies, and other experts. When your child comes up to you at the "wrong" moment to play some silly game or play out some childlike fantasy, don't be so quick to turn down the invitation. Play does not always follow a schedule. Watch a playful child or pet cavort and allow yourself the luxury of time to laugh and join in.

Play through imagination. Play with words, play with ideas, play with humor and your point of view.

Listen for laughter. Laughter is a physiological mystery, but we know that it's good for you. Watch for the comedy in life and surrender to laughter.

Play with others. Sharing a good time enlarges the experience of celebration and adds to the inspiration available to all involved.

Principle Five: Recognize Mystery and Awe

Proclaim the mystery of a moment
and stand in awe of it.

People love mysteries. They read them on the beach, in their beds, and watch them endlessly on television and at the cinema. What is this fascination with mystery? I believe that our hunger for published mysteries is due to our unconscious understanding that we are surrounded by mystery in our real life.

We call them coincidences. We call them surprises. We call them dilemmas and perplexing problems. We call them scary things. We call them universal fears and universal aspirations. But they are mysteries.

How does a child grow? It's a mystery. How does a connection with a friend or loved one change our day? It's a mystery. Can we contemplate death? It's a mystery. What is our personal significance in the universe? It's a mystery.

We must learn to respect mystery and the role it plays in our lives. We can use the word without embarrassment and fear of ridicule. Mystery is not just the unknown that awaits discovery. Mystery is also the whole universe that is both known and unknown and how it all works together to create our life and all life, and particularly, how it creates meaning in life.

Mystery and awe form the centerpiece of most religious expression, but you don't need to go to church or temple to access it. Mystery and awe are at the center of our lives, in our relationship with nature and spirit, with one another and with ourselves. Mystery is present in every moment. We have only to look for it and savor it.

I used to walk my dog past a messy grouping of tall flowering plants each year. I would watch from early springtime as these plants grew and grew. They were disorderly. They leaned into the walkway, narrowing the passage and creating an inconvenience at times. I found myself wishing the owner of the property would tie them back.

Then came the day the buds burst forth in brilliant color. The flowers were large and broad and stretched toward the sun. That evening they were gone! No, I finally realized, they were asleep. The petals had closed for the night. The next day they reopened to the sun and closed again at sunset. This would last weeks— many weeks. I came to stand in awe of this display. My dog got a few extra walks during that season each day. There was mystery and awe in the relationship between the flowers and the sun, and then between me and the flowers and the sun. I was responding to the dialogue between the flowers and the sun. I was in a state of awe.

The process of celebration is itself awesome: it moves through our lives much as a great swell moves through the ocean. The swell is born of the various winds, pressures, and configurations of the ocean and atmosphere together. As the water rises, the movement separates the molecules that make up its mass. The increased space among molecules and drops of water permits the infusion of air and water within one another, creating mist and oxygenating the water. As the winds of nature propel the swell over time and place, the swell lifts the water up and over the obstacles that present themselves in its path. Even in the end, as the swell crashes as a wave upon the land and ends its existence, it simply returns to the mass of its history and lives again.

Celebrating life's moments opens the spaces of our mind and soul, and we can be infused with the wisdom of life and impart our own wisdom upon life. When we celebrate life, we are lifted above and over life's obstacles. We can reassemble. We are changed, but we integrate that change into our new self and are enriched by the change. We can move beyond the moment and continue our journey. As much as we may theorize about how and why celebration has this effect, the mystery of it remains. That mystery does nothing to diminish the effect, and the power of celebration remains as constant and indomitable as the ocean swells.

• BECOMING FLUENT IN CELEBRATION •

What started as a happy whim took on a much greater dimension in my life. At fifty years, I decided it was time to learn a second language. I studied French and became quite proficient. I was also quite pleased with myself. This old dog had indeed learned a new trick.

Then unexpected circumstances led to our living weeks at a time in France. What I thought was proficiency was less so once I had to live and use French in France. My language skills began to grow as my experience of French life deepened. I began to awaken to a new level—a new depth—of knowing the joy and richness of both the language and the lifestyle of the French. I realized that true fluency was made up of many more factors than vocabulary and grammar. Those nuances and that richness became available to me once I was immersed in the French language and life in France.

It's the same with celebration. Many of us think we are doing it. (**239** We lift a glass occasionally. We celebrate a birthday. We have a confirmation party or bar or bat mitzvah. We call our friends and family on their special occasions. We think we are fluent in the language and life of celebration, but often we are so focused on the events of life and their more superficial aspects that we overlook the deeper dimensions of the moment and the richer rewards available to us when we invest our attention there.

How fully are you celebrating life for yourself and those around you? Ask yourself:

Am I attuned to life's moments? Little moments as well as big moments present a great opportunity to lend this depth and texture, which is so important, as both the bricks and the mortar, to our lives.

Do I have the vocabulary to name these moments? And do I have the courage to use my vocabulary in the moment, regardless of awkwardness or derision?

How much do I know my history? Do I know our family history? Do I know my cultural history? Do I know our religious history? Do I feel free to use that history accurately, without secrecy, and including the history that is not as positive and polished as I would like? Can I speak of history in a personal and familiar manner that lends present tense to the past? Have I taken the time to fill in the blanks in my knowledge about the various histories I need to know in order to celebrate my life and the lives of the ones around me?

Am I prepared to share? How am I at initiating and sharing these moments I recognize and name? How willing am I to share the history that is summoned up by those moments? Sharing is one of the most idiosyncratic aspects of modern life. We live among so much abundance and accessibility of what we feel we need, that we have atrophied our capacity to share. Sharing takes effort, initiative, sometimes courage, and definitely the readiness to give up in order to get.

What is my attitude about mystery? Can I admit that I really don't know something and that the knowledge or origin of the phenomenon is beyond my grasp? Do I shrug "I don't know" to dismiss the moment, the question, or the person? Or do I say it and mean "I'm okay about not knowing. It doesn't frighten me. As a matter of fact, there is something wonderful about the relationship between not knowing and discovery that keeps me vibrant."

Can I talk about mystery? Can I speak of mystery with wonder and awe? Do I ever admit wonder and awe without embarrassment? Do I celebrate the mystery of our universe and feel the awe it inspires?

Do I seek to learn everything the moment can teach me? Am I a seeker or a follower of trend and tradition? Seekers are people of courage, who are willing to find out what there is to be found out. Do I have the courage to find out that there is more to a moment or time in life than I thought? Am I prepared to accept new insights and new possibilities, even if they raise new questions in my life?

For every question you can answer with an honest yes, your access to the celebrated life is wide open. The others represent underdeveloped aspects of celebration in your life, opportunities available to you for enriching your experience of life if you choose to cultivate them.

In my travels and my work here and abroad, these principles of celebration have evolved into a successful curriculum for teaching celebration in schools, hospitals, and places of worship. I am convinced, not by faith but by experience, that the power of celebrating moments of life can have enormous power in our lives. I have seen people exhale years of tension—a lifetime of tightly wound anxiety and fear—as a result of feeling that I, or another person in their life, recognizes and names an aspect of their character that has gone unrecognized, or names and shares a universal fear that was not respected in their family, or offers a sense of what is wonderful about them or their life that had gone unnoticed.

I have seen "hyperactive" "avoidant" children relax and attend to the moment when an adult slows down and seeks to know them—really know them. I have seen people die in peace after thrashing about in fear upon being told that they are dying, only to discover that they have it in them to do this well.

I believe that many seemingly intractable international conflicts could at least be set on the road to resolution when the opposing sides are seated—preferably at the dinner table—and forced to listen, truly listen, to each other and share their hurts and fears. I know that people and cultures can recover from the worst sorts of ravaging war and economic distress, if what is good and great and inspired in their culture is named and shared and celebrated.

LIVING WITH CELEBRATION

Money helps. Money is necessary for nations to recover from devastating trauma, but money alone cannot do the job. People will stay wounded even when the economy heals unless they are celebrated as individuals and as a culture.

The capacity to celebrate is inborn—natural. For that reason, it is accessible, yet easily overlooked, and thus elusive. The power of celebration lies in the shared mental and spiritual energy of the moment. It truly knows no bounds except the bounds of our own skepticism and timidity. True courage is the courage to celebrate *all* of life—the good and bad, the small and large, the simple and complex, the knowable and unknowable. If we allow ourselves to lose that natural, essentially human capacity, if we live discouraged lives, then humankind will not advance but instead risk extinguishing itself with its own inventions. If we have the courage to celebrate then we will enrich all life and continue to advance humankind.

(Celebrating Children:
Our Turn as Parents)

There is always one moment in childhood when the
door opens and lets the future in.

GRAHAM GREENE, *THE POWER AND THE GLORY*

(1940)

Whether you experienced life as a celebrated
child or an uncelebrated child, if you have children of your own
now, it's your turn. As parents, we have the ultimate power, responsibility, and privilege to create a celebrated life for each of
our children. Every loving parent wants to do this. If you were a
largely uncelebrated child, then your challenge is to start from
scratch, to celebrate your son or daughter even though you have
little or no experience from which to draw. If you are fortunate
enough to have been a largely celebrated child, then you have
handier access to those life skills and emotional tools, but the
task is the same, and you, too, start from scratch. The challenge
we all share is to see our children for who they are, *centered in
their own realm of being and possibility,* rather than seeing them

for whom we want them to be, objects of *our* expectations and dreams.

In the previous chapter, "Living with Celebration," I offered a practical guide for bringing the elements of celebration to everyday living, in our relationship with ourselves and with all those whose lives we touch. As parents, our path is no different. In the space of the relationship we have with a child, we must open ourselves to the richness they bring to bear on the moment. We must share the moment, inviting their expression, contributing our own. We must recall and recount, sharing the stories, and in appropriate ways, the secrets of our time and of their own beginnings. And with our children, we must embrace life's mystery and give them the words for awe.

Beyond those markers of a celebrated life, any more detailed instructions for parenting can lead you down a wrong path as easily as a right one. There are so many variables, combinations, and permutations in a relationship between a parent and a child. As we've seen in earlier chapters, any moment comes loaded with a different history and meaning for each participant in it. Our response, as parents, to any given moment with our child reflects as much from our past as it does from the activity of the moment. Our child, too, brings history and expectations to the moment. Something as simple as a time-out for a four-year-old may be experienced by one child as an uninvited but useful break in the action, while another child may be frightened by the sense of isolation.

We learn so much more—about ourselves *and* our children—when we stop looking for right answers and begin to think below the eyebrows, with our hearts and souls. We need to get beyond the intellectual how-to frame of mind and move instead into the shared moment, and into the heart of our child for inspiration and answers. This is the celebratory process. So let's talk not so much about how to parent in a given circumstance, but how to think in a way that enables you to celebrate your child's life, no matter what the circumstances.

• THE FAMILY CIRCUS: THREE RINGS AND A TRAPEZE •

Life is a circus. Parents are the ringmasters. Each of us is the master of ceremonies, the emcee, in the circus that is our child's world. To a child, no matter what age, the world is a magical, mysterious, wondrous place. It is filled with strange people doing strange things, ambulating in and out of view. Beasts prance before our children's eyes *and within their minds.* Some are friendly beasts and some are scary. This includes children from the very young to those well into adulthood. All ages have their beauties and their beasts. The beasts of young childhood are simply replaced by the beasts of adolescence to be followed by the beasts of adult life and finally the beasts that we face at death.

(245

A parent organizes all this commotion, much as the master of ceremonies organizes the activities of the three-ring circus, so that it is not overwhelming and so that it is comprehensible. We carry our children into the wondrous circus of life, exposing them to, and pointing out, first the simpler friendly performances, and gradually the more complicated acts, including some that are frightening. We draw their attention to what's going on and identify it—name the performances—and help our children distinguish what is important to glean from the moment. Fears and fantasies, connections and conflict, delight and disappointment—we put these and other feelings and actions into context:

> *"People get angry at each other and that's normal, they disagree. We all disagree about something sometime. What's important isn't that we disagree, but that we talk it out and work it out."*

"It's natural to be disappointed that you didn't make the team, but if it's important to you to keep playing basketball, let's talk about it and see what other possibilities there are in the community."

"Going to the museum with Uncle Bob wasn't your first choice, but you can find something to enjoy if you look for it. And he really appreciates the fact that you're going to spend the time with him. It's like giving him a present."

"Sometimes people are unfair and we can correct it, and other times we just have to live with it. Your teacher may seem a little unfair, but she's trying to make a point, and this is one of those times you're just going to have to live with it."

"Dad lost his job, and while he's looking for a new one it means we have to live with a little bit of uncertainty in our lives. We're not used to that so it might feel a little scary, but we're really okay. It may take some time, but things will work out."

Fear has a large presence in a child's perceptions. We can allay fears, not with lies or avoidance, but by putting fear in perspective, and by being unafraid to talk about it. "Oh, I have that one, too," is a most comforting message for a child. We all have the same menagerie of beasts, but our children don't know that until we, as their masters of ceremonies, beckon them onstage with us and share the experience. The parent emcee points out how wild, scary beasts can be tamed and even ridden with grace and elegance. The wild, scary beasts in the interior of a child's mind will hide unless they are recognized, named, and shared so that a child does not feel too alone with such scary monsters. All fears and scary things loom large in the dark. When we shine the light of day upon them they become smaller and manageable.

"Are you afraid of trying new things? I am, too. It's so easy to keep doing what we know how to do, but then we cannot grow and gain new experience. So I just take a deep breath and try. You never know what'll come of it, but you can always be proud of yourself for trying." (**247**

"Flying and tall buildings are both exciting and scary these days. The scariest part of each is that we have no control over the terrible things that can happen. We must think about how many people fly in airplanes and work or live in tall buildings each day to place the scary part in perspective. We must do both in order to live a modern life. We must learn to live with risk and become smart about it."

Above all, as masters of ceremonies, we must respect our audience. Genuine respect is a good basic rule for all interpersonal interaction, including with our children. Respect is the foundation of a celebrated childhood, and it is the basic prerequisite for celebrating your child. In any moment, think first: *does this action respect the person that is my child, or is that respect missing?*

A friend tells the story of one ordinary night, when a moment turned on that awareness:

Helen was at the end of a long day, with a long night of housework ahead, when she went in to read a bedtime story to her five-year-old daughter. As she read the story aloud, her daughter interrupted every few lines with questions, comments, or exclamations. The story was long enough to begin with, but now it grew longer with each interruption. Helen's patience was getting short. Finally, exasperated, she shut the book sharply, and glared at her daughter.

"We'll *never* finish the story like this!" she snapped. "Do you want to interrupt, or do you want me to read you a story? Take your pick!"

Her daughter stopped midword, startled, and then she wilted. Her shoulders drooped, her eyes looked sorry, and she pressed her lips together in a grim little line of silence. They looked at each other glumly. The sudden quiet stretched like a canyon between them.

In that instant, a wave of memory and feeling swept through Helen's mind, and she recalled her own history as "the chatterbox" in her family, her parents' occasional impatience, but more often, their openness to her continuing commentary. She felt their presence, and felt the weight and the privilege it is to be a parent; felt her luck as a child, and her good fortune now, to be sharing this most tender moment of the day with her own child. She felt grateful, even tearful, that her life had brought her to this moment in time, awed by the timelessness of a child's need and a parent's power. All this passed through her mind in an instant. Helen took a deep breath, and let it out slowly. She felt transformed.

Watching her daughter's small, stony face, she opened the book, then reached and touched her daughter's hand. First, she apologized, without offering excuses. Then she said the words that were to become a familiar declaration in the years to come: "Tell me what's on your mind," she said. "I like to hear your thoughts."

Children have a sense of themselves as fully vested individuals in the moment and need to feel respected in that way. They don't— or shouldn't—experience themselves generically; for instance, as being just a child Mom has to put to bed before she can do laundry or work brought home from the office, or a dependent who must be fed and driven around town. We celebrate our children when we show an interest in their individual perception of events, their feelings, their hopes and dreams. With respect, we can listen and respond at the level they are ready to understand.

• LIFE'S BALANCING ACT: ACTION, REFLECTION, AND TRANSITION •

As masters of ceremonies, we can see to it that the circus program includes intermissions—deliberate transitions and quieter times for reflection between moments of action. We know that when infants become overstimulated by too much activity or intensity, if we provide a soothing, quieter moment, then they can calm themselves. Children never outgrow their need for an opportunity to reflect between acts, a chance to absorb what they've seen or heard or done, and think about what comes next. The overscheduled child is at risk of losing this centering time, but as emcees we can see to it that there is a pause in the action, time to transition from one experience, one emotion, one moment, to another.

When my sons were growing up, and as prone to temper outbursts as anyone their age, the rule at our house was that it was okay to storm off in a huff, if need be, but once they were finished with their angry moment, then we had to follow up with another kind of moment, one of reflection and reconciliation. I respected that they had to leave the room, but we knew that next we would have another moment dedicated to setting things straight. I had to go by the same rules and learned my line well from practice: "I'm over being angry. Now we can talk."

The rich background of life grows in the quieter, reflective time. Without it, the circus spins out of control, too much, too fast, too scattered. The intermissions give us time to let go, to regroup, to gather our thoughts or wander in them, to experience anticipation, and the process of transition from one experience to another.

"This divorce process has been all about breaking our family apart, and I know it has been long and hard on you and your sister. Now that the divorce is final, it's time to turn our attention to the family we are, instead of the one we're not, and do all we can to support one another and strengthen what we have."

"This has been a busy week for all of us. Let's order pizza, rent a movie, and veg out for the evening."

"You seem upset with Ben. It's hard when friendships hit a bump, but a big part of friendship is helping each other through these kind of moments. Give yourself a chance to cool off, and think about taking the initiative in mending the relationship. It's likely that he needs your help out of this disagreement and will appreciate it."

"Your relationship as a couple moved pretty quickly from a few dates to this talk now of getting an apartment together. It seems to me that it could be helpful to have one more step before you sign a lease—spend a lot more time together and a lot more mornings together."

I love the old southern saying, "Sometimes I sits and thinks, and sometimes I just sits." We can see to it that the circus of our children's lives includes times for action, times for reflection, and times for just being.

In the
moment

A good master of ceremonies knows how to move on and off the stage. The goal of the parent emcee is to carry the attention of the audience into the moment and then let the audience *be* in the moment, making of the moment whatever they wish. Only then can children engage *themselves* and make the moment their own. This is the only way they can know their own power and bring back from that experience something to be shared further as they return to the drama or the comedy of their own life. When we fail to realize that the moment ultimately belongs to our child, when we make the mistake of seeing our child as an extension of ourselves, then we are celebrating only ourselves—not our children. In these moments, a child is uncelebrated, deprived of the victories as well as the defeats of life.

Mary took her son, Todd, to the ballet for the first time to see *The Nutcracker*. "Look at those men, they are the soldiers," she pointed out. "Oh, look at the Christmas tree grow. Can you see the ballerinas dancing on their toes? Isn't the music just beautiful?" Her excited commentary defined every moment. Todd enjoyed the ballet, but it was hard to tell where his mother's experience of the moment left off and his own experience began. By directing her son less, and giving him more space in their conversation to make his own observations, he would have experienced the bullet and his own reactions to it in a more meaningful way.

Joe was sure that his daughter Katie had the makings of a star soccer player on their junior high team. He was there for every one of her games, cheering her on, but also coaching her loudly from the sidelines. He shouted at the referees when they made a call he didn't like. He shouted at Katie when she fumbled or failed to stop the other team from advancing. He also was her loudest fan when she scored or stopped the other team from scoring. After several years of this, Katie was having mixed feelings about continuing in the sport. She enjoyed *playing* soccer, but her dad's constant coaching and his histrionics at the game took the fun out of it. She wasn't sure anymore whether she was in the sport to please her father or herself. She worried that if she stopped, she would disappoint her father, and he would think of her as a loser. Katie's involvement in soccer had ceased to be about Katie. Her father had become a prominent, and problematic, player in her soccer experience.

There are parents, like Katie's father, who can turn any aspect of a child's life into a serious competition the *parent* doesn't want to lose. Their child must read first or better than the other kindergartners. Their child must do gymnastics or soccer younger and better than their peers. Grades, sports, musical, or other artistic endeavors, even community service, *everything* becomes an arena in which the child's experience is secondary to the parent's satisfaction. It is the overly invested parent who claims center stage and uses it to stand in judgment. As caring adults, we blanch when we see the red-faced parent screaming from the sidelines of a children's sport event. Some children are more resilient than others to this harassment. But for an impressionable child—even someone *else's* child who is witness to the scene—it can take just one of these experiences to traumatize their natural system of play.

The parent master of ceremonies steps out of the spotlight and invites a child to be the central figure onstage in his or her own life.

In the
moment

It is our obligation and joy as parents to discover our child's nature and talents and to celebrate that about them. Their nature and talents may be quite different from our own, but as emcee, it is not our aim to turn our children into an audience for our lives or into caricatures of children as we would have them be. We celebrate our children when we let them move into their own experience of the moment and bring their insights to bear on us, and within the family.

I once treated a retarded adult child of two lovely people. They had managed their grief at the birth of this child and gone on to find out what *she* could do, and worked with it. She did a lot for a woman with an IQ of 58. With help separating from her parents, she became an emancipated woman, living in a supervised, independent home under the care of a retarded citizens association, and worked, earned a living, voted, and visited her parents weekly for outings to Sunday school and church. They discovered what was special about their daughter and celebrated it.

Another patient was less fortunate. "I am my father's son," Frank confessed. "I became a doctor to please him and be like him. Now I'm a successful radiologist, I'm wealthy, I'm the father of six, and I'm miserable. I never discovered myself. I just discovered *him*."

• ACKNOWLEDGING LIFE'S SUSPENSE, DRAMA, AND COMEDY •

In the end, there is only so much we can do as parents. Even a master of ceremonies cannot dictate the content of the acts. We can't guarantee outcomes in the drama or comedy of life. There is pain and frustration in life. We can call attention to it and point out our own experience, but we cannot protect our child from that. A real high-wire act carries suspense because a real fall can occur.

"Part of growing up is starting school. I must leave you here where you'll learn and meet other children and make new friendships. I know that it is scary and that you would prefer not to be left here right now, but there is no other way to help you become a big boy or big girl. Just remember, at the end of the school day we will have so much to talk about."

"It would be nice if all tests were fair, but that's not real-istic. Life is full of unfair moments, and all those mo-ments are tests of some sort. The real tests are not the facts that we might have learned better with a bit more study, but that we can learn some sort of lesson from the failure."

"Friendships can hurt as much as they can be wonderful. That is true of love in all its forms, but the alternatives are worse; we cannot thrive alone in life."

"I was not the most handsome or the smartest or the best athlete, but I had to move into the world as I was and take my chances. I now laugh that I was lucky to be born not too handsome, too rich, or too smart, because I have come to value all that I have accomplished in love, work, and play by virtue of my own effort."

Yes, we can put a net far beneath, but we cannot remove the danger and anxiety of the act. Knowing our limitations and being open about them is at least honest, and at best respectful and in-spiring.

Every child's relationship with risk is different and requires a different response from us as parent emcees. One child will need encouragement to take intellectual, emotional, and even physical risks, while another will need to work on controlling the reckless impulse to do so.

My son Josh was a serious child. He could have fun; he could play. But he was a perfectionist. He hated making mistakes. This seriously limited his fun, particularly at play. When he was in his first preschool class, his teacher commented on this. "Josh does not tolerate mistakes very well," she said. Oh, we knew this to be too true. We had seen this emerge at home from early on. He was born too observant and too interested in developing skill levels. He would get very cranky as new developmental milestones approached. His mood would not lighten until that milestone was mastered. We could breathe easily until the next challenge to his young expertise.

The preschool teacher gave us good advice: "Make a big deal of your mistakes," she recommended.

"I don't make many," I said, only half-joking, I admit.

"Well then, make them up!" she demanded. "Josh needs to know that mistakes are part of life and can be as much fun as mastery."

That night, at our dinner table, I gave it a shot. It had to be a mistake that Josh, at four, would appreciate. "Oh, you should have seen the mess I made today when I spilled my drink all over the place," I said.

Josh was wide-eyed. He wanted to know every detail. That was the beginning of this important life lesson we now understood we needed to add to our own repertoire.

Josh remained a serious young man. He relished mastery. Finally came the time in young adulthood when we had to confront his inhibition regarding play and sport. Despite the fact that his mother and I were gym regulars, he did not ever visit the gym. He refused our invitations, as well as those from friends who worked out. I couldn't remain silent. I mentioned the importance of physical exercise. Josh sadly admitted he knew this but hated the idea of the gym. More than self-conscious about his level of fitness, he dreaded the exposure of his incompetence at workout skills.

We arrived at a strategy. Josh would work out with a trainer with whom he could be comfortable, not looking at others in the gym, just focusing on the trainer. He could look up and out once he felt more competent. One day, Josh called enthusiastically to report that he had completed his first workout.

"How did the exposure issue work?" I asked.

"Easy, I kept my glasses off and couldn't see anyone!" he exclaimed. It worked. Josh gained skill and eventually became a fellow gym rat.

Josh didn't like his unformed instinct. It was a matter of his nature. He was a naturally born perfectionist, and it may be that my own tendency that way had added a bit to it. As he learned to be more open to the possibility of the moment—which included the risk of not being perfect—whole new arenas of life opened for him—arenas of instinct and power, slightly less formed and controlled.

That wise preschool teacher had led us to the center of the ring and reminded us of our job description. It was up to us, as ringmasters, to find ways to invite our son into the arena called risk taking while respecting his nature and leaving him free to find his own way of entering that action.

• THE EMOTIONAL THEATER: KNOWING WHERE THE ACTION IS •

In a child's life, the circus of events moves from the outside to the inside and back outside again rather quickly, and it is important for the master of that ceremonies to know on which stage the action is at a given time. Is the moment being felt most significantly as an *inside moment*, about internal feelings, or an *outside moment*, having more to do with external circumstances? It's important for us to make this distinction because it has everything to do with whether we understand how our child is experiencing a moment, how best to communicate with them about it, and how to interpret their responses. Pointing out in practical terms how easy it is to skate is not helpful when your child is cowering in the corner of his mind because he is afraid of humiliating himself or disappointing others. The same is true when the real action is outside the child's mind and a parent misaddresses it as an inside issue.

Barb was concerned that her teenage son was becoming socially withdrawn, after he had opted not to go to several different dances and parties at his school. He was a successful student and had friends who came to the house, but he seemed to avoid socializing in groups. Finally, when he sidestepped an invitation to a classmate's birthday party, she expressed her concerns and urged him to be "more social." He gave a vague response defending his choice, but when she began talking about the need for him to "overcome this social shyness," he interrupted to set her straight. "Alcohol, smoking, drug use, and other stuff you really don't want to know about" were part of the party culture at his school, he said, and he preferred to steer clear of it. He wasn't having "social problems," as his mother feared. He was making thoughtful choices about where and with whom to socialize.

This wasn't the inside moment Barb had assumed it was. It was more of an outside moment, a matter of situation. Once Barb understood the reasons for her son's choices, she was able to shift her parenting energy from concern about social shyness to appreciation that her son was thinking for himself and making wise choices.

It's not always easy to discern an inside moment from an outside moment. We rely heavily on observation and intuition, and finally on conversation with our children, in which we ask, listen, share, and reflect. Sometimes we'll be right on target, other times not. We try again. *Eventually, our children will forgive us for our mistakes, but they will find it harder to forgive us for ignoring the problems they suffer or for being dishonest or hypocritical.*

• TIMING: KNOWING WHEN THE ACTION IS •

The master of ceremonies must develop a sense of timing, to discern *when* to point to the new action, or when to let the current action finish playing out; *when* to move onto the scene or to leave; *when* to name the moment, and *when* to share personal reflections with a child. There are times in a child's life when they are open and receptive to a parent's voice, and other times when they don't want to hear from anyone, or cannot hear beyond their own inner voice or the clamor of the peer group.

We cannot make a child feel open and receptive. All we can do is try to help organize the child's mental and emotional experience of the moment, of the phase of life they are traversing. A sense of timing requires empathy, the capacity to find within ourselves the other person's experience. Sometimes it is the same type of experience, sometimes an analogous one. Sometimes it is nothing like what we imagined.

Timing and respect are all we can bring to the moment, and they are enough. In the context of concern or conflict, or of adversity, if a child isn't ready to talk about it, or isn't open and receptive to what we have to say, then at least we can recognize that and name the moment in *those* terms.

> *"It's clear that you're not ready for a conversation about this right now. You might want to tell me when and if you*

are ready to talk about things. I can't tell when that will be, and I don't want to impose on you, but I do notice that you are having a problem and would like to share with you any way I can help."

Timing starts from the first moments of the parenting experience. With an infant, we try to sense what is needed, what helps and what does not. We try, and the response we get helps us know if we sensed the moment correctly or not. No matter how old our child is, that technique doesn't change, though the words and complexity of our children grow. I used to tell gatherings of parents of diabetic children (my expertise was as a father of one) that they had better develop a shared vocabulary with their child about many aspects of life, including diabetes, before adolescence, because during adolescence the hormonal storm prevents a child from taking in much information or engaging in fruitful conversation.

For any of us, there are times when the best place for the master of ceremonies is not onstage at all, but to the side. We aren't needed to introduce every phase, every new arena of activity. Our children move into new experiences in school and in the community. We might not hear about all they are doing, but we see that they have moved on from one experience to another and are growing. We can let this happen, with joy, and not interfere. We can note it and inquire, but most of all listen for their cues and respect their timing.

• LIFE: DO WE GIVE IT FOUR STARS? •

Finally, as a master of ceremonies, a parent must really be convinced of the beauty and fineness of the circus itself. Why should a child learn about the complexities of life if the master of ceremonies doesn't care? You might as well say, "I wish you well tonight.

We have a lot of acts on the program, and some are good, but most are pretty mediocre. Just sit and bear it." That won't work in the circus or in our child's life. We must convey an enthusiasm for life and for our children's lives.

Adult enthusiasm for living is not a given. Many people have never thought about life in terms of it being *worth living*. That question requires that we ask ourselves whether we're wasting that worth, wasting life. Some people are living simply because they were born and survived and grew up and graduated and found a job and bring home a paycheck. As parents, they have a hard time passing on to a child that life *is* worth living, worth getting excited about. Children need to sense from us that this is a *good* circus, a worthwhile adventure, and that it is possible to find your place in it. We can each find our passions and our aptitudes, and make our own act, contribute our value to life, to the circus.

• THE FAMILY BIG TOP: LIVING IN CELEBRATION, FAMILY-STYLE •

If our intent is to celebrate our child, to create a celebrated childhood for that child, then we cannot ignore the context for that celebration—the family itself. Family is the arena in which the celebrated childhood begins and flourishes. "Happy families are all alike; every unhappy family is unhappy in its own way," wrote Leo Tolstoy in *Anna Karenina*. The resemblance of "happy families" to one another is the internal celebratory process that allows them to deal with life in general, and with the individual lives of each family member, so that each can grow and develop to the best of their abilities. Each family member feels celebrated at the same time as the family, as a whole, and processes issues and events with respect for one and all.

How do you know if you're doing that? How does that look?

In the
moment

In celebration, a *family takes life in, rather than keeping life out.* The family is open to life and finds a way to help each member face challenges and use events as an opportunity to better know themselves as individuals and as a family.

In celebration, *a family develops a vocabulary for life and invents it as the need for new words and concepts arise.* Not all events in the life of a family or an individual in a family are easily identified and named, but in celebration a family finds the words to name the moment and the feelings of the moment. It is important to name elements and events in life because without a name we have no way to refer to the event or element we need to address. A name demystifies the moment, event, or element at hand. A parent loses his or her job and the vague sense of malaise that casts a shadow over a family can be quite scary and confusing to all until it is spoken: "Dad has lost his job." It is still scary, but now it can be discussed and fears can be processed. Self-esteem can be preserved, and the family can be enlisted in the project of dealing with the new reality.

In celebration, *a family talks.* I have never heard of a family running out of things to say, if all is allowed to be spoken about. A family that wants to deal with life talks about life. The time and place can be quite different for every family, reflecting the family lifestyle, but every family lifestyle must provide for it. For my family it was the dinner table. For some it is a coffee shop, a neighborhood park, Friday evening after dinner, at bedtime, or during a family drive. It is not the setting for talk, but the act of it, the fact of it, that makes big and little, good and bad, things gain their rightful proportion in life, and their proper place in the matrix of our psyche.

In celebration, *a family laughs together.* Humor helps us develop a sense of humility, sometimes delight, and a way of finding allegory or a meaningful story in life's events. A family that can laugh together can survive anything.

In celebration, *a family cries together.* Crying is a sign of life, from the first cry of a newborn baby, affirming that it is alive and breathing on its own, to the exclamations of joy and sorrow that sound throughout our lives. We must be able to cry together if we are to feel safe and learn to accept the helplessness that we all feel—helplessness in the face of loss, disappointment, or pain—and recognize it as no less a part of the celebrated moment.

In celebration, *a family tells the truth.* Remember that secrets and lies, and the unspoken, kill celebration by preventing the openness that invites connection and transformation. In a family that lives in celebration, a parent can admit he has failed or she is flawed; a child can criticize a parent without fear. If a parent has lost a job, or is ill, or if conditions require the family to adjust, then adjustments can be made in a climate of honesty, in which every member is respected and valued and known, perhaps in new ways.

In celebration, *a family plays together.* Family members have permission to act out one another's roles and enjoy one another's imaginations, dreams, passions, or interests. From our youngest days and throughout our lives, play allows us to practice or experiment with new ideas and ways of being, within a safe context. Children can test their power in a safe context without censure, without fear of being hurt or hurting or humiliation. Children can lead the action, trying out the responsible role of parents, and letting parents step into the role of children. Through play in the family, our children develop the language and skills for all roles. They learn empathy, boys for girls, girls for boys, and between child and parent.

In celebration, *a family works together.* Moms work and dads work, whether in an office or the home. Children need to support parents working, just as parents support the family. Maybe Dad needs some space. Maybe Mom needs a respite. Beyond assigned individual tasks, the experience of working together celebrates each member's value and contribution. In the larger world, we must work in our lives, work at jobs, at relationships, at building community, at being dependable and getting a job done. We must be able to do it alone and in contact with others. The lessons of work, like most lessons, are best learned in the early stages of family.

• FAMILY IN PROCESS: A SUDDEN SCARE AND A STRATEGY FOR SUCCESS •

When my younger son, Aaron, was five years old, he collapsed at school one day. He was rushed to the hospital and admitted in a near coma state. The word came back; it was diabetes. My wife, Jane, and I were devastated. His older brother Josh, at eight years of age, was a bit jealous of the attention suddenly riveted on Aaron. "Maybe I could just have a broken leg," he suggested, although his complaints were a thin mask for the shock he felt at this sudden, frightening turn of events.

Jane stayed over that first night in the hospital, keeping watch over our semicomatose child. She cried a lot, and she tried to imagine the life ahead for Aaron and for our family, but she had no markers in her experience to aide her imagination. I took Josh home and put him to bed. As I left his room, my throat tightened suddenly and I thought I was either about to vomit or scream. I moved quickly into my own room, and in my own bed put my face in the pillow and screamed: *"Momma!"* I wanted—I needed—her to fix things. But she had been dead for many years, and no one could fix this one.

The next day, we sent Josh to school, and I went to the hospital to relieve Jane, and to sit with Aaron. He was coming out of the coma, awake but quiet, his eyes worried and weary. I watched him drift in and out of sleep. In one wakeful stretch, I lifted him onto my lap and told him what the doctors had said. I told him about diabetes and how he would have to have shots each day and have his blood sugar measured a few times each day. We both cried a lot.

Then I heard myself saying, "You know, Aaron, there is some good news in all of this." Aaron looked up through teary eyes and said, "Yeah, what?"

"Well, you know this is tough to live with. I think the only way to do it is to cheat—we're going to find the wiggle room in this thing. We're going to practice cheating. You can cheat smart or you can cheat stupid. We're going to become a family who learns how to cheat smart."

I'm not sure where the inspiration came for that thought, but it transformed the moment from one of disaster and fear, to one that young Aaron could understand: a family challenge, and one for which his dad already had an intriguing strategy. Jane returned and found us laughing softly. We told her about the "good" news, and she laughed with us. A little while later, she turned to me and said, "We'd better learn how to give shots, too."

And so we began the process of incorporating this new fact into the family life and the life of each individual member of our family. In this crucible moment of crisis and uncertainty, one thing was certain: we would never be the same, but we would share becoming different.

The boys decided between them that, from now on, dinner would not be accompanied by TV or radio in the background. They would talk, as they always did, but without distraction. There was an unmistakable sense of gravity in the air, and there was also a sense that there was a lot that had to be processed.

Most nights were typical talk about their day. But once in a while the conversation was amazing. One evening at dinner, Josh was picking on Aaron as any older brother would do. Finally, in frustration, Aaron cried out, "Okay! I know—I should have died and not been such a geek!" He ran from the table, crying.

Josh, now in tears himself, screamed back, "You can't do that to me; it's unfair!"

Jane left the table to follow Aaron, and Josh and I sat in the silence for a moment. "You're right," I said. "That was unfair."

Jane was telling Aaron a similar thing. "Josh was wrong to pick on you, but you were wrong to tell him you should have died. That's not true, and it's unfair to fight that way." They returned to the dinner table and we continued the meal in a subdued way.

Then quietly, Josh said to Aaron, "The next time I pick on you, you can punch me on the arm, even my throwing arm. But the next time you tell me you should have died, I'm gonna punch you in the pancreas, or whatever is left of it."

They both broke down in laughter. They were beginning to absorb—to process—their new lives. It was a new chapter in their lives as brothers, and a new chapter in our family story.

As masters of ceremonies in the family circus, we don't need to be perfect. We just need to be present and committed to celebrating our children and life within our families as best we can. If I have given the impression that raising a child is all about the celebration of good times, I apologize. It is not. There is much to worry about, much to anguish over, many bad moments. But, as I have written about earlier in this book, celebration isn't about either good or bad times only. Celebration is a process—a lens—through which we look at life and live life. It is about both good and bad times.

In raising children we inevitably encounter both. We all hope for more good than bad, but even that is not always our destiny. What the lens of celebration offers us is a way to see and embrace even the bad moments of our children's lives and our life with them. It doesn't hurt to say, "This is a bad moment." It can help everyone involved. It is the pretense that it is *not* a bad moment that hurts. I don't know how many "bad" children would be turned around if they were celebrated; I suspect many but not all. But even a problem child stands to gain more from hearing the bad moments truthfully named, than from seeing them ignored or covered up.

If we are to maintain our own dignity as parents and as people we must fully and honestly share in all the moments of our child's life. We cannot select out only the good ones. We will find honor, respect, self-respect, even joy in the celebration of all moments of our children's lives—even the worst. Why is it important to remember the bad times in human history? It is because by embracing the lowest of points in human history, we offer a background for the most noble. In the individual lives of our children we do the same. As masters of ceremonies, we create context and invite possibility. That is the gift of a celebrated childhood, and that is the legacy we pass on to our children.

(A Legacy of Celebration)

I wanted a perfect ending. Now I've learned, the hard way, that some poems don't rhyme, and some stories don't have a clear beginning, middle, and end. Life is about not knowing, having to change, taking the moment and making the best of it, without knowing what's going to happen next.

GILDA RADNER

When I was in medical school, there were many daunting tasks to learn. Before we ever worked with patients, we medical students practiced certain laboratory procedures on one another. With practice came competence, and one by one, we would find ourselves teaching, and learning from, one another. I remember the first time my professor called me forward to demonstrate a procedure I had mastered. "Welcome to the see one, do one, teach one club," he said.

"See one, do one, teach one" is a fitting instruction for many of life's most important skills, including the way we learn how to celebrate life and create a legacy of celebration. The desire for celebration is innate in all humans, but as with all innate human capabilities, it develops in the context of experience. We need to learn and practice, and we need to mentor those around us. Our children are watching us, listening to us; what are they learning from us?

A friend in his fifties said he knew he had ascended to a place of some respect in his large, extended family when he was asked to make the toast at a family reunion dinner. Other members of the family had come to appreciate his ability to articulate the specialness of a moment. It gave him great pleasure to serve in this role of speaker of the house, he said, continuing a family tradition of openly recognizing occasions and one another. He also enjoyed calling upon the children in the family to "do the honors" from time to time, and he could see how each child relished his or her opportunity to speak and define the moment.

Whether we are eloquent speakers or not, we have the opportunity to both practice and teach celebration in everyday ways. We can choose to take note of a moment, to call a friend to report a rainbow, or pause to give someone our full attention. We can take the initiative in marking a moment as special, and putting it in words for others. It may feel awkward at first, but the more you do it the more natural it will feel, and the more you inspire others to bring celebration to life. When we do this, we not only enrich our experience of the moment, we also model a life of celebration for others, and we create a legacy of celebration for our children and all those around us.

Throughout this book I have spoken about naming moments, telling stories, and embracing mystery with a sense of awe. Legacy is the final point I wish to make. We each live in the midst of creating a legacy, our own and the larger legacy of which ours is a part. Our legacies will differ in size, scope, direction, and impact. But make no mistake, the most quietly lived life contains its own legacy.

All the stories go into our legacy. The stories that preceded us and created us and launched us and raised us, and then the stories that we created, and the stories that we leave behind in our children, our friends, our neighbors—all the stories come together to create our legacy.

Yet how many of us are aware that we are generating a legacy in the way we live our lives each day? I daresay, few of us think about it. And that is a loss, too. Life can have a whole other cast if we acknowledge the fact that we are living a project—the creation of a legacy. Relationships can take on a new dimension when we see them as part of the creation of a personal and joint legacy. Celebrating life and creating life's legacy are indivisible.

The celebrated life is contagious. Our spouses, children, relatives, friends, colleagues, neighbors, and fellow citizens can "catch" the inspiration to live with celebration. They will be enlightened by our capacity to celebrate our life and our life with them. From this, too, the following generations will be touched and affected.

Ultimately, legacy is about stories and connection. I have spoken about stories, but to turn stories into a legacy one must connect to others and convey these stories in some form. This could be done by telling the story, or by living the story, or by writing about or performing the story. A legacy conveys the summation of a person's story or the story of an epoch. With connection in mind, the telling, living, writing, and performing of a story take on a whole different dimension and meaning. The story being listened to and heard completes the sense of legacy.

Ultimately we must celebrate ourselves. We are the celebration of our histories—our natural history, cultural history, family history, and human history. In celebrating ourselves we affirm our place in history, our existence, our identity, our potential. If we can affirm our place in history, we can affirm ourselves as part of time. We become part of all time, including the future.

Create a legacy of celebration. Celebrate yourself in a way that affirms your identity, your history, your presence, and the possibility you envision for your life. Celebrate others in the same way. The large life is not determined by the size of a bank account, the prefixes or suffixes attached to a name, the stamps on a passport, or by lengthy résumés, as some would have you believe. The largeness of a life is determined by the focus we bring to the moments of life and our willingness to create a legacy of celebration for those whose lives we touch.

Acknowledgments

Since this book represents a culmination of sorts of all the formative people and events in my life, it would be easy to write yet another book of acknowledgment. However, to acknowledge those whose influence are not directly mentioned in the text, I would like to start with my friend Judith Viorst. Judy is an accomplished author, poet, playwright, and a master of friendship. It is my profound wish for everyone to have a friend like Judy. She was also my classmate in psychoanalytic education and the person who taught me to write. With her rigorous red pencil and gentle ways of telling me how horrible my writing was, she coaxed me to a place where my writing matched my voice. I shall, forever, be grateful for her loving friendship and her wisdom and her friendly persuasion.

Teresa Barker and I started with a professional relationship. She is an amazing writer, editor, reader, and conceptualist. Her task was great. She had to learn my ideas and my voice. She did both. She not only learned both, but she sometimes did both better than I could do. She was able to let me write and forced me to write beyond my own sense of my ability. She was able to edit with a light hand both technically and psychologically. You the reader are indebted to her also. She was able to be your "ombudswoman" and stop me from making leaps that would have left you behind wondering. In time our relationship became a friendship. We shared the joys and frustrations of the writing process. We shared our expertise. I am proud to share this book with her and cannot conceive of having written it without her.

To Drs. Donald and Helen Meyers who lent me their magnificent villa in the South of France where I found my muse. To Gail Ross, Esq., my literary agent, who recognized the potential for a book out of my notes and wisely guided me through my virgin literary voyage. To Henry Ferris, my editor at William Morrow/HarperCollins, whose grace and sense of timing proved exactly right for this book.

And, finally, to Jane, my wife, who has shared thirty-three years of my life and contributed in so many ways that cannot be enumerated. She has been the major constant in my life—my center. The many times I might have let a moment pass, she said, "Do it." Gratitude has it limits. Whatever lies beyond gratitude is what I feel for her.

—HLR

This has been joyful work, and I am grateful to Harvey for his wisdom, spirit, and laughter, and to Jane for her good humor; to Gail Ross for her matchmaking; to Henry Ferris for his intuition; to Liz Leibowitz, Kathy Flaherty, and Leah Nakamura for their inspiration; to my parents for the gift of our family life; and to my own husband and children—Steve, Rachel, Rebecca, and Aaron—for including the story of this book in the days of their lives.

—THB

ACKNOWLEDGMENTS

About the Authors

HARVEY L. RICH, M.D., has been a clinical psychiatrist, psychoanalytic teacher and lecturer, and psychoanalytic consultant for almost thirty years. Founder and first president of both the Washington Psychoanalytic Foundation and the American Psychoanalytic Foundation, Dr. Rich has been a prime shepherd and consultant on the creation of more than fifteen similar foundations throughout the country. He also has served as a consultant to the World Bank and U.S. Department of State in postconflict civil reconstruction, participating in missions to Angola, Peru, and Croatia. He has taught on the faculty of the Washington Psychoanalytic Institute, Georgetown University Medical Center, and the Wilford Hall Medical Center in San Antonio, Texas, where he is a distinguished professor of psychiatry for the major air force training hospital in the United States. He is also a published essayist in the *Washington Post* on psychoanalytic issues of everyday life. Dr. Rich lives with his wife in Washington, D.C.

TERESA BARKER is a veteran journalist and book cowriter, whose collaborations include *Girls Will Be Girls: Raising Confident and*

Courageous Daughters (Hyperion, 2002) by JoAnn Deak, Ph.D.; *Speaking of Boys: Answers to the Most-Asked Questions About Raising Boys* (Ballantine, 2000) by Michael G. Thompson, Ph.D.; *Raising Cain: Protecting the Emotional Lives of Boys* (Ballantine, 1999) by Michael G. Thompson, Ph.D., and Dan Kindlon, Ph.D.; *The Creative Age: Awakening Human Potential in the Second Half of Life* (Avon, 2000) by Gene Cohen, M.D., Ph.D; and *The Mother-Daughter Book Club: How Ten Busy Mothers and Daughters Came Together to Talk, Laugh, and Learn Through Their Love of Reading* (HarperCollins, 1997) by Shireen Dodson. Prior to becoming a book writer, Barker was a feature writer, news reporter, and editor, at different times specializing in health, education, legal affairs, and family life for publications including the Chicago *Tribune* and *Sun-Times, Time* magazine, *Advertising Age,* the Nashville *Tennessean,* the Memphis *Commercial Appeal,* the Eugene (Ore.) *Register-Guard,* and the Dubuque (Iowa) *Telegraph-Herald.* Barker lives with her husband and three children in Wilmette, Illinois.